The Moral Foundations of Civil Rights

Maryland Studies in Public Philosophy

Series Editor: The Director of The Center for Philosophy and Public Policy
University of Maryland, College Park

Also in this Series

Values at Risk
Edited by Douglas MacLean

To Breathe Freely
Risk, Consent, and Air
Edited by Mary Gibson

The Good Lawyer
Lawyers' Roles and Lawyers' Ethics
Edited by David Luban

The Security Gamble
Deterrence Dilemmas in the Nuclear Age
Edited by Douglas MacLean

The Border That Joins
Mexican Migrants and U.S. Responsibility
Edited by Peter G. Brown and Henry Shue

Boundaries
National Autonomy and Its Limits
Edited by Peter G. Brown and Henry Shue

Conscripts and Volunteers
Military Requirements, Social Justice, and the All-Volunteer Force
Edited by Robert K. Fullinwider

Energy and the Future
Edited by Douglas MacLean and Peter G. Brown

Liberalism Reconsidered
Edited by Douglas MacLean and Claudia Mills

Income Support
Conceptual and Policy Issues
Edited by Peter G. Brown, Conrad Johnson, and Paul Vernier

The Moral Foundations of Civil Rights

Robert K. Fullinwider

Claudia Mills

ROWMAN & LITTLEFIELD

Publishers

ROWMAN & LITTLEFIELD

Published in the United States of America in 1986
by Rowman & Littlefield, Publishers
(a division of Littlefield, Adams & Company)
81 Adams Drive, Totowa, New Jersey 07512

Library of Congress Cataloging-in-Publication Data

The Moral foundations of civil rights.

  (Maryland studies in public philosophy)
  Includes index.
  1. Civil rights—Moral and ethical aspects.
I. Fullinwider, Robert K., 1942-
II. Mills, Claudia. III. Series.
JC571.M777   1986   172   86-13761
ISBN 0-8476-7507-6
ISBN 0-8476-7511-4 (pbk.)

88 87 86
10 9 8 7 6 5 4 3 2 1

Printed in the United States of America

Contents

Preface

THE CENTER FOR PHILOSOPHY AND PUBLIC POLICY was established in 1976 at the University of Maryland in College Park to conduct research into the values and concepts that underlie public policy. Most other research into public policy is empirical: it assesses cost, describes constituencies, and makes predictions. The Center's research is conceptual and normative. It investigates the structure of arguments and the nature of values relevant to the formation, justification, and criticism of public policy. The results of its research are disseminated through workshops, conferences, teaching materials, the Center's newsletter, books published in the Maryland Studies in Public Philosophy series, and other publications.

The chapters in this book originated in a conference on the moral foundations of civil rights policy held in October 1984 at the University of Maryland to commemorate the twentieth anniversary of the Civil Rights Act of 1964. The conference was supported by grants from the Ford Foundation and the Prudential Foundation. The views expressed by the authors are, of course, their own and not necessarily those of the foundations supporting the conference, of the Center, or of the institutions or agencies for which the authors work.

Special thanks are due to David Luban, from whose initial idea the conference eventually sprang and who co-directed it, and to Lori Owen, who managed its arrangements expertly. Thanks are also due to Susan Mann, Carroll Linkins, and Louise Collins for preparation of this book.

Robert K. Fullinwider
Claudia Mills

vii

SECTION I

Race

PART ONE

Beginning and Ending

1

Race and Equality: Introduction

Robert K. Fullinwider

THE CHAPTERS IN THIS BOOK emerged from a conference to honor the twentieth anniversary of the Civil Rights Act of 1964. The Civil Rights Act was a remarkable watershed in American social legislation and race relations, unleashing changes across society whose effects have yet to be reckoned. It provided broad legal machinery for a sustained assault against racial discrimination (and, although it was an afterthought at the time, against gender discrimination as well).

The act contained sweeping prohibitions of racial discrimination in public accommodations, public facilities, federally assisted programs, and employment. It promised federal technical assistance to states in desegregating their public schools, mandated a survey of registration and voting statistics, and established the Community Relations Service. It gave to the Department of Justice extensive enforcement powers and created, in addition, a new enforcement agency, the Equal Employment Opportunity Commission. The provisions of the act rested on diverse legal grounds, including the federal government's right to regulate the use of its funds, the right of Congress to regulate interstate commerce, and the right of Congress to enforce the Fourteenth Amendment.

The Civil Rights Act passed into law ten years after the Supreme Court's ruling in *Brown* v. *Board of Education*, a decade marked by tumultuous school desegregation in the South, sit-ins, marches, demonstrations, and freedom-rides—and by mob violence, "massive resistance," murder, and legal mayhem. Bull Connor, Ross Barnett, and George Wallace, no less than James Meredith, Martin Luther King, and James Farmer, brought about a crystallization of political consensus to do something about civil rights. The Civil Rights Act became law at a moment of broad agreement on the necessity for governmental action to discard policies of official racial separation and to act against egregious denials to blacks of basic liberties and

3

opportunities. From this broad consensus emerged not only the Civil Rights Act, but its progeny: the Voting Rights Act of 1965, Executive Order 11246 of 1965, the Education Amendments of 1972, the Equal Employment Opportunity Act of 1972, and hundreds of state and municipal civil rights laws and ordinances.

Nevertheless, the broad consensus around the unacceptability of official policies of racial separation and the intolerability of denying basic political and civil liberties to blacks masked underlying fissures and fault lines in the way Americans understood race relations and perceived the problems of discrimination. As the initial legal and social barriers to black progress were cleared away, public divisions emerged over evolving policy. School desegregation suits against northern cities and desegregation orders involving school busing provoked a backlash. New concepts of discrimination evolving from case law led to legal actions against many of the largest and most distinguished business firms in the country, producing protracted and acrimonious litigation and extensive changes in the employment practices of the affected firms, frequently to the displeasure of their labor unions. The executive order subjecting all federal contractors to extensive affirmative action regulations produced confusion and controversy about "goals" and "quotas," preferential treatment and "color-blind" policy.

The breakdown of consensus has been manifested most dramatically in recent years by the explicit efforts of the Reagan administration to dismantle fifteen years of policy on affirmative action and by the increasingly fragile relations between blacks and Jews, who had been long-time allies in the civil rights struggles.

Because so much of the recent controversy about civil rights is framed in moral terms, an underlying motif of the conference from which this book emerged was whether a reexamination of the moral foundations of civil rights policy would clarify matters and produce some ground for rebuilding a consensus. But do the divisions over affirmative action, busing, and other civil rights controversies actually reflect deeper moral differences? What are the issues that produce friction?

The Meaning of Discrimination

According to the simple and innocent aspirations of Congress in 1964, the Civil Rights Act would turn the full force of law against the "whites only" sign in the motel window, the segregated departments in the textile factory, the "colored entrance" at the movie house, the "no blacks hired" policy at the automobile dealership. The act would prohibit racial discrimination, but Congress did not bother to define "discrimination." Against worries that this could cause difficulties, the Senate floor managers of the Civil Rights Act were sanguine: "It has been suggested that the concept of discrimination is vague. In fact it is clear and simple and has no hidden meaning."[1] But by 1972, the Supreme Court had found in Title VII of the Civil Rights Act a notion of unintentional discrimination,[2] and Congress was talking about the complexity, not the simplicity, of discrimination:

> During the preparation and presentation of Title VII of the Civil Rights Act of 1964, employment discrimination tended to be viewed as a series of isolated and distinguishable events, due, for the most part, to ill-will on the part of some identifiable individual or organization. . . . Employment discrimination, as we know today, is a far more complex and pervasive phenomenon. Experts familiar with the subject generally describe the problem in terms of "systems" and "effects" rather than simply intentional wrongs. . . . The forms and incidents of discrimination . . . are increasingly complex. Particularly to the untrained observer, their discriminatory nature may not appear obvious at first glance.[3]

In other words, far from being transparent and obvious, discrimination requires "trained observation" to spot!

Because Congress did not define "discrimination," the courts had to do so in applying the Civil Rights Act. They were soon faced with cases that pushed them toward conceptualizing discrimination not just as a consequence of a deliberate act or policy *designed* to exclude or hinder blacks, but also as a consequence of acts or policies that have the *effect* of excluding or hindering blacks, regardless of their original aim or design. For example, an employer who segregated blacks and whites into different departments prior to the Civil Rights Act might drop that policy to comply with the law, but his transfer and seniority rules, while neutral on their face and not specifically intended to work against blacks, would have the effect of locking black employees into their old, low-paying departments, i.e., have the effect of continuing to penalize older black employees for having been the victim of the employer's past discrimination. Unless such rules were upset, the employer's old discrimination would be allowed to "carry-through" into the present, even though he had abandoned his overtly discriminatory policies. Courts began to attack such rules, and the "effects" test of discrimination was born. The test was soon extended to cover practices that worked a hardship on black employees not by carrying through the employer's own past discrimination, but by carrying through the effects of past discrimination in general. Thus, the *Griggs* standard in 1971 made illegal those employment practices that especially disadvantage blacks and that cannot be justified as "business necessity," regardless of their intended purpose.

The idea that rules and practices that maintain and support the racial separation and exclusion produced by past discrimination can count as present discrimination is not an unreasonable one, especially in a world built around the exclusion of blacks and able, like a spinning top, to maintain its inertia even after the discriminatory hand is lifted from it. Nevertheless, the effects test introduces into the legal definition of discrimination a considerable elasticity, greatly enlarges its scope of application, and detaches it from the paradigmatic cases of deliberate discrimination around which consensus was built. The effects test can be used not only to require a business to stop using an invalidated aptitude test or an irrelevant height requirement for selection of workers, but potentially to prevent a state from subjecting teachers to minimum competency exams because a disproportionate number of black teachers fail.[4] In the end, the effects test comes down to a judgment about whether it it reasonable to make an institution, firm, or government forgo convenient, efficient, traditional, profitable, or even quality-improving practices in order that blacks will have more opportunities. This is the kind of judgment that will, in a wide range of cases, generate disagreement rather than agreement.[5]

Affirmative Action and Racial Preferences

The flashpoint of the most intense public and political controversy is affirmative action. Affirmative action programs have generated confusion, misunderstanding, resistance, hostility, and political backlash. The term "affirmative action" has a dual provenance. It occurs in Title VII of the Civil Rights Act in a remedial context. Section 706(g) of Title VII tells a court what to do when it has found an employer guilty of discrimination: it "may enjoin the employer from engaging in such unlawful employment practice, and order such *affirmative action* as may be appropriate, which may include, but is not limited to, reinstatement or hiring of employees, with or without backpay . . . , or any other equitable relief as the court deems appropriate."[6] Courts would require offending employers to make whole the victims of their discrimination and, in those cases involving deeply entrenched discriminatory practices, order a restructuring of employment practices and, frequently, the hiring of a fixed number or percentage of blacks.

The other occurrence of the term "affirmative action" is in Executive Order 11246, issued a year after Title VII. The order applies to all federal contractors and requires each to include as a contract stipulation that he

> will not discriminate against any employee or applicant because of race, color, religion, sex, or national origin. The contractor will take *affirmative action* to ensure that applicants are employed, and that employees are treated during employment, without regard to their race, color, religion, sex or national origin.[7]

In the one case, affirmative action is what an employer does to make up for his past discrimination. In the other case, affirmative action is what an employer does in order not to discriminate. Affirmative action in the two cases may not prescribe the same course of action, or even compatible courses.

The executive order left it to the secretary of labor to set out rules to implement affirmative action. With one eye to the developing Title VII case law, the Department of Labor first tackled the construction industry. Beginning with the Philadelphia Plan in 1967 (modified in 1969), it imposed (or elicited) a number of regional plans aimed at integrating the construction industry. The Philadelphia Plan involved numerical "goals" for the involvement of blacks in the lucrative craft jobs from which they had been excluded, and this feature was upheld by federal courts in 1970 and 1971.[8] Utilizing the strategies and ideas worked out in its construction industry plans, the department at the end of 1971 issued Revised Order No. 4, a detailed set of regulations covering all other federal contractors, from airplane manufacturers to universities. Thus were born the "goals and timetables" that became a part of the fabric of most business firms, manufacturers, utilities, and educational institutions.

The revised order never succeeds in disentangling two quite separate, though very close, concepts. The first is that of a *goal* in the dictionary sense, as something you aim at. The second is that of a *prediction*, that is, of what you expect to happen. Revised Order No. 4 tells the contractor that "in establishing the size of his goals and the length of his timetables, he should consider the results which could reasonably be expected from his putting forth every good faith effort to make his overall affirmative action program work," a program whose objective "is equal employment opportunity."[9] Here is the germ of one concept of "affirmative action goal." The contractor *aims* at nondiscrimination, and in order to assess his progress in achieving this aim, predicts how many blacks he would employ over a period of time were he successful in achieving nondiscrimination. Such a prediction ("goal") gives him, and the government, a standard by which to evaluate a program after it has been in operation for some time.

But the germ of a different concept is also present. Contractors are to take stock of their "underutilization" of minorities, and affirmative action goals "must be designed to correct any identifiable deficiencies." This implies the goals *are* what the contractor aims at, not the predicted by-product of his aiming at something else. The scenario here is of the contractor aiming to achieve proportional representation, which is not the same thing as aiming to achieve equal opportunity.[10]

The second concept of goals immediately raises the specter of racial preferences. If a contractor cannot meet his goals without taking the race of applicants or employees into account, then he will (must) meet them *by* taking race into account.

Revised Order No. 4 seeks to head off this interpretation by declaring that affirmative action plans are not "intended to encourage or permit the granting of preferential treatment to any individual or to any group because of race, color, religion, sex or national origin of such individual or group."[11] This disclaimer guided some early official interpretations of affirmative action. Thus, Stanley Pottinger, whose Office of Civil Rights in the Department of Health, Education, and Welfare (HEW) had responsibility for applying Revised Order No. 4 to institutions of higher education, sought in 1972 to assure universities and colleges that affirmative action did not call for preferential treatment. He offered an interpretation of goals consistent with the first concept noted above:

> Universities are required to commit themselves to defined, specific steps that will bring the university into contact with qualified women and minorities and that will ensure that in the selection process they will be judged fairly on the basis of their capabilities. Universities are also required to make an honest *prediction* of what those efforts are likely to yield over a given period of time, assuming that the availability of women and minorities is accurately approximated, and assuming that the procedures for recruitment and selection are actually followed.
>   This *predictive* aspect of Affirmative Action could be called any number of things. . . . They happen to be called "goals."[12]

But other affirmative action efforts exemplified the second concept. When the Department of Labor, along with the Equal Employment Opportunity Commission (EEOC) and the Federal Communications Commission (FCC), entered into a consent decree in 1973 with AT&T—a decree founded on the executive order program as well as on Title VII and FCC regulations—the "goals" and "targets" were incorporated into the company's Model Affirmative Action Plan as straightforward requirements, not predictions, and forced the company to use extensive sexual and racial preferences.[13]

Two different concepts of "goals" were embodied from the very start in the revised order, and this Janus-faced aspect of affirmative action has produced policy confusion ever since. Field offices of the Labor Department and HEW gave uncertain and conflicting interpretations of the affirmative action regulations. Heavy-handed enforcement activities were not uncommon and generated hostility. "Deficiencies" were identified whose "correction" would apparently require employers to hire blacks at rates proportionately greater than their availability. And "availability" itself, upon which goals were to be founded, was a matter hotly disputed and variously interpreted. When one university mathematics department noted that there were hardly any black Ph.Ds in mathematics, it was told (informally) by an HEW official to drop the requirement for the Ph.D.[14] And official efforts to distinguish "goals" (good) from "quotas" (bad) were often mealy-mouthed and confused.

Critics of affirmative action saw the regulations as intellectually dishonest and the disclaimers of discriminatory intent as disingenuous: goals was just another word for quotas. Or they conceded that goals need not imply quotas, but would nevertheless be treated as if they did by employers who wanted to avoid troublesome explanations to the government; or they held that whatever the actual concept of goals embedded in the revised order, the iron law of bureaucracy would produce a system of quotas. In any case, the critics viewed affirmative action as involving substantial, and unacceptable, uses of racial preferences.

This brings us to the heart of the matter. Can it be legitimate to use racial preferences? Why?

How to Think About Race

Discussions about race quickly become discussions of principle and right. But it is unclear, often, exactly what principle or principles are at stake, and how one should understand the role of principles and of other relevant considerations.

In 1974 the Supreme Court entertained the case of *De Funis* v. *Odegaard* involving a policy of the University of Washington Law School to set aside a certain number of its admissions for minority students.[15] The Anti-Defamation League (ADL) of B'nai B'rith offered a friend-of-the-court brief firmly in opposition to the law school's policy. "For at least a generation," it said,

the lesson of the great decisions of this Court and the lesson of contemporary history have been the same: discrimination on the basis of race is illegal, immoral, unconstitutional, inherently wrong and

destructive of democratic society. Now this is to be unlearned and we
are told that this is not a matter of fundamental principle but only a
matter of whose ox is gored. . . . A state-imposed racial quota is a *per se*
violation of the Equal Protection Clause of the Fourteenth Amendment
to the Constitution because it utilizes a factor for measurement that is
necessarily irrelevant to any constitutionally acceptable legislative purpose. A racial quota is a device for establishing a status, a caste,
determining superiority or inferiority for a class measured by race
without regard to individual merit. . . . Here lies the inherent evil of
quotas that reverse the objective of Anglo-American democracies to
move toward freedom by the rejection of status, measured by immutable factors like race, for assigning an individual his place in our
society.[16]

The brief presents an eloquent, stirring, much-quoted, and obscure
case—obscure because it blends together a variety of considerations
without indicating how they are to be weighed against one another
should they point in different directions. One set of concerns is
captured by the claims that "a racial quota is a device for establishing
status" and that "the use of race is destructive of democratic society."
We have certainly used racial classifications in the past to establish
status or caste, but is this a necessary feature of such classifications?
Past uses of race have been destructive and divisive, but need every
use be? The brief seems engaged here in making empirical and
historical claims—claims that ought to be amenable to some sort of
clarification and limited testing. We can try to imagine different kinds
of racial classifications in different kinds of conditions with different
purposes, and then speculate on the consequences. We can look in
detail at past practices of racial classification to identify what was
wrong in them, how the wrong was brought about, and whether it
was specific to the particular aims of the practices or a function of
features common to any aim. Might it not be possible to imagine—or
even to construct—racial preferences that in specific historical circumstances supported and strengthened democratic society and undermined and diminished caste?

Such questions and inquiries would lead us to look at the actual
effects of affirmative action on institutions, whether those effects
varied in different situations, what courts and government agencies
were trying to accomplish by devising the rules or issuing the orders
they did, and what alternative courses of action might have been
available with what results. Should, however, its historical and empirical concerns be put to rest, the ADL brief still does not seem
prepared to yield its opposition to racial preferences. A second line of
argument there holds such preferences to be "inherently wrong"—
they are wrong as a matter of "fundamental principle."

The principle at issue seems to be a principle of nondiscrimination to the effect: "Do not burden or benefit people on the basis of immutable characteristics." Clearly this principle is not fundamental, however, but derivative. Its acceptability as a principle must lie in its expressing some deeper value of equality or freedom or human dignity; "immutability of characteristics" is by itself a concept without any moral import. More important, it remains unclear what role the principle is supposed to play, what its "logic" is. In the ADL brief, it seems to trump other considerations, and no considerations are allowed to count against it. Regardless of purpose or outcome, all uses of racial preferences are proscribed, apparently, by the principle.

Once the argument devolves to claims of principles and rights— rights to equality or dignity, rights not to be discriminated against— have we reached a ground where common understanding can be forged? Obviously, rights and principles have a place in moral and political thinking, but what place? How shall their presence guide thought? What human realities are they rooted in, what hopes do they speak to? Are they perfect instruments or imperfect guides?

Alexander Bickel, in *The Morality of Consent*, contrasted two ways of political thinking—the "Contractarian tradition" and the "Whig tradition." The former, he said, rests upon "a vision of individual rights that have a clearly defined, independent existence" to which society "must bend." "The Whig model, on the other hand, begins not with theoretical rights but with a real society. . . . Limits are set by culture, by time- and place-bound conditions, and within these limits the task of government . . . is to make a peaceable, good, and improving society." The Contractarian approach "is moral, principled, legalistic . . . weak on pragmatism, strong on theory." The Whig approach, on the other hand, is "flexible, pragmatic, slow-moving, highly political."[17]

Bickel favored the Whig model, whose style he summed up in quoting Edmund Burke: "Every virtue, and every prudent act, is founded on compromise and barter. We balance inconveniences; we give and take; we remit some rights, that we may enjoy others; and we choose rather to be happy citizens, than subtle disputants."[18] Yet, ironically, Bickel was also co-author of the ADL brief in the De Funis case, a brief that is unyielding and adamant in its resistance to the use of racial preferences, and that, in the final analysis, appeals to the very sort of abstract principle that stocks the arsenal of the Contractarian. There is reliance on individual rights that must be protected even if this hinders "improving society"; there is no flavor of compromise, barter, and balancing of inconveniences.

Although the Bickel of *The Morality of Consent* may be reconciled logically with the Bickel of the ADL brief, the tension in tone and emphasis between the two Bickels is real and serves to remind us how difficult it is to think clearly about race. Because the second Bickel was writing as a lawyer and party to a dispute, however, perhaps it is just to give the last word to the first Bickel. If a principle like the principle of nondiscrimination is to enter constructively and fruitfully into our thinking about race, it must be tied not to an abstract right against decisions that rely on immutable characteristics, but to a realistic vision of how we will become a "peaceable, good, and improving society."

Engaging the Debate

The foregoing complications and concerns—and many others as well—form the background for the chapters that follow. The essays are gathered into two groups. The first contains the opening and closing statements made at the conference, offered essentially as they were presented. Both essays, by Drew Days and Derrick Bell, exhibit a marked pessimism about the further progress of civil rights, drawing parallels between our present circumstances and the retreat from legal protection of blacks after Reconstruction. Readers may or may not share the pessimism, but it is a significant fact itself that moderate and thoughtful blacks view the current scene so bleakly.

The second group of chapters constitutes a debate about affirmative action. The first four chapters are versions, variously revised, of presentations by symposiasts Wm. Bradford Reynolds, Richard Wasserstrom, Christopher Edley, and Orlando Patterson. The essays by Wasserstrom and Reynolds directly engage each other on the legitimacy of racial preferences in affirmative action. The chapter by Edley takes up the same issue, but also raises questions about the larger vocabulary within which affirmative action gets discussed. He is worried—and Drew Days expresses a similar concern—that the controversies about discrimination and its remedies are inordinately framed in terms of rights, a mode of analysis that, perhaps, distorts and limits our thinking as much as it aids it. Patterson tackles head on the unspoken presumption behind the conference, namely, that consensus is a good thing. He questions whether consensus is always worth its cost.

The fifth chapter in this group is an edited transcript of the discussions among Reynolds, Wasserstrom, Edley, Patterson, and the audience, following their presentations. It sheds light on the differences at issue. In the last chapter, Robert Fullinwider sharpens some of the points of contention between Reynolds and Wasserstrom.

Notes

1. Interpretative Memorandum on Title VII, 110 *Congressional Record* 7212–13 (1964).
2. *Griggs* v. *Duke Power Company*, 401 U.S. 424 (1971).
3. House Report No. 92–238, Report of the Education and Labor Committee on the Equal Employment Opportunity Act of 1972. *U.S. Code, Congressional & Administrative News* 2137, 2143–44 (1972).
4. *Washington Post*, November 5, 1985, p. A3.
5. Senator Orrin Hatch pushed very strongly at the outset of the Reagan presidency to overturn the effects test and make intent to discriminate an essential element of any legal definition of discrimination. The test is a "pernicious test," he claimed, "one that undermines everything that the civil rights movement has traditionally stood for—by undermining some of the most basic principles of fairness and due process." (*Hearings on the Nomination of Rex Lee and William Bradford Reynolds*, Senate Judiciary Committee, June 14, 24, July 17, 1981, p. 95.) Hatch's point is that basic principles require that a person intend to do wrong before he be found guilty of wrong. Now, such a requirement does underlie much law, especially those parts that are "judgmental," i.e., imply a moral condemnation of the guilty. But large areas of law are also designed to hold people responsible for unintended consequences of their actions. The law holds them accountable even when they are not at moral fault. The laws of accident, product liability, and malpractice do not require that the guilty defendant has intended the harm he has brought about, nor, in the case of strict liability, require that the defendant was negligent or morally derelict.

Senator Hatch's hostility to the effects test rests on his equating a legal finding of discrimination with a moral condemnation: "If we can justify charges of discrimination against people who never had an intent to discriminate whatever, . . . we are calling people racists without proving that they had the bad state of mind to commit racism" (*Hearings*, p. 137). This equation is inappropriate but not altogether ill-founded. As a political term, "discrimination" came by the 1950s to have a pejorative meaning, and the paradigmatic acts of discrimination—those involving deliberate exclusion of blacks—involved an explicit hostility to blacks and an intention to prevent their intermingling with whites or sharing benefits on the same basis as whites, acts that not only merited legal prescription under the Civil Rights Act but moral condemnation as well.

The evolution of the legal definition of discrimination detached it from its direct moral associations, while common understanding of discrimination retained these associations. It is understandable how special confusion and animosity could arise out of government enforcement policy. Companies that might easily have accepted and acted on the accusation that their work rules "provide less latitude for blacks' flourishing than is possible" resented and resisted accusations of "discrimination."

6. 42 U.S. Code 2000e-5(g). Emphasis added. The term "affirmative action" actually has a longer history. Section 706(g) was modeled on parts of the 1935 National Labor Relations Act, 29 U.S.C. Section 160(c). The term also occurred before 1964 in equal employment orders but remained pretty much an uninterpreted dead letter.
7. 42 U.S. Code 2000e, Section 202. Emphasis added. Sex was not included until 1967.
8. *Contractors Association of Eastern Pennsylvania* v. *Shultz*, 311 F. Supp. 1002 (1970); affirmed, 442 F. 2d 159 (1971).
9. 41 C.F.R. 60-2.12(a), 60-2.10.
10. 41 C.F.R. 60-2.10, 60-2.11(b), 60-2.12(g).
11. 41 C.F.R. 60-3.4(c).
12. Stanley Pottinger, "The Drive Toward Equality," in *Sex Discrimination and the Law*, edited by Barbara Babcock et al. (Boston: Little, Brown, 1975), p. 516. Emphasis added. See also 37 *Federal Register* 24687 (1972).
13. For a detailed account of the AT&T program, see Robert K. Fullinwider, *The AT&T Case and Affirmative Action: Case Study and Teaching Note* (Dover, Mass.: Case Publishing Company, 1971), reprinted in part in *Ethics & Politics: Cases and Comments*,

14 ROBERT K. FULLINWIDER

edited by Amy Gutmann and Dennis Thompson (Chicago: Nelson-Hall, 1984), pp. 173–81.

14. Malcolm Sherman, "Affirmative Action and the AAUP," *AAUP Bulletin* 61 (December 1975): 293–94. See also *Federal Higher Education Programs Institutional Eligibility:* Hearing Before the Special Subcommittee on Education of the Committee on Education and Labor, House of Representatives, 93rd Congress, 2nd Session, August–September 1974, Part 2B, 1251–53.

15. *DeFunis* vs. *Odegaard*, 416 U.S. 312.

16. Ann Fagan Ginger, ed., *De Funis v. Odegaard and the University of Washington: The Record* (Dobbs Ferry, N.Y.: Oceana Publications, 1974), Vol. 1, pp. 484–85, 487.

17. Alexander Bickel, *The Morality of Consent* (New Haven: Yale University Press, 1965), pp. 4, 5.

18. Ibid., p. 19.

2

Moral Philosophy and Legal Reasoning

Drew S. Days III

IT IS FITTING that there should be a volume commemorating the twentieth anniversary of the Civil Rights Act of 1964. Many are inclined to forget that this piece of federal legislation has had a profound effect upon the direction our society has taken in the past two decades with respect to civil rights. Let me mention just a few of its broader consequences:

- It was the first comprehensive effort in almost one hundred years by Congress to address pervasive racial discrimination;[1]
- The act was a recognition by Congress that it could not leave to the Supreme Court (which had acted in *Brown* v. *Board of Education*[2] and subsequent discrimination cases after 1954) and the executive branch (President Eisenhower had called out federal troops to ensure desegregation of Little Rock High School in 1957)[3] the enormous task of purging our society of its ugliest and basest instincts;
- It recognized for the first time that any effort to end racism in this country would require, notably in access to public accommodations and employment discrimination, an attack upon certain forms of private conduct as well as governmental practices;
- It provided the impetus for subsequent congressional action against racial discrimination not addressed fully in 1964 (voting rights, for example, which were treated comprehensively in the 1965 legislation),[4] as well as practices that had prevented nonracial groups such as the disabled[5] and the elderly[6] from being fully protected members of the society;
- It also served as the occasion for the Supreme Court to reassess earlier decisions on the meaning and reach of the Civil War amendments and of statutes passed during Reconstruction pursuant to those amendments. In significant respects, this reassessment resulted in

15

broadened interpretations of what conduct was prohibited and what relief was available under these provisions.[7]

On a more personal, less global level, the act has produced benefits for millions of Americans. The most visible sign of our former racial caste system, segregation in places of public accommodation, has been removed. Blacks have found decent jobs, educational opportunity, adequate housing, as well as positions of power and influence in the political process as a consequence of legal and public policy changes brought by the act. Dr. King, the Kennedys, Lyndon Johnson, Medgar Evers,[8] Chaney, Schwerner, and Goodman,[9] and the thousands of blacks and whites who marched, sat-in, lobbied, and litigated changed America for the good in ways too profound ever to be undone.

I

But we would not be discussing the "Moral Foundations of Civil Rights Policy" and the question "Can consensus be restored?" if the last twenty years had been an unmitigated success. Whatever the nature of the national consensus in 1964 or 1968 or even 1972, it is clear that major differences have arisen during the last decade or so over the nature, scope, and direction of continuing civil rights effort.

Given the subject of this book, the reader may wonder why a lawyer, rather than a philosopher or theologian, was asked to provide an opening statement. After pondering this question, I decided that the editors had opted for someone who reflected the nature of the problem rather than someone who was likely to offer any helpful solutions. A lawyer fits this bill perfectly. Lawyers are not trained to think in moral terms; in fact, we have been traditionally discouraged by education and practice from thinking in moral terms. We do not like thinking in moral terms; whether this is a predisposition of those who enter the profession or the result of acculturation is a difficult question that I will not pursue here. We do not like people around us to think in moral terms. Deep down, we believe that "thinking like a lawyer" is a characteristic every intelligent and thoughtful person should admire and want to develop.[10] In any event, lawyers have been remarkably successful in passing on their disdain for moral discourse to the society at large. We are a highly legalistic people. Rarely does a Martin Luther King, Jr., come along who asks, first, not whether something is legal, but whether it is just and morally right, and who is willing to suffer the consequences for violating legal restrictions in the name of a higher moral order.[11]

II

Having trotted out my "qualifications" to discuss the moral foundations of civil rights policy, let me turn to the question of our current national debate over this issue. While everyone was singing "We Shall Overcome" in 1964, any lawyer or legal historian should have anticipated, I can say with the certainty of twenty-year, 20-20 hindsight, that this civil rights consensus was unlikely to endure. For all of this had happened one hundred years earlier. I want to describe three striking similarities between the Civil War/Reconstruction period and the present.

The first involves the process of searching for the intent of the framers of the Civil War amendments and then measuring the constitutionality of legislation or official practice against that intent. Using this approach in 1883, the Supreme Court decided that a Reconstruction Era public accommodations act was unconstitutional. It was authorized, said the Court, by neither the Thirteenth nor Fourteenth Amendment.[12] In 1896, the Court was able to find, in *Plessy* v. *Ferguson*, that the "separate but equal doctrine" did not run afoul of the Equal Protection Clause of the Fourteenth Amendment.[13] Since 1964, the Court has continued this search for the framers' intent, in some instances coming to quite different conclusions from those reached in the last quarter of the nineteenth century. For example, it found, contrary to the conventional wisdom, that Congress was authorized by the Thirteenth Amendment to prohibit not only governmental discrimination, but certain private conduct harmful to blacks, as well.[14]

More recently, the Court and litigants before it have devoted enormous time and energy to determining what Congress intended to achieve under provisions of the modern civil rights statutes. The question has been simply put: "assuming that Congress was constitutionally empowered to prohibit certain practices, did it in fact intend to exercise that power?" Sometimes the Court has reached results that, in my opinion, advance the cause of civil rights;[15] other times it has not.[16] The point I mean to make has less to do with the result than with the process. In its constitutional decisions then and now, the Court asks not what is just and fair, but rather what was meant to be. It did not ask in 1883 how blacks, freed from slavery, made citizens, and given the franchise, could as a matter of morality be denied equal access to places of public accommodation. Nor did the Court ask in 1976 how governmental practices that fell disproportionately upon blacks could be morally defended on the grounds that the Fourteenth Amendment prohibits only *intentionally* discriminatory practices.[17]

Its treatment of statutes has been no different. The Court has been able to conclude, based upon its reading of the legislative history of Title VII of the 1964 Civil Rights Act prohibiting employment discrimination, that Congress intended to outlaw screening devices, such as standardized tests, that have the effect of discriminating against blacks, regardless of the motive of the employer,[18] and to allow voluntary race-conscious programs designed to remedy the effects of discrimination (even racial quotas).[19] But it has decided that Congress did not *mean* to provide any remedy for a "generation of black workers" locked in inferior jobs by seniority systems that incorporate past discriminatory practices in hiring and promotion.[20] These results are not dependent upon morality but upon often disputed statutory interpretations.

Recently, the Court concluded in the *Grove City College*[21] case that Congress did not intend to prohibit discrimination by a recipient of federal funds throughout its operations, but rather to ensure that the specific program supported by such funds be free of bias. Whatever the justifications, tactical or otherwise for so doing, the debate over the unsuccessful congressional effort to overturn the *Grove City College* decision in the proposed Civil Rights Act of 1984 focused upon establishing that Congress's intent was otherwise.[22] Relatively little time was spent upon the immorality of allowing taxpayers' money to support discrimination so long as recipients set up effective accounting procedures to mask their wrongdoing. I do not mean to suggest that courts ought to be free to pick and choose policies that they regard as morally correct regardless of what reasonably can be discerned about the objectives constitutional or statutory provisions were designed to achieve. Nor do I contend that moral discourse has no place in the legal process. In fact, the genius of the 1954 *Brown* decision lies in the degree to which the Supreme Court was able to achieve an appropriate balance between legal authority and morality. Rather, I want to shed light on a process that tends to restrict unduly the way in which society at large discusses questions of morality in the civil rights area.

III

The second similarity has to do with our attention span as a nation. More than a few commentators on foreign affairs have remarked waggishly that the Soviets do a better job than we do at diplomacy because one of their favorite national pastimes is chess, whereas we tend to enjoy poker.[23] While the comparison is meant principally to contrast the methodical quality of their approach with the risk-taking nature of ours, I think it also suggests something about their ability to keep a focus upon what is important, while we tend to be distracted by less important issues, ready to turn in our hand for a new one when things do not seem to be going very well. This characteristic is certainly evident in the field of civil rights, whatever force the comparison may have in foreign affairs. Take Reconstruction. It is difficult to imagine that America could drop, only ten years after the Civil War, all major efforts to help a people who had been in bondage for more than two hundred years and think that it had discharged its moral duty. Civil rights simply became politically unpopular; society turned its attention to other matters.[24]

The task facing our nation in 1964, while not equal to that presented in the 1860s, was exceedingly formidable nevertheless. Yet over the last twenty years, despite overall forward movement, the resources devoted to remedying the effects of past and present racial discrimination have been shockingly inadequate. Indeed, federal agencies charged by statute with enforcing the modern civil rights laws have admitted in open court their inability to do more than the bare minimum, arguing instead for more liberal judicial rules governing *private* enforcement of such laws.[25] Levels of commitment to civil rights enforcement have varied, certainly from administration to administration; but the latitude available for allocating personnel and other resources has been rather narrow no matter what administration was in power.[26] And, on a substantive level, only in the area of voting rights has Congress shown, in my estimation, a willingness and ability to develop new mechanisms to ensure meaningful minority participation in the electoral process in light of changing circumstances.[27] With respect to problems of housing discrimination, on the other hand, rights and remedies that offered hope in 1968, when the Fair Housing Act was passed, have been significantly undermined by the passage of time.[28] Once again, civil rights have become passé. We are told that the *real* issues are inflation, the deficit, terrorism, international human rights, unemployment, tax incentives, and so forth, depending on the speaker.

One standard response then and now to charges of administrative inaction, congressional deadlock, and judicial benign neglect has been that what the Constitution and the civil rights laws require is only equal, not special, treatment for blacks. It was on this basis that President Andrew Johnson vetoed repeatedly, albeit unsuccessfully, most of the post–Civil War legislation specifically designed to aid the newly freed slaves, such as the Freedman's Bureau Acts.[29] It was also part of the Court's reasoning in the 1883 *Civil Rights Cases* decision that to uphold the federal public accommodations act would unduly prolong the status of blacks as "the special favorite of the laws."[30]

Even today, some suggest that Justice Harlan's reference to a "color-blind" Constitution in his classic dissent in *Plessy* reflected his view that what the Fourteenth Amendment required was equal treatment and nothing more.[31] I do not think that this is a correct reading of Justice Harlan's position or the intent behind the Equal Protection Clause. His object in *Plessy* was to tear away the majority's disingenuous assertion that state-mandated segregation in railroad cars was not meant to suggest that blacks were inferior, but was instead an attempt to accommodate the mutual desire of blacks and whites to mingle socially with members of their own race. Justice Harlan, a man who changed from Kentucky slaveholder to forceful advocate for the rights of blacks, was accustomed to looking beyond the forms of justice in search of its substance.[32] Were he alive today, I think he would readily comprehend the necessity for something more than "evenhandedness" in addressing the plight of black Americans.

But even if I am wrong about Justice Harlan and about the Equal Protection Clause, the moral issue put so ably by President Lyndon Johnson in his 1965 Howard University speech remains:

> You do not take a person who, for years, has been hobbled by chains and liberate him, bring him up to the starting line of a race and then say, "You are free to compete with all the others," and still justly believe that you have been completely fair.[33]

IV

The final similarity I want to address is really an extension of my second point. It involves the degree to which blacks are made to feel guilty for pressing their claims and asking for more than an invitation to compete freely "with all the others" after experiencing generations of disadvantage. The charge is that blacks are seeking to improve themselves at the expense of "innocent third parties," whites who had no hand, it is asserted, in the discriminatory practices being challenged.[34]

This is not a new claim. On February 7, 1866, a delegation representing blacks in Illinois, Wisconsin, Alabama, Mississippi, Florida, South Carolina, North Carolina, Virginia, Maryland, Pennsylvania, New York, what were referred to as the "New England States," and the District of Columbia visited the White House.[35] They were there to ask Andrew Johnson's support for their efforts to gain the right to vote under the Constitution. As one member of the delegation, the famous black abolitionist and orator Frederick Douglass, put it, they wanted the president to "favorably regard the placing in our hands the ballot with which to save *ourselves*" (emphasis added).[36] President

Johnson refused their request, pointing out that to do so would unnecessarily disadvantage and upset poor whites in the South who had not been slaveholders. According to him, blacks should be satisfied that slavery had been abolished by the Thirteenth Amendment.[37]

Though the president allowed no full response to these assertions during the meeting itself, the delegation took the opportunity in a subsequent letter to point out that the antagonism between slaves and poor whites prior to emancipation had been fostered by the slaveholders; it was in their interest to keep these two groups at odds. What existed under slavery, they asserted in the letter, would not necessarily follow now that blacks were free. And in any event, they concluded, why should they be denied the vote because slaveholders had left a legacy of ill will between them and poor whites?[38]

In 1984, we have no difficulty in seeing, I would hope, that what Frederick Douglass and his colleagues were seeking was equal, not special, treatment; to quote the delegation's letter, "a state of equal justice between all classes." But President Johnson, and many other whites before and since, did not see it that way. Consequently, we must ask ourselves, if we are serious about moral questions, whether what we think of today as equal treatment and special treatment have any more validity as categories than Andrew Johnson's.

Let me offer a modern analogy. In the 1983–84 Term, the Supreme Court decided the *Stotts* case.[39] That case presented the question of whether a lower federal court violated Title VII by prohibiting layoffs of Memphis Fire Department personnel according to strict seniority. This action had been taken on the grounds that to allow layoffs, using the standard of strict seniority, would cause blacks, recently hired as part of a settlement of their employment discrimination suit, to be disproportionately affected. The Supreme Court ruled that the lower court erred and that Title VII required that seniority be respected. What is instructive about this case and others like it[40] is that they are depicted as contests between blacks who should have no quarrel, not having been actual victims of discrimination, and innocent whites with more time on the job. Yet, nothing in Title VII required Memphis to lay off workers. Rather than seeking other funds or altering its priorities, Memphis decided to pit black and white workers against one another. By maintaining that conflict, employers, like the city of Memphis, avoid being forced to defend the way in which they allocate their resources. And the states and federal government can avoid having to confront the question of why they are offering no assistance to prevent or mitigate these clashes between the values of seniority and affirmative action. The moral question, for me, is not whether blacks or whites have a greater right to scarce jobs, but rather why, whatever their respective claims, they should be unnecessarily placed in conflict.

But even where the competition does not involve scarce resources, such as limited job opportunities, the suggestion that blacks are seeking unfair advantage is made, nonetheless. Hence, a justice of the Supreme Court could feel at ease equating the minority set-aside provisions of the federal Public Works Employment Act of 1972 with the laws of Nazi Germany that attempted to separate Jews from non-Jews on a genetic basis.[41] Such extravagant claims tend to obscure rather than illuminate the real moral questions presented by the explicit use of race in allocating benefits and burdens.

Conclusion

What all this means is that I am asking us as a society to attempt to do more than lawyers are comfortable doing because of professional training and experience. If we spend most of our time debating whether the Fourteenth Amendment allows Congress to reach private discrimination, whether the Equal Protection Clause of the Fourteenth Amendment is "color-blind," whether Title VII requires proof of discriminatory intent, or whether Congress intended Title IX to be program-specific in the way that the *Grove City College* decision defines that term, we will be unlikely to reach agreement on these questions. We will have ignored underlying moral issues and lost our way once again.

Notes

1. Civil rights legislation in 1957 and 1960, the first since Reconstruction, addressed principally problems of discrimination in voting. The history of those laws is discussed in *South Carolina* v. *Katzenbach*, 383 U.S. 301 (1966).

2. 347 U.S. 483 (1954).

3. *Cooper* v. *Aaron*, 358 U.S. 1 (1958).

4. Voting Rights Act of 1965, Pub. L. No. 89–110, 79 Stat. 437 (codified as amended at 42 U.S.C. 1971, 1973 through 1973bb–1 (1976 & Supp. V. 1981).

5. See, for example, Section 504 of the Rehabilitation Act of 1973, 29 U.S.C. 794, which prohibits discrimination against "otherwise qualified handicapped individual(s)" in federally assisted programs.

6. Age Discrimination in Employment Act of 1967 (ADEA) 29 U.S.C. 621 *et seq.*

7. One example is *Griffin* v. *Breckenridge*, 403 U.S. 88 (1971), where the Court held that a Reconstruction Era statute, 42 U.S.C. 1985(c), reached private conspiracies to interfere with civil rights. In so doing, it departed from a 1951 decision which seemed to restrict the statute's reach to acts of governmental officials. *Collins* v. *Hardyman*, 341 U.S. 651 (1951).

8. NAACP Field Secretary in Mississippi, assassinated in June 1963.

9. Civil rights workers murdered in Mississippi in the summer of 1964. Their deaths

resulted in a successful federal prosecution for civil rights violations. *United States* v. *Price*, 383 U.S. 787 (1966).

10. Literature on the amorality of the legal profession is legion. Richard Wasserstrom's "Lawyers as Professionals: Some Moral Issues," *Human Rights* 5, no. 1 (1975–76) is a particularly thoughtful consideration of this question.

11. Martin Luther King, Jr., "Letter from Birmingham City Jail" (1963).

12. *Civil Rights Cases,* 109 U.S. 3 (1883).

13. 163 U.S. 537 (1896).

14. *Jones* v. *Alfred H. Mayer, Co.,* 392 U.S. 409 (1968) (private discrimination in housing prohibited by 1866 statute.)

15. *Monell* v. *Dept. of Social Services,* 436 U.S. 658 (1978) (municipalities not totally immune from suits claiming civil rights violations).

16. *General Building Contractors Association, Inc.* v. *Pennsylvania,* 458 U.S. 375 (1982) (discriminatory intent required to establish violation of 1866 law).

17. *Washington* v. *Davis,* 426 U.S. 229 (1976).

18. *Griggs* v. *Duke Power,* 401 U.S. 424 (1971).

19. *United Steelworkers of America* v. *Weber,* 443 U.S. 193 (1979).

20. *Teamsters* v. *United States,* 431 U.S. 324 (1977).

21. *Grove City College* v. *Bell,* 104 Sup. Ct. 1211 (1984).

22. See Stacy E. Palmer, "2 House Panels Back Bill That Would Clarify How Civil-Rights Laws Apply on Campuses," *Chronicle of Higher Education,* May 30, 1984, p. 17, col. 2.

23. See Eugene Victor Rostow, "The Russians' Nuclear Gambit," *The New Republic,* Feb. 20, 1984, p. 17.

24. See, generally, K. M. Stampp, *The Era of Reconstruction 1865–1877* (New York: Vintage Books, 1965), pp. 187–215 for a description of the "Compromise of 1876" and the demise of Reconstruction.

25. See, for example, *Cannon* v. *University of Chicago,* 441 U.S. 677 (1979), where the Department of Health, Education and Welfare urged the Supreme Court to grant a private right of action under Title IX of the Education Amendments of 1972, Pub. L. 92–318, 86 Stat. 373, 20 U.S.L. 1681 *et seq.* on the grounds, among others, that its administrative resources were inadequate to handle the claims of sex discrimination in employment.

26. United States Commission on Civil Rights, *Civil Rights: A National, Not a Special Interest,* pp. 34–36 (1981).

27. The 1965 Voting Rights Act was amended in 1970, 1975 and, most recently, in 1982. This latest amendment extends certain provisions of the original act into the next century. Voting Rights Act Amendments of 1982, Pub. L. No. 97–205, 96 Stat. 131 [codified at 42 U.S.L.A. 1971, 1973, 1973b, 1973c, 1973aa-1a, 1973aa–6 (West Supp. 1983)]

28. Joel L. Selig, "The Justice Department and Racially Exclusionary Municipal Practices: Creative Ventures in Fair Housing Act Enforcement," *University of California at Davis Law Review* 17 (1984): 445.

29. See generally, A. Avins, *The Reconstruction Amendments Debates,* pp. 136–49 (2d ed. 1974).

30. *Civil Rights Cases,* p. 25.

31. Wm. Bradford Reynolds, "Individualism v. Group Rights: The Legacy of Brown," *Yale Law Journal* 93 (1984): 995, 996.

32. See Alan F. Westin, "John Marshall Harlan and the Constitutional Rights of Negroes: The Transformation of a Southerner," *Yale Law Journal* 66 (1957): 637.

33. Commencement Address, "To Fulfill These Rights," June 4, 1965, *Public Papers,* 636.

34. Alan Freeman's article, "Legitimizing Racial Discrimination Through Antidiscrimination Law: A Critical Review of Supreme Court Doctrine," *Minnesota Law Review* 62 (1978): 1049, discusses this development fully.

35. The details of this meeting are provided in E. McPherson, *History of the Reconstruction,* p. 52 (1875).

36. Ibid.
37. Ibid., pp. 54–55.
38. Ibid., pp. 55–56.
39. *Firefighters Local 1784* v. *Stotts*, 104 Sup. Ct. 2576 (1984).
40. *Boston Firefighters Local 718* v. *Boston Chapters, NAACP*, 52 U.S.L.W. 3934 (July 5, 1984).
41. *Fullilove* v. *Klutznick*, 448 U.S. 534–535 n. 5 (1980) (Justice Stevens, dissenting).

3

Civil Rights in 2004: Where Will We Be?

Derrick Bell

WITH A TITLE LIKE MINE, I recognize the need to begin with a disclaimer. Despite the suggestion that I have come into supernatural powers, I am not the Jeane Dixon of the American racial scene, nor will what follows be a session of transcendental peeping into the mist-shrouded boudoir of the future.

Even so, the light of experience generated in the two decades since those heady days of what we called "The Movement," and the lessons racial history has provided over 200 years, casts sufficient light to enable predictions about the future that should prove more accurate than a wild and unruly surmise.

To begin, it requires no mystical power to see the error in the commonly held view that the long effort by blacks to gain freedom and civil rights in this country constitutes a long, unbroken line of steady progress. Rather, what is denominated "progress" has been a cyclical phenomenon in which rights are gained, then lost, then gained again, in response to economic and political developments in the country over which blacks exercise little or no control.

Recently, a person knowledgeable about civil rights criticized my observation as overly pessimistic, if not cynical, and suggested that, at the least, a spiral was a better representation of black progress than my cycle. Whether one prefers my cycle or my friend's spiral, we can agree that just as today's events can be discerned in the developments of 1964, so the origins of conditions likely to exist in 2004 are lurking in what is happening this year.

To put it quite gently, there is little optimism in the civil rights community at present and every reason to believe that the cycle or spiral, if you will, is heading toward a period that is still more bleak.

There are the obvious signs:

- The great campaign to desegregate the public schools has bogged down, while a majority of poor children of color are receiving inferior educations whether or not they attend schools with white children.
- Barriers to effective employment discrimination litigation grow sufficiently to enable all but the most idealistic to realize that Title VII will not come close to eliminating racism in the workplace.
- The federal Voting Rights Act has been renewed and strengthened and the number of black and Hispanic elected officials continues to climb, but the real political potential of blacks can perhaps be measured by the treatment Jesse Jackson received at the 1984 Democratic National Convention.

  As *Chicago Tribune* reporter Monroe Anderson assessed the situation, Mondale, fearful of a white backlash in the South and an anti-Jesse-Jackson Jewish desertion in the North, treated the black vote the way a snake handler treats a python. He explained, "The Democratic Party has that vote on a pole with a loop around its neck so that it can't get too close but can't get away, either."[1]
- The concept of affirmative action has left the realm of the controversial and is now deemed almost un-American in all sectors of American society save those liberal gatherings where the idea can be worn like a badge without any real concern by its advocates that they will ever be even mildly inconvenienced by its operation.

* * *

It is not that the years since 1964 have brought no improvement in schools, employment, housing, public accommodations, and other areas of civil rights concern. The change has been dramatic and meaningful for those blacks with the skills and training needed to benefit from them. But besides deliverance from the gross indignity that so pained every black person living in an officially segregated America, the racial reforms are, at best, an abstraction for those victims still denied or unable to obtain access to economic opportunity. For roughly one-half of the blacks now entitled to the protection of more civil rights laws than at any other time in American history, the economic devastation is as frightening as it is discouraging:

- The poverty rate for blacks is nearly three times the rate for whites, and the unemployment rate for blacks is more than twice the rate for whites.
- Under the combined attack of economic disadvantage and a still rampant racism, the black family is being destroyed. As the black academics who met at Tarrytown in 1981 and 1982 observed, the combination of forces has weakened a family fabric that until 1960 had enabled a remarkable 75 percent of black families to include both husband and wife. Today, 48 percent of black families with related children under 18 live in female-headed households where in 1979

the median income was only $6,610 compared with close to $20,000 for all families.

All of this is common knowledge. The question is how could the great expectations we shared as we celebrated the enactment of the Civil Rights Act of 1964 become the great trepidation of 1984, which is likely to become the great desperation of 1985 and beyond? In search of an answer, I was drawn again to three observations about the course of racism that have proved accurate in the past and are not likely to lose hard-gained validity in the next twenty years.

All who jubilantly believed that racism in America would end with our victory in World War II, or when the Supreme Court decided *Brown* v. *Board of Education*, or when the federal civil rights acts became law in 1964 and 1965, ignored the warnings of these three men.

First, in 1932, the theologian Reinhold Niebuhr wrote prophetically:

> It is hopeless for the Negro to expect complete emancipation from the menial social and economic position into which the white man has forced him, merely by trusting in the moral sense of the white race. . . . However large the number of individual white men who do and who will identify themselves completely with the Negro cause, the white race in America will not admit the Negro to equal rights if it is not forced to do so. Upon that point one may speak with a dogmatism which all history justifies.[2]

Second, W. E. B. DuBois, in his first and most famous book, *The Souls of Black Folk*, predicted in 1903 that "the problem of the twentieth century is the problem of the color line, the relation of the darker to the lighter races of men in Asia and Africa, in America and the islands of the sea."[3]

Fifty years later, in a new edition of the book, he wrote:

> I still think today as yesterday that the color line is a great problem of this century. But today I see more clearly than yesterday that back of the problem of race and color, lies a greater problem which both obscures and implements it: and that is the fact that so many civilized persons are willing to live in comfort even if the price of this is poverty, ignorance and disease of the majority of their fellowmen; that to maintain this privilege men have waged war until today war tends to become universal and continuous, and the excuse for this war continues largely to be color and race.[4]

Third, and by way of providing a motivation for the truth in the predictions by DuBois and Niebuhr, public policy expert Tilden W.

LeMelle expressed serious doubt that the United States is capable of legislating and enforcing laws to combat racial discrimination.[5] Writing in 1971, he observed that history presents no instances where a society in which racism has been internalized to the point of being an essential and inherently functioning component of that society ever reforms, particularly a culture from whose inception racial discrimination has been a regulative force for maintaining stability and growth and for maximizing other cultural values. LeMelle predicted that this country will act effectively against racism only when that racism is perceived as posing a serious threat to the country rather than serving as the useful regulator it has been.

These statements are strengthened through the scrutiny provided by illustration. For it is true that blacks have never received rights gratis. Not only was a struggle required for every gain, but the civil rights struggle had to coincide with outside events or conditions that made it necessary to grant blacks rights in order to further interests of greater importance to whites, or at least to those whites who set policy.

Here is a truth often obscured by the fact that white society—quite capable of ignoring the racism-caused suffering of blacks for generations—is also fully capable, when a racial reform is finally adopted, of hailing that reform as motivated by that sincere, if somewhat tardy, racial justice which, we are told, is the blessed proof of the nation's commitment to freedom and justice for all.

Forgotten is the self-interest without which black distress would have continued despite the most eloquent, or poignant, pleas for relief. Blacks, either genuinely magnanimous in racial victory, or inured to the hypocrisy of whites on racial matters, accept the reasons offered without question, a tradition-laden courtesy soon forgotten as black people move on to the next racial goal—one that all too often turns out to require a rewinning of ground already won.

A few major illustrations of this phenomenon should suffice:

—The northern states abolished slavery in the years following the Revolutionary War because slavery provided unwanted competition with white labor. The presence of slaves raised fears of slave revolts, and accompanying the efforts of abolitionists who believed slavery was an evil was the far more general belief that there was no place for blacks in the new world.

—The Emancipation Proclamation was signed by a reluctant Lincoln because it would clear the way for the recruitment of blacks in the armed forces, perhaps disrupt the labor force in the South, and strengthen ties with abolitionists in Europe, who would prevent England and France from siding with the Confederacy.

—The Thirteenth Amendment served to end the threat that slavery would continue to undermine the growing industrial society with its exploitation of "wage slaves." Its enactment also facilitated the discharge from the military of thousands of black soldiers who were understandably suspicious of new rules that barred mustered-out soldiers from keeping their rifles.

—The Fourteenth and Fifteenth Amendments were intended by the Radical Republicans to prevent the North from winning the Civil War and losing the peace. Predictably, the former slaves would vote for their liberators and not for their former masters.

—The Supreme Court's decision in *Brown* v. *Board of Education*, while the fruit of a decade of difficult litigation by civil rights lawyers, was likely helped as much by the challenge of Communism faced by America in the wake of its victory in World War II. The self-interest argument was set out in the *amicus curiae* brief filed by the federal government in the *Brown* case. It warned the Court:

It is in the context of the present world struggle between freedom and tyranny that the problem of racial discrimination must be viewed [for] discrimination against minority groups in the United States has an adverse effect upon our relations with other countries. Racial discrimination furnishes grist for the Communist propaganda mills, and it raises doubts even among friendly nations as to the intensity of our devotion to the democratic faith.[6]

In keeping with the well-settled traditions of racial reform, the Supreme Court's opinion in *Brown* did not suggest any self-interest motivations. Rather, it spoke of the need to provide black children, at long last, with the equal educational opportunity that somehow had been denied them during all those dreary "separate but equal" years. But the absence of documentary evidence will not convince me that the Court or many of its members had not heard and did not recognize the obvious fact that the nation could no longer afford to maintain the racial compromise of constitutionally supported segregation struck in the nineteenth century that had become an international embarrassment and contained all the ingredients for domestic disaster.

* * *

I realize that this will seem to many an all too deterministic view of history. Many will need to believe that the idea of equality is embedded deep within the American ethic, even if its pretensions far exceed its practice. But the truth about the real motivations for each of what have been deemed civil rights gains is revealed by the speed in which the commitments are revoked, repealed, or forgotten as soon as the self-interests of whites are served.

To a far larger extent than we could have imagined, the nation is relegating the civil rights laws and policies it adopted during the turbulent 1960s to precisely the same fate as befell the post–Civil-War amendments and the federal civil rights statutes enacted to enforce them. When the need for the black vote faded in the wake of the post-Reconstruction reapproachment between North and South, new political and economic arrangements were effected that placed American blacks in the position of sacrificial lambs.

For like lambs, blacks lost their entitlement to federal protection as the catalyst in a deal in which both northern and southern whites gained at the expense of blacks. It was an almost eerie repeat of the deadlock on the slavery question during the Constitutional Convention where the founding fathers sacrificed the rights of blacks, free as well as slave, to ensure that the new government could get a start. As Staughton Lynd has put it:

> Unable to summon the moral imagination required to transcend race prejudice, unwilling to contemplate social experiments which impinged on private property, the Fathers, unhappily, ambivalently, confusedly, passed by on the other side.[7]

But surely, someone will object, the general guideposts of history cannot be turned into a detailed blueprint for the future. There is no possibility that blacks can again be deprived of their basic rights of citizenship, as occurred in the 1880s and 1890s. But if we have referred to the progress made in the latter part of the twentieth century as the Second Reconstruction, is it impossible that this period of growth will end as did its nineteenth-century predecessor? As historians like Professor James M. McPherson have been at some pains to point out, the percentage of gains made by blacks in the two decades after 1860 in literacy and school attendance, in registration and voting, in land ownership and income, and in public offices held was greater than at any time since.[8]

The racial reformation of the late nineteenth century could not survive the economic and political winds that blew through the country in those times. In the 1880s, the cries of the American working class for labor rights, free silver, a graduated income tax, and protection against the worst impositions of big business were countered by an ideology embracing the established order of things and the immutability of prevailing social patterns.

The spokespersons for corporate enterprise, which included the influential social scientists Charles Darwin, Herbert Spencer, and William Graham Sumner, championed a system that supported natural rights and racial purity and equated wealth and power with virtue. The Supreme Court, sympathetic to conservative interests, became in these decades the major protector of propertied interests. Having recast its image and reputation after the debacle of *Dred Scott,* the Court expanded its role from interpreter to a principal maker of law and became the central paradox in a paradoxical age of conservative reform. It espoused individual rights at the expense of the individual and acted on behalf of public interest through the protection of private enterprise.

Within this framework, racial law became an important conduit for the preservation and legitimization of the established order. Shaken by fears of a powerful coalition of white Populists and blacks, white conservatives in the South turned to disfranchisement as well as to legal separation in social and economic spheres. The courts in the main cooperated in this racial subordination movement.

Today, the growing disparity in the statistical indicia of economic status between blacks and whites provides a most painful proof that the advent of racial equality remains a future event. And some observers are concluding that the doctrine of equality not only has failed to liberate blacks, but has become the replacement for official segregation as the means for maintaining white domination.

They assert that while slavery and segregation rested on the need to exploit white as well as black labor, wealth in this country is now produced through the exploitation of technology. Society, which no longer needs their basic labor, feels free to offer long disadvantaged blacks and poor whites "equal opportunity" to jobs, schools, housing, and public accommodations that they are ill-prepared to accept or are unable to afford. As has happened throughout the history of this country, poor whites relieve their economic-based frustrations and fears against blacks rather than against upper-class whites whose ranks, despite the heavy odds, they still hope to join.

Professor Sidney Willhelm predicts that the myth of equality within a context of oppression will simply provide a veneer for more oppression. The redundancy of blacks in the marketplace and the growing socioeconomic gap, Professor Willhelm fears, place the continued existence of black life in America at risk.[9]

The prediction is chilling, but Willhelm points out that many blacks are already outcasts in the labor market and poverty-stricken in the midst of plenty. Future ghetto uprisings could provide the excuse for police and other officials to eliminate blacks who resist military rule

over their communities. And, warns Willhelm, military occupation
will not recognize class distinctions. All blacks, regardless of class,
will be viewed as and treated like the enemy.

*   *   *

To summarize an admittedly pessimistic scenario, the following is
possible to foresee:

- Civil rights law enforcement will continue to be deemphasized, both
  in response to the prevailing mood of whites that enough has been
  done for blacks, and because existing law does not effectively reach
  the discrete discrimination that many continue to experience, but
  fewer and fewer are able to prove.
- Even though advocates of the women's movement do not intend this
  result, white women will increasingly replace blacks as the group
  entitled to priority concern in civil rights activities. I use the term
  "white women" because while black women are subjected to sexist
  practices, racism remains their preeminent problem. Even now, we
  see universities and businesses hiring and promoting more white
  women than blacks because white women are far more likely to have
  all the traditional (academic and cultural) qualifications than blacks,
  male or female. Having hired or promoted some white women,
  employers point to these statistics as proof of their conformance with
  affirmative action policies.
- The plight of underclass blacks, beyond the help of even basic civil
  rights laws, will continue to worsen in the absence of a general
  economic collapse that would require government job and other
  assistance to relieve suffering among larger sectors of the society than
  the black community.
- Middle-class blacks, already isolated from poor blacks in both the
  workplace and the neighborhood, will be hard pressed to provide
  either leadership or organized support to slow the slide of the black
  masses toward the inevitable destruction that is already under way.
  And in the absence of either political or economic pressures to
  manifest a token black presence, the positions and status of much of
  the black middle class will also be placed in jeopardy.

  A black bank executive, government official, or law school dean is a
  convenient symbol of the equality so much hailed on the Fourth of
  July and so little practiced during the rest of the year. But the felt need
  for such symbols has already declined markedly, with the likely result
  that in ten years only blacks with markedly superior skills matched by
  strong assimilationist tendencies will survive in what for so long
  were, and may become again, jobs for white folks only.
- Political power without economic potential, like a body without food,
  can remain active and alive for only a limited period. We learned that
  in the nineteenth century. Unless the growing gap in income and
  unemployment between blacks and whites can be arrested, the black
  vote will decline and with it the number of black elected officials.

In this regard, we should not read the increases in both the number of black voters and their political power as a demise of white opposition to blacks exercising the franchise or holding public office. Schemes both simpleminded and sophisticated are being used to discourage the black voter and dilute the effectiveness of the black vote. These efforts are hindered but not discouraged by the renewed Voting Rights Act of 1982, one of the few bright spots on the fast-fading civil rights litigation scene.

I do not think it too partisan a statement to suggest that if conservative Republicans remain in office, my assessment of the next two decades will be much worse than the bleak prospects I have outlined. If the Democrats return to power, conditions will be somewhat, but not much, better. For neither party has any inclination to risk power by advocacy of the kind of reform required to alter substantially the cyclical gain and loss of citizenship rights and status that has been the fate of blacks from the earliest days of this country to the present.

The cycle of racial reform and repression in the nineteenth century has been duplicated with remarkable similarity in the twentieth. For example:

- The Emancipation Proclamation was signed in 1863, and the *Brown* decision was handed down in 1954.
- The Civil War amendments and federal civil rights laws intended to enforce them were enacted in 1865–1871. The modern civil rights statutes were enacted from 1964 to 1968.
- The Hayes-Tilden Compromise was signed in 1877. The Supreme Court decided *Washington* v. *Davis* in 1976.
- The Supreme Court invalidated many of the nineteenth-century civil rights laws in *The Civil Rights Cases* in 1883. The Reagan administration cut back on civil rights law enforcement in 1980–1984.

Certainly these comparisons are approximate. Some progress can be expected even when times are hard, and the progressive periods are never without setback; but in general, while I may be deemed a pessimist, on the available evidence my conclusions cannot be dismissed as foolishness. And based on that available evidence, it is not unreasonable to predict that in the absence of intervening circumstances, the civil rights status of blacks in 2004 will be an updated version of what they were in 1904, which is to say almost nonexistent.

Civil rights laws will be on the books in 2004—just as they were at the dawn of this century—when lynching and terrorizing of blacks was commonplace; when labor exploitation through sharecropping or a labor contract system was the rule; and when justifications for widespread pernicious racist policies flowed from the courts, the sciences, and even the church.

All the old patterns are again falling into place. Some may be more optimistic than I that our more enlightened, sophisticated society will not allow a repetition on the verge of the twenty-first century of what happened 100 years ago, but the events of the last decade, I submit, do not support these hopes.

But all is not lost. We had not expected in the optimistic period twenty years ago the need at this point to seek opportunity from adversity. As we do, we can be buoyed by the fact that it is not the first time and is likely not to be the last. There is activity likely to prove more productive than bemoaning our fate.

For example, the effort required to avoid the simple repetition of past mistakes is worth taking and can pay rich dividends. We learned at great cost that segregation, with all its malevolent manifestations, was not the real evil afflicting blacks. It was rather a convenient policy vehicle through which the real evil, racism, could be projected. By directing our major resources to the elimination of segregation, we enabled those who had benefited most from Jim Crow policies slyly to substitute and get us to advocate a new vehicle, equal opportunity, which enabled the same old racial subordination to continue under a more acceptable guise.

In the future, we must recognize the importance of ever-changing political and economic conditions to our struggle and be ready to take advantage of trends through which white society can advance the cause of racial justice while serving interests to which they give more priority. Indeed, as during the sit-in era of the 1960s, our activism can highlight the manner and means by which racial justice can stabilize an otherwise disruptive environment.

The advice of Harlem activist Preston Wilcox, that "no one can free us but ourselves," can serve to dispel the false belief that civil rights progress requires a friendly president or a supportive Supreme Court. As we learned in the 1960s, an activist program gained the support of an ambivalent President Kennedy and held the votes of a wavering Supreme Court.

On the social front, we must organize and do whatever is necessary to reverse the poverty-based devastation of poor black families. Even those not motivated by humane considerations should act out of gratitude. For it was the ghetto uprisings in the late 1960s and early 1970s as much as the civil rights litigation and legislative lobbying that brought about many of the policies that have benefited better pre-pared blacks. One need not advocate violence, and I do not, to recognize that the frustration-induced rioting in the ghettos led many to move who would otherwise have remained immobile.

And on the litigation front, even if no major new breakthroughs are forthcoming, there will be plenty of work for civil rights lawyers in simply resisting the erosion of hard-won gains. But court efforts should not all be defensive.

Just as the NAACP organized a major movement in the early 1930s that eventually toppled the "separate but equal" doctrine, civil rights organizations must begin the long hard work needed to gain constitutional recognition of the one right that counts in this money-oriented land: the right to an equal economic opportunity, including entitlement to work (not welfare) at a reasonable wage. We have learned that equality without an income is a contradiction in terms.

The task, I fear, may make the effort that led to *Brown* seem like a small undertaking indeed, but we must begin. And we must somehow try to enlist in this crusade the millions of white working and nonworking poor who continue to resist black-led initiatives, including those that would benefit them as much as blacks. Overcoming the deeply held belief that being white is enough to guarantee a fair shake in this society will not be easy, but Jesse Jackson's Rainbow Coalition showed that a beginning could be made. And we must continue this effort for, as some street brother has remarked, "until poor white folks get smart, we black folks will never get free."

There is then only one thing that we can guarantee for certain about the condition of civil rights in 2004, and that is that blacks and whites concerned about real equality will still be doing whatever is required to survive and, as the old spiritual urged, "trying to make heaven our home"—right here.

Notes

1. Monroe Anderson, "Blacks Must Regain Spirit of 1972 Gary Convention," *The Oregonian*, September 1984.

2. Reinhold Niebuhr, *Moral Man and Immoral Society* (New York: Scribner's, 1932), pp. 252–53.

3. W. E. B. DuBois, *The Souls of Black Folk*, (Chicago: A. C. McClurg, 1903), p. 23.

4. W. E. B. DuBois, *The Souls of Black Folk*, 26th ed. (New York: Fawcett Publications, 1961), p. xiii.

5. Tilden W. LeMelle, Foreword, in Richard Burkey, *Racial Discrimination and Public Policy in the United States* (Lexington, Mass.: Heath Lexington Books, 1971), p. 38.

6. See quote in Albert P. Blaustein and Clarence Clyde Ferguson, *Desegregation and the Law* (New York: Vintage Books, 1962), pp. 11–12.

7. Staughton Lynd, "Slavery and the Founding Fathers," in *Black History*, edited by Melvin Drimmer (Garden City, N.Y.: Doubleday, 1968), pp. 119, 131.

8. James M. McPherson, "Comparing the Two Reconstructions," *Princeton Alumni Weekly* (February 26, 1979), pp. 16, 18.

9. Sidney Willhelm, *Black in a White America* (Cambridge, Mass.: Schenkman, 1983).

PART TWO

Affirmative Action, Equal Opportunity, and Consensus

4

Stotts: *Equal Opportunity, Not Equal Results*

Wm. Bradford Reynolds

No one disputes that "affirmative action" is a subject of vital significance for our society. The character of our country is determined in large measure by the manner in which we treat our individual citizens—whether we treat them fairly or unfairly, whether we ensure equal opportunity to all individuals, or guarantee equal results to selected groups. As assistant attorney general, I am faced daily with what seem to have emerged on the civil rights horizon as the two predominant competing values that drive the debate on this issue—that is, the value of equal opportunity and the value of equal results. I have devoted a great deal of time and attention to the very different meanings these concepts lend to the phrase "affirmative action."

Typically, to the understandable confusion of almost everyone, "affirmative action" is the term used to refer to both of these contrasting values. There is, however, a world of difference between "affirmative action" as a measure for ensuring equality of opportunity and "affirmative action" as a tool for achieving equality of results.

In the former instance, affirmative steps are taken so that all individuals (whatever their race, color, sex, or national origin) will be given the chance to compete with all others on equal terms; each is to be given his or her place at the starting line without advantage or disadvantage. In the latter, by contrast, the promise of affirmative action is that those who participate will arrive at the finish line in prearranged places—places allocated by race or sex.

I have expressed on a number of occasions my conviction that the promise of equal results is a false one. We can never assure equal results in a world in which individuals differ greatly in motivation and ability; nor, in my view, is such a promise morally or constitu-

39

tionally acceptable. In fact, this was well understood at the time that the concept of "affirmative action" was first introduced as a remedial technique in the civil rights arena. In its original formulation, that concept embraced only nonpreferential affirmative efforts, such as training programs and enhanced recruitment activities, aimed at opening wide the doors of opportunity to all Americans who cared to enter. Thus, President Kennedy's Executive Order 10925, one of the earliest to speak to the subject, stated that federal contractors should "take affirmative action to ensure that the applicants are employed, and that employees are treated during employment, without regard to their race, creed, color, or national origin."

This principle was understood by all at that time to mean simply that individuals previously neglected in the search for talent must be allowed to apply and be considered along with all others for available jobs or contracting opportunities, but that the hiring and selection decisions would be made from the pool of applicants without regard to race, creed, color, or national origin—and later sex. No one was to be afforded a preference, or special treatment, because of group membership; rather, all were to be treated equally as individuals based on personal ability and worth.

This administration's commitment is to what Vice Chairman of the Civil Rights Commission Morris Abram calls the "original and undefiled meaning" of "affirmative action." Where unlawful discrimination exists, we see that it is brought to an abrupt and uncompromising halt; where that discrimination has harmed any individual, we ensure that every victim of the wrongdoing receives "make-whole" relief; and, where affirmative steps in the nature of training programs and enhanced recruitment efforts are needed, we require such steps to be taken to force open the doors of opportunity that have too long remained closed to far too many.

The criticism, of course, is that we do not go far enough. The remedial use of goals and timetables, quotas, or other such numerical devices, designed to achieve a particular balance in race or sex in the work force, has been accepted by the lower federal courts as an available instrument of relief, and therefore, it is argued, such an approach should not be abandoned. There are several responses to this sort of argumentation.

The first is a strictly legal one and rests on the Supreme Court's recent decision in *Firefighters Local Union No. 1784* v. *Stotts*, 104 S. Ct. 2576 (1984). The Supreme Court in *Stotts* did not merely hold that federal courts are prohibited from ordering racially preferential layoffs to maintain a certain racial percentage, or that courts cannot disrupt bona fide seniority systems. To be sure, it did so rule, but the

Court said much more, and in unmistakably forceful terms. As Justice Stevens remarked during his August 4, 1984, commencement address at Northwestern University, the decision represents "a far-reaching pronouncement concerning the limits on a court's power to prescribe affirmative action as a remedy for proven violations of Title VII of the Civil Rights Act." For the *Stotts* majority grounded the decision, at bottom, on the holding that federal courts are without *any* authority under Section 706(g)—the remedial provision of Title VII—to order a remedy, either by consent decree or after full litigation, that goes beyond enjoining the unlawful conduct and awarding "make-whole" relief for actual victims of the discrimination. Thus, quotas or other preferential techniques that, by design, benefit nonvictims because of race or sex cannot be a part of Title VII relief ordered in a court case, whether the context is hiring, promotion, or layoffs.

A brief review of the opinion's language is particularly useful to understanding the sweep of the decision. At issue in *Stotts* was a district court injunction ordering that certain white firefighters with greater seniority be laid off before blacks with less seniority in order to preserve a certain percentage of black representation in the fire department's work force. The Supreme Court held that this order was improper because "there was no finding that any of the blacks protected from layoff had been a victim of discrimination."[1] Relying explicitly on Section 706(g) of Title VII, the Court held that Congress intended to "provide make-whole relief only to those who have been actual victims of illegal discrimination."[2]

Specific portions of the legislative history of the act were cited in support of this interpretation. For example, Hubert Humphrey, the principal force behind passage of Title VII in the Senate, had assured his colleagues during consideration of the statute that:

> [t]here is nothing in [the proposed bill] that will give any power to the Commission *or to any court* to require hiring, firing or promotion of employees in order to meet a racial "quota" or to achieve a certain racial balance. That bugaboo has been brought up a dozen times; but it is nonexistent.[3]

Moreover, the Court recognized that the interpretive memorandum of the bill entered into the Congressional Record by Senators Clark and Case stated unambiguously that "Title VII does not permit the ordering of racial quotas in business or unions."[4]

After *Stotts*, it is, I think, abundantly clear that Section 706(g) of Title VII does not tolerate remedial action by courts that would grant to nonvictims of discrimination—at the expense of wholly innocent employees or potential employees—an employment preference based solely on the fact that they are members of a particular race or gender. Quotas, or any other numerical device based on color or sex, are by definition victim-blind: they embrace without distinction, and accord preferential treatment to, persons having no claim to "make-whole" relief. Accordingly, whether such formulas are employed for hiring, promotion, or layoffs, they must fail under any reading of the statute's remedial provision.

There are equally strong policy reasons for coming to this conclusion. The remedial use of preferences had been justified by the courts primarily on the theory that they are necessary to cure "the effects of past discrimination" and thus, in the words of one Supreme Court Justice, to "get beyond racism."[5] This reasoning is twice-flawed.

First, it is premised on the proposition that any racial imbalance in the employer's work force is explainable only as a lingering effect of past racial discrimination. The analysis is no different where gender-based discrimination is involved. Yet, in either instance, equating "underrepresentation" of certain groups with discrimination against those groups ignores the fact that occupation selection in a free society is determined by a host of factors, principally individual interest, industry, and ability. It simply is not the case that applicants for any given job come proportionally qualified by race, gender, and ethnic origin in accordance with U.S. population statistics. Nor do the career interests of individuals break down proportionally among racial or gender groups. Accordingly, a selection process free of discrimination is no more likely to produce "proportional representation" along race or sex lines than it is to ensure proportionality among persons grouped according to hair color, shoe size, or any other irrelevant personal characteristic. No human endeavor, since the beginning of time, has attracted persons sharing a common physical characteristic in numbers proportional to the representation of such persons in the community. "Affirmative action" assumptions that one might expect otherwise in the absence of race or gender discrimination are ill-conceived.

Second, and more important, there is nothing remedial—let alone equitable—about a court order that requires the hiring, promotion, or retention of a person who has not suffered discrimination solely because that person is a member of the same racial or gender group as other persons who were victimized by the discriminatory employment practices. The rights protected under Title VII belong to individuals, not to groups. The Supreme Court made clear some years ago that "the basic policy of Title VII requires that courts focus on fairness to individuals rather than fairness to classes."[6] The same message was again delivered in Stotts. As indicated, remedying a violation of Title

VII requires that the individual victimized by the unlawful discrimination be restored to his or her "rightful place." It almost goes without saying, however, that a person who is *not* victimized by the employer's discriminatory practices has no claim to a "rightful place" in the employer's work force. And according preferential treatment to *nonvictims* in no way remedies the injury suffered by persons who have in fact been discriminated against in violation of Title VII.

Moreover, racial quotas and other forms of preferential treatment unjustifiably infringe on the legitimate employment interests and expectations of third parties, such as incumbent employees, who are free of any involvement in the employer's wrongdoing. To be sure, awarding retroactive seniority and other forms of "rightful place" relief to individual victims of discrimination also unavoidably infringes upon the employment interests and expectations of innocent third parties. Indeed, this fact has compelled some, including Chief Justice Burger, to charge that granting rightful place relief to victims of racial discrimination is on the order of "robbing Peter to pay Paul."[7]

The legitimate "rightful place" claims of identifiable victims of discrimination, however, warrant imposition of a remedy that calls for a sharing of the burden by those innocent incumbent employees whose "places" in the work force are the product of, or at least enhanced by, the employer's unlawful discrimination. Restoring the victim of discrimination to the position he or she would have occupied but for the discrimination merely requires incumbent employees to surrender some of the largesse discriminatorily conferred upon them. In other words, there is justice in requiring Peter, as a kind of third-party beneficiary of the employer's discriminatory conduct, to share in the burden of making good on the debt to Paul created by that conduct. But an incumbent employee should not be called upon as well to sacrifice or otherwise compromise his legitimate employment interests in order to accommodate persons *never wronged* by the employer's unlawful conduct. An order directing Peter to pay Paul in the absence of any proof of a debt owing to Paul is without remedial justification and cannot be squared with basic notions of fairness.

Proponents of the so-called remedial use of class-based preferences often counter this point with a twofold response. First, they note that the effort to identify and make whole all victims of the employer's discriminatory practices will never be 100 percent successful. While no one can dispute the validity of this unfortunate point, race- and gender-conscious preferences simply do not answer this problem. The injury suffered by a discriminatee who cannot be located is in no way ameliorated—much less remedied—by conferring preferential treatment on other randomly selected members of his or her race or sex. A person suffering from an appendicitis is not relieved of the pain by an appendectomy performed on the patient in the next room.

Second, proponents of judicially imposed numerical preferences argue that preferences are necessary to ensure that the employer does not return to his or her discriminatory ways. The fallacy in this reasoning is self-evident. Far from *preventing* future discrimination, imposition of such remedial devices *guarantees* future discrimination. Only the color or gender of the ox being gored is changed.

It is against this backdrop that the Court's decision in *Stotts* assumes so much significance in the "affirmative action" debate. The inescapable consequence of *Stotts* is to move government at the federal, state, and local levels noticeably closer to the overriding objective of providing all citizens with a truly equal opportunity to compete on merit for the benefits that our society has to offer—an opportunity that allows an individual to go as far as the person's energy, ability, enthusiasm, imagination, and effort will allow—and not be hemmed in by the artificial allotment given to his or her group in the form of a numerical preference. The promise is that we might now be able to bring an end to that stifling process by which government and society view their citizens as possessors of racial or gender characteristics, not as the unique individuals they are; where advancements are viewed not as hard-won achievements, but as conferred "benefits."

The use of race or sex, in an effort to restructure society along lines that better represent someone's preconceived notions of how our limited educational and economic resources should be allocated among the many groups in our pluralistic society, necessarily forecloses opportunities to those having the misfortune—solely by reason of gender or skin color—to be members of a group whose allotment has already been filled. Those so denied, such as the more senior white Memphis firefighters laid off to achieve a more perfect racial balance in the fire department, are discriminated against every bit as much as the black Memphis firefighters excluded from employment. In our zeal to eradicate discrimination from society, we must be ever vigilant not to allow considerations of race or sex to intrude upon the decisional process of government. That was precisely the directive handed down by Congress in the Civil Rights Act of 1964 and, as *Stotts* made clear, the command has full application to the courts. Plainly, "affirmative action" remedies must be guided by no different principle. For the simple fact remains that wherever it occurs, and however explained, "no discrimination based on race [or sex] is benign. . . . no action disadvantaging a person because of color [or gender] is affirmative."[8]

Notes

1. *Firefighters Local Union No. 1784* v. *Stotts*, 104 S.Ct. 2576, 2588 (1984).

2. Ibid., at 2589.

3. 110 Congressional Record 6549 (1964) (emphasis added).

4. Ibid., at 6566 (emphasis added by the Court).

5. *University of California Regents* v. *Bakke*, 438 U.S. 265, 407 (Justice Blackmun, concurring).

6. *Los Angeles Department of Water & Power* v. *Manhart*, 435 U.S. 702, 708 (1978).

7. *Franks* v. *Bowman Transportation Co.*, 424 U.S. 747, 781 (1976) (Justice Burger, dissenting).

8. *United Steelworkers of America, AFL-CIO* v. *Weber*, 443 U.S. 193, 254 (1979) (Justice Rehnquist, dissenting).

5

One Way to Understand and Defend Programs of Preferential Treatment

Richard Wasserstrom

PROGRAMS OF PREFERENTIAL TREATMENT make relevant the race or sex of individuals in the sense that the race or sex of an applicant for admission, a job, or a promotion constitutes a relevant, although not a decisive, reason for preferring that applicant over others. In my discussion of these programs I will consider only preferential treatment programs concerned with preferring a person who is black over one who is white, but what I have to say will be illustrative of a way to approach and assess comparable programs in which members of other ethnic or minority groups, or women, are concerned.

My thesis is a twofold one. First, such programs can very plausibly be seen to be good programs for us to have in our society today because they help to make the social conditions of life less racially oppressive and thereby more just, and because they help to distribute important social goods and opportunities more equally and fairly. Second, these programs can be seen to help to realize these desirable aims without themselves being in any substantial respect unjust—without, that is, taking an impermissible characteristic into account, violating persons' rights, failing to give individuals what they deserve, or treating them in some other way that is unfair.

The positive case for such programs begins with the following claim about our own society: we are still living in a society in which a person's race, his or her blackness rather than whiteness, is a socially significant and important category. Race is not, in our culture, like eye color. Eye color is an irrelevant category in that eye color is not an important social or cultural fact about individuals; nothing of substance turns on what eye color they have. To be black rather than white is not like that at all. To be black is to be at a disadvantage in terms of most of the measures of success or satisfaction—be they economic, vocational, political, or social. To see, in a very crude and rough way, that this is so one could conduct a thought experiment. If one wanted to imagine maximizing one's chances of being satisfied with one's employment or career, politically powerful rather than powerless, secure from arbitrary treatment within the social institutions, reasonably well off economically, and able to pursue one's own goals and develop one's own talents in ways that would be satisfying to oneself, and if one could choose whether to be born either white or black, wouldn't one choose to be born white rather than black?

If this claim about the existing social reality of race is correct, then two further claims seem plausible. The first is that there is in place what can correctly be described as a system of racial oppression. It is a racial system in that the positions of political, economic, and social power and advantage are concentrated and maintained largely in the hands of those who are white rather than black. It is an oppressive one in that some of these inequalities in social burdens and lessened opportunities are unjust because of the nature of the disadvantages themselves—they are among those that no one ought fairly be required to confront or combat in any decent society. And it is an oppressive one in that others of these inequalities are tied to race in contexts and ways that make such a connection itself manifestly unfair and unjust. But the primary and fundamental character of the oppression is in what results from these and related features and is not reducible to them. The oppression has to do, first, with the *systemic nature* of the unequal and maldistributed array of social benefits, opportunities, and burdens, and it has to do, as well, with *how* things are linked together to constitute an interlocking, mutually reinforcing system of social benefits and burdens, ideology, and the like which, when tied to race as they are, make it a system of *racial* disadvantage and oppression—and, for all of these reasons, a decidedly and distinctly unjust one.

Now, if this be granted, the next claim is that even if it is assumed that the intentions and motivations of those occupying positions of relative power and opportunity are wholly benign and proper with respect to the pursuit of the wrongful perpetuation of any unjust racial oppression toward blacks, it is likely that the system will perpetuate itself unless blacks come to occupy substantially more of the positions within the major social institutions than they have occupied in the past and now do. Thus, to have it occur that blacks do come to occupy more of these positions of power, authority, and the like is *a* way, if not *the* way, to bring about the weakening, if not the destruction, of that interlocking system of social practices, structures, and ideology that still plays a major if not fundamental role in preventing persons who are black from being able to live the kinds of lives that all persons ought to be able to live—lives free from the burdens of an existing, racially oppressive system.

If this is so, then the case for programs of preferential treatment can be seen to rest upon the truth of the claim that they are designed specifically to accomplish this end, and upon the truth of the claim that they do accomplish it. They do succeed in introducing more blacks into the kinds of vocations, careers, institutional positions, and the like than would have been present if these programs had not been in place. In this respect there is, I believe, little question but that the programs have worked and do work to produce, for example, black judges and lawyers where few if any existed before, and to produce, more generally, black employees in businesses and in places within the other major structures and hierarchies where few if any were present before. And this can be seen to be especially important and desirable because changes of this sort in the racial composition of these institutions have mutually reinforcing consequences that can reasonably be thought to play an important role in bringing about the dismantling of the existing system of racial disadvantage and oppression.

They do so, first, by creating role models for other black persons to identify with and thereby come to see as realizable in their own lives. They do so, second, by bringing members of this historically excluded and oppressed group into relationships of equality of power, authority, and status with members of the dominant group. This is important because when relationships of this kind are nonexistent or extremely infrequent, as they are in the system of racial oppression, the system tends most easily and regularly to sustain itself. Third, changes in the racial composition of the major social institutions work, as well, to make it possible for blacks, with their often different and distinctive but no less correct views of the nature of the complex social world in which we all live, to participate in such things as the shaping of academic programs and disciplines and to participate in the definition, focus, and direction of significant social, legal, economic, and related institutional policies, and in deliberations and debates concerning their supporting justifications. And they do so, finally, by making it more likely that there will be the more immediate and meaningful provision of important services and benefits to other members of that group who have up until now been denied fair and appropriate access to them.

Thus, the primary claim in support of these programs is that, in what they do and how they work, they can be seen to play a substantial role in weakening the system of racial oppression that is still in place and that makes a person's blackness have the kind of pervasively deleterious social meaning and significance that it ought not. The aim of these programs is to eliminate this system and to produce a society in which race will cease to matter in this way; and on this view of things it may be superficially paradoxical but is, nonetheless, more deeply plausible to believe that such can be significantly accomplished by taking race into account in the way these programs do.

What should be apparent is that, in some large measure, there are empirical claims involved here, and to the degree to which there are, disagreements about the justifiability of preferential treatment programs can be located and settled by attending to their truth or falsity. Thus, if such programs produce or exacerbate racial hostility, or if they lead to a reduced rather than an enhanced sense of self-respect on the part of blacks, then these are matters that count against the overall case for these programs. But I do not, myself, think the case against them can be rested very easily upon such grounds, and I do not think that, when it is, the evidence is very convincing and the arguments very plausible. Nor are such programs typically opposed on grounds of this sort. Instead, the main ground of principled opposition has to do with what is thought to be fundamentally wrong with them: with the fact that they are unjust, inconsistent with important ideals and principles, and violative of persons' basic rights. In what follows, I will seek very briefly to indicate why this is not so and how my way of understanding and justifying these programs can help to bring these matters, too, into a different and more proper focus.

The first argument that is both common and close to the core of the cluster of objections to these programs is this: if it was wrong to take race into account when blacks were the objects of racial policies of exclusion, then it is wrong to take race into account when the objects of the policies differ only in their race. Simple considerations of intellectual consistency—of what it means to have had a good reason for condemning those social policies and practices—require that what was a good reason then be a good reason now.

The right way to answer this objection is, I think, to agree that the practices of racial exclusion that were an integral part of the fabric of our culture, and which still are, to some degree, were and are pernicious. Yet, one can grant this and also believe that the kinds of racial preferences and quotas that are a part of contemporary preferential treatment programs are commendable and right. There is no inconsistency involved in holding both views. The reason why depends upon a further analysis of the social realities. A fundamental feature of programs that discriminated against blacks was that these programs were a part of a larger social universe in which the network of social institutions concentrated power, authority, and goods in the hands of white individuals. This same social universe contained a complex ideology that buttressed this network of institutions and at the same time received support from it. Practices that prevented or limited the access of blacks to the desirable social institutions, places, and benefits were, therefore, wrong both because of their direct consequences on the individuals most affected by them, and because the system of racial superiority that was constituted by these institutions and practices was an immoral one, in that it severely and unjustifiably restricted the capacities, autonomy, and happiness of those who were members of the less favored category.

Whatever may be wrong with today's programs of preferential treatment, even those with quotas, it should be clear that the evil, if any, is simply not the same. Blacks do not constitute the dominant social group. Nor is the prevailing ideological conception of who is a fully developed member of the moral and social community one of an individual who is black rather than white. Programs that give a preference to blacks do not add to an already comparatively over-abundant supply of resources and opportunities at the disposal of members of the dominant racial group in the way in which exclusionary practices of the past added to the already overabundant supply of resources and opportunities at the disposal of whites. Thus, if preferential treatment programs are to be condemned or abandoned, it cannot be either because they seek to perpetuate an unjust society in which the desirable options for living are husbanded by and for those who already have the most, or because they realize and maintain a morally corrupt ideal of distinct grades of political, social, and moral superiority and inferiority—in this case grades or classes of superiority and inferiority tied to and determined by one's race.

A related objection that fares no better, I believe, has to do with the identification of what exactly was wrong, say, with the system of racial discrimination in the South, or with what is wrong with any system of racial discrimination. One very common way to think about the wrongness of racial discrimination is to see the essential wrongness as consisting in the use of an irrelevant characteristic, namely race, to allocate social benefits and burdens of various sorts, for, given this irrelevance, individuals end up being treated in an arbitrary manner. On this view, the chief defect of the system of racial segregation and discrimination that we had and still have is to be located in its systemic capriciousness. Hence, on this view, what is wrong and unjust about any practice or act of taking any individual's race into account is the irrational and arbitrary character of the interest in and concern with race.

I am far less certain that that is the central flaw at all—especially with our own historical system of racial segregation and discrimination. Consider, for instance, the most hideous of the practices, human slavery. The primary thing that was wrong, I think, with that institution was not that the particular individuals who were assigned the place of slaves were assigned there arbitrarily by virtue of an irrelevant characteristic, i.e., their race. Rather, the fundamental thing that was and is wrong with slavery is the practice itself—the fact that some human beings were able to own other human beings—and all that goes with the acceptance of that practice and that conception of permissible interpersonal relationships. A comparable criticism can be made of many of the other discrete practices and institutions that comprised the system of racial discrimination even after human slavery was abolished.

The fundamental wrongness in taking race into account in this way has to do, perhaps, with arbitrariness, but it is the special arbitrariness attendant upon using race in the constitution and maintenance of any system of oppression so as to make that system a system of racial oppression. The irrationality, arbitrariness, and deep injustice of taking race into account cannot, I think, be isolated or severed from the place of a racial criterion in the very constitution of that system which becomes both a system of *oppression* and a system of *racial* oppression in and through the regular systematic use of that criterion. Whatever may be said about the appropriateness of regarding race as relevant in other contexts, the arbitrariness of taking race into account has a special and distinctive bite of injustice when race becomes the basis for fixing persons' unequal positions, opportunities, and status in this kind of systemically pervasive fashion. When viewed in the light of existing social realities and in the light of this conception of the wrongness of a racially oppressive system, the central consideration is that contemporary programs of preferential treatment, even when viewed as a system of programs, cannot plausibly be construed in either their design or effects as consigning whites to the kind of oppressed status systematically bestowed upon blacks by the dominant social institutions.

A third very common objection is that, when used in programs of preferential treatment, race is too broad a category for programs designed to promote, in a legitimate way in our present society, conditions of fair equality of opportunity and full equality with respect to political and social status. The objection presupposes that whatever the appropriate or relevant characteristic, it is not race.

Instead, almost always it is taken to be disadvantaged socio-economic status.

This objection, too, helps to bring into focus the mistaken conception of the social realities upon which a number of the central objections to preferential treatment programs depend. While socio-economic status unquestionably affects in deep and pervasive ways the kinds of lives persons can and will be able to fashion and live, it is, I think, only a kind of implausible, vulgar Marxism, or socio-economic reductionism of some other type, that ultimately underlies the view that, in our society, socio-economic status is the sole, or even the primary, locus of systemic oppression. Given my analysis of the social realities, blackness is as much a primary locus of oppression as is socio-economic status. And if so, it is implausible to insist, as this objection does, that socio-economic status is central while race is not. Race is just the appropriate characteristic to make directly relevant if the aim is to alter the existing system of racial oppression and inequality, or otherwise to mitigate its effects. Socio-economic status is an indirect, imperfect, unduly narrow and overly broad category with which to deal with the phenomena of *racial* oppression and disadvantage, in precisely the same way in which race is an indirect, imperfect, unduly narrow and overly broad category to take on the phenomena of *socio-economic* oppression and disadvantage.

The final objection I wish to introduce concerns the claim that these programs are wrong because they take race into account rather than taking into account the only thing that does and should matter: an individual's qualifications. And qualifications, it is further claimed, have nothing whatsoever to do with race. Here, I can mention only very briefly some of the key issues that seem to me to be at stake in understanding and assessing such an objection.

First, it is important to establish what the argument is for making selections solely on the basis of who is the most qualified among the applicants, candidates, and the like. One such argument for the exclusive relevance of qualifications—although it is seldom stated explicitly—is that the most qualified persons should always be selected for a place or position because the tasks or activities connected with that place or position will then be done in the most economical and efficient manner. Now, there is nothing wrong in principle with an argument based upon the good results that will be produced by a social practice of selection based solely upon the qualifications of the applicant. But there is a serious problem that many opponents of preferential treatment programs must confront. The nature and magnitude of their problem is apparent if their objection to my way of justifying these programs is that any appeal to good and bad results is the wrong *kind* of justification to offer. For if that is the basis of their objection, then it is simply inconsistent for them to rest their case for an exclusive preoccupation with qualifications upon a wholly analogous appeal to the good results alleged to follow upon such a practice. In any event, what is central is that this reason for attending only to qualifications fails to shift inquiry to that different kind of analysis having to do with justice that was originally claimed to be decisive.

Second, given the theses offered earlier concerning how the increased presence of blacks in the positions of the major social institutions changes the workings of those institutions, it is anything but obvious why a person's blackness cannot or should not appropriately be taken into account as one of the characteristics which, in any number of contexts, genuinely should count as an aspect of one's qualifications for many positions or places at this time in our social life. And preferential treatment programs can, therefore, often be plausibly construed as making just the judgment that a person's blackness is indeed one of the relevant characteristics helping to establish his or her overall qualifications.

Third, even if this way of looking at qualifications is rejected, a further question must still be addressed with respect to any or all of the characteristics of the more familiar sort that are thought to be the ones that legitimately establish who is the most qualified for a position: is the person who possesses these characteristics, and who is, hence, the most qualified, to be selected because that is what he or she deserves, or for some other reason? If persons do truly deserve to be selected by virtue of the possession of the characteristics that make them the most qualified, then to fail to select them is to treat them unjustly. But I am skeptical that a connection of the right sort can be established between being the most qualified in this sense and deserving to be selected. The confusion that so often arises in thinking about this issue comes about, I think, because of a failure to distinguish two very different ways in which the linkage between qualifications and desert might be thought to be a sound one.

The first way is this. If there is a system of selection in place with rules and criteria that specify how to determine who is the most qualified and therefore is to be selected, then there is, of course, a sense in which the most qualified, as defined by those criteria, do deserve to be selected by virtue of their relationship to those rules and criteria. But this sense of desert is a surface one, and any resulting desert claim is very weak because it derives its force and significance wholly from the existing criteria and rules for selection. In this same sense, once preferential treatment programs are established and in place, as many now are, these new programs can also be understood to establish alternative grounds and criteria for selection; as such, they stand on the same footing as more conventional systems of qualification and selection. In the identical manner, therefore, these new programs also give rise to surface claims of desert, founded now upon the respect in which those who best satisfy those criteria have a claim that they deserve to be selected because that is what the rules of these programs provide should happen.

What this suggests, I believe, is that the real and difficult question about the possible linkage between qualifications and desert has to be sought elsewhere, for that question has to do with whether those who possess certain characteristics deserve, in virtue of their possession of those characteristics, to have a selection procedure in place which makes selections turn on the possession of those characteristics. If they do, then those who possess those characteristics do deserve in a deep, nonsurface way to be selected because of their qualifications. But now the problem is that being the best at something, or being the most able in respect to some task or role, does not, by itself at least, seem readily convertible into a claim about what such persons thereby genuinely deserve in virtue of things such as these being true of them. Perhaps a theory of desert of the right sort can be developed and adequately defended to show how and why those who are most able deserve (in a deep sense) selection criteria that will make them deserving of selection (in a surface sense); however, given the difficulty of connecting in any uniform way the mere possession of abilities with things that the possessor can claim any credit or responsibility for, and given the alternative plausibility of claims of desert founded upon attributes such as effort or need, the intellectual task at hand is a formidable one, and one that opponents of preferential treatment programs have not yet, I think, succeeded in coming to terms with in a convincing fashion.

Nonetheless, as was suggested earlier, there may be good reasons of other sorts for being interested in persons' qualifications—reasons which have to do, for example, with how well a predefined job or role will be performed and with the relative importance of having it done as well as possible. These reasons point directly to the good that will be promoted by selecting the most able. Still, a concern for having some predetermined job or role performed *only* by the person who will be *the best* at performing it is something that itself must be defended, given the good that is otherwise done by programs of preferential treatment (construed, as they must be within this objection, as programs which make race a relevant, but non-qualification-related criterion for selection). And the plausibility of that exclusive concern with performance will vary greatly with the position and its context. Sometimes this concern will be of decisive, or virtually decisive, importance; when it legitimately is, preferential treatment of the sort I have been defending should play a very minor or even nonexistent role in the selections to be made. But in many contexts, and most of them are the ones in which preferential treatment programs operate, no such exclusive concern seems defensible. In the case of admission to college or professional school, of selection to a faculty, or of selection for training or employment, the good that is secured in selecting the most qualified person, in this restricted sense, is at most only one of the goods to be realized and balanced against those other, quite substantial ones whose realization depends upon the implementation of such programs. In sum, therefore, preferential treatment programs are presumptively justifiable insofar as they work to dismantle the system of racial oppression that is still in place, although it should not be; and their justifiability is rendered more secure once it can be seen, as I think it should be, that they are not unjust either in themselves or as constitutive elements of any larger system of racial oppression.

6

Affirmative Action and the Rights Rhetoric Trap

Christopher Edley, Jr.

WHY CAN'T WE REACH CONSENSUS on affirmative action?[1] The question is a bit daunting, and discussions about affirmative action always make me feel stuck. We have a crisis in persuasion, to which almost everyone responds by attempting to increase the volume or the complexity of their arguments. Few people seem to change their minds, however.[2] Rather than take the question as an invitation to reargue the merits of affirmative action, therefore, I want to explore whether there is something in the nature of the arguments being made on all sides that *causes* us to be stuck. My conclusion is that we will remain stuck until we adopt a different strategy of persuasion, a strategy that does not depend so completely on express claims of moral and legal rights.

The Dispute Is Not "Merely" About Means

At a very simple level, the explanation of robust disagreement over affirmative action is easy: in the wake of the civil rights enlightenment of the '60s, there is broad consensus on the aspirational ideal, but disagreement over means. That ideal, stated succinctly, is that racial difference ought not mean disadvantage.[3] This is the essential racial-justice goal, with affirmative action simply one means of attaining that goal. This disagreement over "mere" means can be regarded as a technical detail about which reasonable people, like-minded as to goals *ex hypothesi*, can reach accommodation if only they will communicate effectively about their differing instrumental calculations.

There are three important errors in this rosy formulation. The first and most limited one is that the supposed empirical dispute about

56

affirmative action arises to some extent because of the differing vantage points of the empiricists: black and white observers will see things differently because their perceived worlds are different. A black may sense an oppressive climate of discrimination and "otherness" in a given setting, while the white will dismiss such claims as overreactions and hypersensitivity.

The second critique is also simple. The supposed empirical dispute about the instrumental correctness of affirmative action is thought to be resolvable because it is an argument about objective "facts" rather than about subjective "values." But facts and values are not neatly separable. My familiar claim here is that there is a value dispute lurking in the empirical dispute—indeed, dominating it. The crux of the conflict has less to do with different estimates of how long it will take for race-blind hiring to produce equitable minority representation in a work force, and more to do with how urgently one wants to make progress, including especially one's willingness to pay the required price for that progress.[4]

Third, and most important, racial justice is only one of several ideals which describe the kind of community we want. The defining of appropriate forms and limits to affirmative action is not merely a problem of instrumental calculations to pursue a stated goal. Those calculations require subjective, controversial choices, and *the* goal is, in fact, several sometimes inconsistent goals, requiring (inter- and intra-personal) subjective, conflictual accommodations. (By "subjective" I mean significantly subject to dispute based on our individual differences in preferences, values, and perceptions.)

Thus, conflict over affirmative action is not simply an empirical dispute about instrumental means to achieve some well-understood and broadly accepted end. This could not be the case, because a helpful distinction between means and ends is impossible in such a value-laden and dispute-ridden field. Moreover, the conflict is an inescapably moral one that has been predominantly couched in terms of legal and moral *rights,* as though such rights are norms supplying objective tests for what would otherwise be merely willful, political preferences of this or that legislator or judge.

Rights-Based Arguments Are Deeply Problematic

But arguing about rights hardly offers a means of resolving the dispute, for claims of rights, especially in this context, are notoriously controversial and anything but objective. And so, with the appeal to "rights," much of the hoped for objective basis for agreement is undermined. The knock-'em-dead, objectively compelling, rights-based argument to end the conflict hasn't been found because it can't exist.[5]

We have seen an explosion of rights rhetoric in recent years, as political and legal advocates in our culture have become adept at stating positions and demands in the rhetoric of rights. Not only has the rights-privilege distinction been abandoned in constitutional doctrine and eroded in political discourse, the rights-"stake" distinction is fast becoming a dead letter. This is perhaps most clear in the evolution of standing doctrine, where even Burger Court retrenchment has left undisturbed the basic expansion of standing to obviate the need for plaintiff to claim an effect on a legally protected right—there need only be a genuine stake in the outcome.[6] In political discourse, the point is clearer still as advocates increasingly seem to frame support for an interest group's stake in a controversy in terms of rights. For example, farmers have an asserted right to price supports; present and even prospective homeowners have a right to the mortgage interest deduction on their federal tax returns; commercial and recreational interests have asserted rights to exploit fish, wildlife, and other natural resources without colorable legal claims to do so.[7]

The accelerating use of rights rhetoric in politico-legal discourse—the devaluing of rights currency—underscores important features of the dilemmas inherent in rights-based theories. First, most rights are, by their nature, alienating because they erect barriers around the individual or group,[8] ostensibly to provide protection against hostile state or individual acts. But such barriers separate the individual or group from the community, for better or worse. This separation has several dimensions. A right with antimajoritarian force protects the minority from democratic consensus by placing the group outside the reach of that consensus, and perhaps outside the community's processes of consensus-formation or reform. In other words, to the extent that a right trumps the community's democratic processes, those processes and the sense of community they create are impaired. We usually consider this desirable on net, but it has its costs.

Relatedly, by asserting the right to stand apart from the majority or consensus view, the holder of an antimajoritarian right is boycotting the continuing, dialectical process of community formation and self-definition of which democratic processes are a part. Thus, while the familiar and positive picture of rights is that they provide an escape valve for those occasions when democratic processes go awry, the flip side of the coin is that they distort structures of inclusion, participation, and accountability. Members of a community are the same in that each enjoys a set of rights, but any individual asserting a right becomes different and alien by insisting on exemption from some collective purpose or judgment.

Resorting to Analyses of Fault and Causation Presents Another Face of the Same Problem

If we are properly skeptical about the power of rights-based analyses to dissolve value-laden conflict such as that surrounding affirmative action, what other modes of analysis are available? The common law framework for liability which stresses individual fault and causation is closely related to, if not derived from, rights-based theories. The common law generally presumes that everyone has a "right" not to be a "victim" of private or state action unless one has been at "fault." An extreme version of this can be found in the writing of Charles Fried, whose essential position is that in order to protect liberty we must impose liability only in cases in which the defendant intended the act, because the voluntariness implicit in intention provides the moral justification for invading the personal sphere.[9] For Fried, liability must proceed from moral choice, and moral choice requires intention, not merely volition. While there are of course exceptions within the common law, those exceptions clearly have the burden of justification.[10]

This framework has precisely the same difficulties as rights rhetoric. First, as to subjectivity, it is clear that in negligence, for example, determining the relevant standard of care and the permissible length of causal chains is a judgment which can in no useful way be termed objective. No rigid application of preformed neutral rules will provide easy answers to interesting cases. Second, as to alienation versus community, the emphasis on fault and causation as prerequisites for loss-shifting is in form a recognition that each of us has a right not to have costs imposed on us if we had nothing to do with the injury. But such a prerequisite for personal responsibility is at odds with the alternative personal duty to help discharge responsibilities owed by the community, where obligations are defined by community aspirations rather than by personal autonomy. Thus, the required proof of personal fault and causation simultaneously protects the defendant from state-enforced loss-shifting and shields him from responsibility for the problem of the needy plaintiff-citizen. As with antimajoritarian rights claims, a barrier is created between the individual and the community.

There is another connection between the rights strategy and the fault-causation strategy, but this time on the victim side. To the extent that rights are conceived as protective devices *for* individuals *against* others and the community (acting through the state), it has been argued that rights belong to individuals rather than to groups. "Groups do not have rights," is a common response to minority demands for affirmative action or other remedies. The individualist conception of rights thus serves to divide and alienate members of the minority group one from another. An alternative, group-based conception of rights would have the opposite effect, emphasizing the shared social experience of the group. Thus, in the affirmative action context, rather than searching for evidence that individual would-be beneficiaries of affirmative action were themselves subjected to discrimination (by this employer) or disadvantage (through illegal acts of nondefendants), one might focus instead on the social condition and opportunities of the group. John Ely has used the phrase "virtual representation" in another context to assess the reasonableness of indirect political representation and participation as legitimate democratic devices;[11] in the racial context the phrase might be "virtual victimization."

A digression seems in order. To a great extent various social welfare interventions of governments can be seen as struggles to throw off the yoke of rights and personal fault analysis in preference for collective choice and community self-realization. Odd testimony for this proposition is the extreme libertarian objection to such government actions; the communal goal of, say, redistribution is an infringement of (an autonomous, alienated conception of) liberty. Suffice it to say that arguments for redistribution from "haves" to "have nots" are more easily made if the "haves" do not have legitimated claims of faultless innocence and a consequent "right" to be *left alone.* In other words, however much redistributive measures, including racial justice, may be advanced by the rhetoric of rights (a voting right, a fair housing right) or fault/causation (disadvantage, reparations), these rhetorical strategies at the same time create costs and limits to full realization of the redistributive goal—costs and limits which have political, doctrinal, and perhaps moral significance.

Thus, the claim that justice and morality demand that the black worker recently hired in a program to reverse decades of black exclusion should be protected from layoff, to the detriment of more senior white workers, has some force if and when it evokes a certain aspiration for society. In that aspiration, lingering effects of past discrimination are finally eliminated, and blacks are free to achieve without the myriad handicaps of historical deprivations and contemporary prejudgments.[12] But this moral vision is not fruitfully expressed in terms of rights, because of our ready ability to identify opposed rights of the black and white workers, and our inability to order convincingly those competing claims.[13] The reciprocal check-mating is inescapable, hence, a draw. But neither side will abandon the game; nor could they.

The Ontology of Victims

Perhaps the favorite argument these days is that many discrimination remedies, especially quotas, create a new class of victims, victimized because they happen to be white. It's a clever attack, since Americans usually (not always) love victims, and our legal system tries to favor them with relief. Courts, however, consistently reject such sweeping logic. Chief Justice Burger, never accused of extremism in these matters, has written that "a 'sharing the burden' by innocent parties" is permissible if the remedy is carefully tailored.[14] That view is sensible, because virtually every form of collective action entails some elements of sacrifice from many. Usually the sacrifice is by the less politically powerful, but sometimes a principle or a law forces the majority to sacrifice in aid of the minority.

Public policy decisions almost always hurt some and help others. When the new highway is built over there instead of over here, a few people get financial compensation for condemnation of their property as required by the Fifth Amendment to the Constitution. But people injured by the traffic, the noise, or the fact that another neighborhood gets the commercial benefits just have to bear the loss. Have your taxes been raised to finance some government program you oppose or that doesn't help you except in the most remote sense (a new strategic bomber, welfare benefits, dairy price supports)? Too bad. When you pay insurance premiums but never have occasion to file a claim, tough luck. It's all part of the overhead of living in a community and engaging in collective activity.

In this context of public policy choices that burden certain individuals or groups, the moral content of "victim" is quite different from the criminal model that comes most readily to mind, and different even from the tort context, dominated as tort is by the concepts of fault, duty, and privilege.

We can imagine several ways of analyzing the assignment of social burdens. The first approach, *culpable causation,* emphasizes that the state should let a loss lie where it falls, unless there is a specific defendant at fault in the sense of having caused the injury. In the affirmative action area, the victim of reverse discrimination will argue that he is not at fault. He hasn't done anything, so why impose costs on him?[15] If background events far beyond this white person's control, including past events, have disadvantaged the black applicant, the state should let the consequential losses lie. The black should be required to find a culpable, discriminating defendant to bear the costs of any remedy. But the disadvantaged black might well ask why this should be so. In what sense is the disadvantaged, faultless white the victim of black aspirations, rather than simply finding himself on the expensive side of a proposition about redistribution, made necessary by the fact that both the disadvantaged black and the innocent white find themselves dealing with a problem bigger than all of us?

A second approach might be labeled one of *collective correction*. In it we might instead emphasize some collective responsibility to address dangers and injuries. This may be a collective expression that we're all in this together and costs of corrective action are to be broadly distributed rather than heaped on the unlucky (innocent). It's an acceptance of *responsibility for healing* the damage. There is also the possibility of collective acceptance of responsibility for the injury itself, in the sense of *blame*. But the two are distinguishable. Accepting responsibility for healing need not entail accepting blame and the associated moral judgment; conversely, accepting blame would definitely suggest some moral obligation to help heal—a collective version of the culpable causation framework, as in arguments for reparations.[16]

Still a third approach—some might view it as a pragmatic advance on the first two—is *interest accommodation*. Rather than the winner-take-all vision of moral calculation, rights-based litigation, or raw majority power, the interest-accommodation vision would emphasize the search for common ground, community, and compromise. Perhaps black workers and white workers can each give a little, rather than insisting that one side has all the entitlements and the other side must bear all the costs. For example, in the situation where layoffs of last-hired workers threaten to obliterate gains from affirmative action, some commentators have suggested job-sharing or wage reduction schemes. This is a familiar model of pluralist politics, rather than a model of moral calculus. As such, its results seem contingent, indeterminate, and subjective. It is not a conventional *legal* approach, because it lacks the trappings of Rule of Law "objectivity." This subjective, nonlegal character is troubling to us. Interest accommodation is attractive, however, because it offers an honest characterization of the judgments and tasks implicit in the culpable causation and collective correction frameworks. This honesty has its advantages, but also its costs—including a cost in terms of legitimacy, if, for example, the parties to the dispute have it in their minds that reified, determinable "rights" are at stake. Accommodation does not square with the objective demands of justice, yet in truth the search for objectivity, as in culpable causation, offers only illusory certainty.

The Collectivist Break with Private Law Categories

If affirmative action and remedies for racial injustice are approached with an emphasis on collective arguments distinct from familiar patterns in private law, new possibilities might arise. Before the *Stotts* decision by the Supreme Court, federal Courts of Appeals in the First and Sixth Circuits had ruled that, in a situation of threatened layoffs, seniority rules of last-hired, first-fired could be modified at the expense of white workers in order to preserve some of the recent minority employment gains brought about by court-approved affirmative action plans.[17] There are suggestions in those opinions that white workers benefited from the employer's earlier discrimination, and suggestions as well that there are social costs to be borne in the struggle to end racial injustice, and the white workers are bystanders who have to help pay those costs. There is, of course, timidity in these assertions. But the attractiveness of embracing a framework unlike the personal rights/culpable causation approach of private law is noteworthy, even though it was ultimately rejected by the Supreme Court in *Stotts*. I believe the attractiveness is rooted in a conception of antidiscrimination policy as a problem of understanding and structuring social categories, not private rights, and therefore a matter more appropriate for "collectivist" modes of analysis. Except for a few academics, it is customary to ignore the theoretical conceptions of property, contract, and tort as matters of social category and culture. Instead, these are too often analyzed as legal attributes or claims tied to the individual, rather than matters contingent on social organization or policy. Seeing antidiscrimination as part of a category of discourse different from private law enables the court to reach for a different calculus of remedies.

It will be asked whether the collectivist kinds of judgments made overt by my paradigms of collective correction and interest accommodation are "appropriate" for judges, as opposed to legislatures or administrative agencies established by legislatures. The conventional view is that this concern has to do with judicial role as defined by feasibility or institutional competence. The basic view about institutional competence (usually unsupported by genuine comparative empirical work) is boot-strapped into arguments stated in the form of separation of powers "principles" of various sorts. But the core instinct is that judges aren't as good at making the kinds of judgments implied in the more collectivist schemes. I think, however, the anxiety about the kind of doctrinal restructuring I have sketched has more to do with modes of permissible reasoning than with demonstrated institutional competence. The rhetoric of causation, rights, and duties is thought of as judge-like; the rhetoric of pluralist accommodation is not consistent with objectivity and the Rule of Law and is therefore the province of the political branches. So the allocation of dispute resolution and rule formulation to courts and legislatures respectively is less dependent on the nature of the problem or the feasibility of resolving it with judges or legislators and more a matter of the mode of analysis we perceive to be entailed. Yet, if one sees that these modes of analysis (politics, rule-of-law, fairness, and instrumental efficiency) are inextricably linked—even impossible to describe in isolated purity—then one also can see that the sharp assignment of each mode of analysis to its institutional pigeonhole is the wrong way to think about the problem.

Forms of Argument about Quotas

So, we should put aside the wishful thought that the disagreement over affirmative action is based on mere differences in empirical judgments about the instrumental need for racial preferences. And we should put aside the naive view that a proper understanding of "rights" as now captured in legal doctrine (or plausibly accommodated by it) will solve the problem. This is no modest task, politically or intellectually, for it requires that we rethink the great many familiar notions to which I have already referred, such as the pretense of shared definitions of racial justice, or reliance on fault-based liability, and try to come up with an alternative way of reasoning and persuading. To what extent do our current ways of debating affirmative action recapitulate the problematic and unresolvable divisiveness inherent in these concepts I would have us put aside?

Consider these general lines of argument—arguments that find their way into both legal analysis and political discourse:

- Proponents of affirmative action are concerned with results and substance; opponents with opportunity and procedure.
- Proponents stress the public role of the state and the social importance of group identity and rights; opponents stress autonomous, private spheres of action, and individual identity and rights.
- As a special case of the preceding, proponents emphasize welfare and reparations; opponents emphasize fault and injury.

With the underlying dispute drawn along these lines, it is no wonder that consensus is elusive. How can the dispute be resolved if the contenders understand the problem as one of choice between equally incoherent alternatives? *The disagreement must be understood in different terms.* To explore why this is so, let us consider the three broad forms of rhetoric *seriatum.*

Opportunity versus Results; Procedure versus Substance

Opponents of quotas are said to be committed to equal opportunity, while proponents are concerned with equal results. This disagreement has the trappings of a dispute between those who want to make sure that the foot race is "fair," and those who pay attention to the winners and losers. One group has an eye, it seems, on the process rather than the outcome: they want to make sure that the contest is not fixed, and that a neutral, on its face, criterion, "fleetness," controls the result.[18] The alternative is to put aside the difficult (I would say impossible) search for unbiased process and neutral rules, and examine instead the distribution of winners and losers. Having embraced the unavoidable problem of subjective choice, you may decide it's the wrong game.

It is now fairly common for law teachers to demonstrate to students that they should be especially wary of doctrinal arguments based on supposed neat distinctions between substance and procedure. In most circumstances, something that seemed procedural can be recast as substantive, and vice versa. At the very least, any problem that at first glance appears to be quite largely the one can, on close inspection, be seen to contain important elements of the other. Thus, the seemingly "procedural" notion of equal opportunity has "substantive" content of enormous significance: opportunities available to different individuals or groups must be compared, and a value-laden decision must be made as to what constitutes "equality." This entails deciding which differences to ignore, and which to count. Grounding this dispute on the opportunity-results distinction has the same conceptual and practical problems as the procedure-substance distinction itself: both sets of distinctions are problematic whenever things get interesting.

A truer explanation of the dispute lies in a conflict about whether the measure of "equal" opportunity ought to reflect the meaningful disadvantages worked by the lingering poisons of slavery.

A case in point is the large body of employment discrimination law that has grown up around Title VII of the 1964 Civil Rights Act, as interpreted by the Supreme Court in the leading case of *Griggs* v. *Duke Power Co.*[19] For our purposes, the key insight in that large body of case law is that employment tests and qualifications that are

statistically shown to have a racially disparate impact must be pre-
sumed to constitute proof of employment discrimination *even though
they are facially neutral*. The employer must then rebut the presumption of discrimination with proof that the test or qualification is job-
related.[20] In this genre of employment discrimination suit, therefore,
it is not sufficient for a defendant to say or even prove "I am not a
racist," where "racist" is meant, in the narrow sense, a racial suprem-
acist. Title VII and *Griggs* represent a decision that facially neutral
criteria that have a disparate impact because of lingering effects of
past societal discrimination, even without proof of present intentional
racism, will be deemed discriminatory. As such, this aspect of antidiscrimination law collapses the distinction between process (the facially
neutral employment criterion) and substance (the racially disparate
effect). It is, therefore, controversial among those who oppose effects
tests by denying the conceptual relatedness of procedure and substance.

Private versus Public; Individual versus Group

Another characterization of the affirmative action dispute is that
opponents believe a sphere of private autonomy must be preserved
against encroachments by the state, that private interests and values
should be subordinated to public will only under extraordinary
circumstances. Proponents of quotas, on the other hand, are ready to
displace the primacy of individual autonomy with emphases on
group identity and government coercion.

This argument, distinguishing public and private, is coherent only
in the extreme form of libertarianism, if then. Once we admit the
possibility of collective action to pursue social welfare goals, we
cannot help but blur the attempted definitions of individual and
community spheres.[21] When the state acts to advance or protect the
interests of individual X, but must do so at the expense of individual
Y, the latter may perceive the action as an incursion on his or her
autonomy. But X's perspective is quite different. Whose view is
correct? Neither. The public-private distinction is of little use in
answering the question; the issue is one of power and fairness, and it
cannot be addressed with absolute rules such as radical individual
autonomy. We gave that up long ago when we came into the cave
together to escape saber-toothed tigers and the cold.

On the other hand, we did not surrender *everything* to the state.
The opposite extreme view, that the public sphere absorbs the private, is no more tenable than radical individual autonomy. If we must
choose to side with X or Y, and we sensibly refuse to embrace extreme

views of the citizen's life, then we must argue about the messy, bloody dispute at hand. The context is almost everything.

Thus, the civil rights dispute cannot profitably or honestly be lifted to the plane of dispute about individual and state, despite recurrence of that tension in countless other areas of the law—or perhaps *because* of that recurring and undisolvable antinomy. The typical opponents of aggressive affirmative action, including goals, are concerned not with the possibility or appropriateness of government intervention in some general, theoretical case: they don't mind tort, bankruptcy proceedings, highway construction, or reasonable environmental protection. Their problem is with the moral and social case for intervention *on behalf of minorities*. The problem is not individual versus state. It's black versus white.

Fault versus Welfare; Injury versus Reparations

In a related rhetorical mode, quota opponents want to base legal and social policy on notions of individual rights and wrongs, while proponents are willing to press claims based on supposed group interests. Thus the black person benefits from the quota by virtue of being black, rather than by virtue of some individualized interest. Likewise, the white worker or job applicant who is disadvantaged by an affirmative action program, perhaps only remotely, has been penalized without the familiar demonstrations of personalized fault and proximate causation which inform so much of our legal order.[22]

Here, too, it is easier to characterize the disagreement than to make sense of it, because line-drawing problems abound and implicate deeper disagreements. As to the injury-fault inquiry, it is not an overreaching of moral analysis to argue that descendants of slaves are currently burdened by a legacy of disproportionate poverty, lingering prejudice, and all their incidents; that whatever contributory responsibility an individual black person may have for his or her own condition, a very substantial residuum is rooted in the outrages of enslavement, Jim Crow, and all the rest. One's life chances are still strongly affected by one's skin color. Surely *that* is injury enough. The culpable fault of the individual white person confronted with affirmative action is in some respects the flip side of the coin. Is theirs an entitlement to the undisturbed enjoyment of the fruits of past injustice, or can that enjoyment be taxed ever so slightly to destroy the legacy?

This decision is, as I have suggested, not solely a matter of inquiry into the rights of the individual. It involves a consideration of the individual's responsibilities as a member of a community, as a coinhabitant of the cave. The disagreement is both empirical and value-based. Does the significance of the slavery residuum rise to a level deserving political and legal attention? Does the white "victim" possess a precious autonomy that should immunize him or her from the demands of a community aspiration, in this case racial? The questions are moral choices, not logic chopping about injury, fault, or causation.

Rhetorical Styles—Summation

It appears that these axes of debate track the three conceptual puzzles I explored earlier. The rhetorical dispute of opportunity versus results *is* the unworkable contrast between instrumental means and racial justice ends. The conflict between the regime of private autonomy plus fault-based liability versus the regime of communalism plus welfare *is* the stalemate of rights-talk.

Again, imagine instead an emphasis on *collective historical correction* for wrongs suffered by blacks—wrongs reflected in and implemented by the state, not just by certain old or dead individuals. This alternative conception of fairness proceeds from a conviction that there is a collective responsibility to repair injuries inflicted *by the collective*, quite apart from pinning blame on particular people; in other words, society has a duty to provide a remedy. For these purposes, privity—connectedness substantial enough to trigger liability—flows from community.

Several years ago in his detailed analysis of reparations, Professor Borris Bittker of Yale Law School suggested that the appropriate solution to these problems is a public fund to compensate victims.[23] But political society is democratically controlled not by victims, but by perpetrators and beneficiaries, including descendants of perpetrators. The majority declines to establish Bittker's public fund, yet recognizes, by statute, legal causes of action for discrimination. Courts have no one before them to bear the burden of remedy except the individual defendants and associated third parties such as white workers. Now what? Within the framework of collective historical correction it is natural to argue that such defendants and their associates have a social-contract obligation to bear some of the costs.

Finally, I note that as a purely descriptive matter society as a whole is not approaching affirmative action and quotas within either the culpable causation or collective correction frameworks. There is no collective moral judgment being made, only a series of private ones. (Could it be otherwise?) The practical process is one of *rights accommodation*, which graciously recognizes many interests—the black victims, the whites enjoying the status quo, the blacks and whites who hope to enjoy the status quo—and seeks to strike compromises which will be "fair" because they are "political." That is, the remedy will not be too offensive to any particular group, assuming they are reasonable, and the range of achievable remedies will in fact change over time as attitudes of the various groups evolve to reflect changing norms. Thus, school desegregation remedies, which in 1955 might have seemed far too intrusive to be politically supportable, were by 1975 entered into voluntarily. (And by 1985 the Justice Department was trying, with little success, to reopen and dismantle those remedies.[24])

Attempting Persuasion without Rights Rhetoric: Rhetorical Persuasion versus Experiential Conversion

I am not arguing that rights are unimportant. Even in their bloodless positivist form, they are an undeniable component of justice and an indispensable tool of advocacy.[25] I have, instead, tried to show how and why rights rhetoric is necessarily an unreliable strategy of persuasion, specifically in the affirmative action debate, and especially now. But what alternative or additional strategies are available?

My point of departure is a loose analogy to the religious concept of conversion. When and how does a person decide to embrace a religion like fundamentalist Christianity, or a cause like nuclear disarmament? I once asked a cardinal of the Catholic Church why he was so confident that racially motivated violence and intolerance could be overcome in certain communities. He said, "Because I believe in the possibility of conversion." When I asked why he is so confident in that belief, he replied, "Because Christ has risen." Charitably, he allowed me to press him for an answer that might be more reassuring to those lacking his religious faith. He continued, in essence, by voicing confidence in human nature.

What he may have had in mind is a collection of things: our search for a stable civil community; our inquiring and flexible natures; and, growing out of those two, our human ability to adapt our conceptions of community and self over time in reaction to experiences and reflection.

The kind of conversion I have in mind cannot plausibly be accounted for in terms of the power of some specific piece of evidence or rational argument that tips the balance and makes someone understand the "Word of God" or the potential horror of nuclear devastation. It will not be some particularly well-crafted argument about rights that finally persuades the apartheid supporter in South

Africa that his or her society is diseased. There may be political, economic, or military developments that coerce acceptance of a new moral order, but the actual conversion of the moral universe of that South African will come about through transformative experiences—whether those are sought out or thrust upon him. Of course those experiences may well include rational arguments, among them rights-based arguments. But the power will be from a collection of such experiences, because rights rhetoric alone will have difficulty doing anything more than legitimating what is already that person's moral reality.

The integrationist tenet about the withering away of racial injustice might be stated in a manner consistent with my theme here. Rubbing shoulders—in classrooms, workplaces, social settings—will be persuasive on the question of racial equality in a way that an argument that blacks have a *right* to be equal probably cannot be. Rather than an argument about rights, the rubbing of shoulders will provide an experience *proving* equality. This, at least, is the integrationists' hope.[26] Rights rhetoric, in a sense, codifies this tenet. It does not inspire it.

The civil rights movement in the United States is also suggestive. The moral transformation brought about in the two decades following *Brown* is one of the more remarkable accomplishments in American history. Racial discrimination passed from the status of entrenched state policy to the target of nearly universal moral condemnation. Was it rights rhetoric that converted millions of Americans, or was it experience in combination with that rhetoric? The power of those television images are enormous—the growling dogs, fire hoses, and "Bull" Connor; the dignity of Martin Luther King, Jr.; the focus of President Kennedy and other white leaders on inequalities ranging from child mortality to retirement income. My contention is that these experiences had at least as much to do with the process of conversion as did rights rhetoric, because it was the experiences and images that led people to reimagine the kind of community they wanted.[27] And that community did not include ugly racism and innocent children condemned to dispiriting disadvantage.

To be more precise, the conversion may involve reimagining both the membership of the community and the terms of social relations within the community. White tolerance of racial injustice and inequality will continue so long as blacks are "other" and social relations are strictly stratified—thus, the power of the integrationist tenet concerning social transformation. Law and litigation may in some places be only codification or reification of socially transformative shifts in the vision of community held by elites in the judiciary, the legislature, or the media. That process of reification in turn reinforces the transformative vision and propels it beyond the intellectual and social elites.

This is, of course, only one possibility. There is no fixed relationship between the legitimating and transformative functions of law. It depends on the moment, the problem, the other social forces, even the individuals on hand. My point is that whatever one's view of the *past* importance of rights rhetoric in either motivating or merely codifying social transformation, as a *theoretical and practical* matter *today*, the strategically "correct" role for rights rhetoric is up for grabs. It may well be a trap, keeping us from persuading each other into a new consensus.

Self-Conscious Strategies for Creating Community

If this notion of conversion and moral development generated through experiences is a plausible one, what are its implications for strategies of persuasion? Short of a blueprint, some possibilities suggested by postliberal writing have attempted to emphasize communal values and ends in a framework that acknowledges and seeks to avoid the alienated conception of rights, and that does not adopt the search for objectivity as its principal mission. Emphasizing the connectedness of people (rather than a notion of autonomous liberty) is consistent with my previous arguments that conversion is most likely to come about as a part of reimagining community membership and relations. A sense of connectedness, therefore, must be the goal of the experiences we must self-consciously construct in order to accomplish the transformative conversion. It is the integrationist ethic writ large and extended, but without any implication of a self-denying assimilation.[28] It is a strategy that, to extend the cardinal's thought, both depends upon and nurtures the human spirit in its qualities of curiosity, bonding, and caring.

What kinds of practices would be consistent with this, given the objective of moving toward consensus on affirmative action? To begin, there must be more shared experiences with the "other." For example, black and white members of Congress on opposite sides of the issue should spend time with each other's constituents—richly textured and intimate time, not stilted panel discussions. Black and white workers facing together the conflict between affirmative action and layoffs should try to understand each other's experiences and perspectives rather than *only* drawing the battle lines and arguing about "rights." More shared experiences might promote understanding and thereby create the possibility for different answers to the very real problems. The same kind of approach would be appropriate for people in almost every context: newspaper editorial boards, school administrators, parents of children in integrated school systems, police officers. You can't feel a sense of community with someone you don't know. The point is not that exposure will make us see that our similarities are more significant than our differences, which may not even be true in particular circumstances. Exposure will, however, give us a better understanding of our differences and promote acceptance or accommodation of them. This strategy of constructing transformative experiences may require a fancy theory of psychodynamics to seem academically plausible. Viewed more concretely, however, this is a program of concerted, grass-roots politics, not a call for multiracial encounter groups. Politics usually flows from a sense of community, but it can also be a force in creating a community.

In another vein, there has been a persistent "packaging" problem for the civil rights and antipoverty movements in the last fifteen years. The message has lost the attention of the American people, while other messages have come to the fore in mass organizing or political agendas: environment, arms production, capital formation, tax reduction, "Christian" education, "basic" education, abortion.

Crudely put, Madison Avenue skills are an important part of persuasion. Yet the civil rights movement has within its cadres of experts far more people who understand the problems of proving discriminatory intent under the Fourteenth Amendment to the Constitution than it has people who understand how to organize a media campaign to focus attention on black unemployment, voter registration, or victimization by crime. We have, thankfully, no figures who are as widely visible, scarily legitimate, and therefore morally compelling as Sheriff "Bull" Connor with his dogs, or the White Citizens' Councils. What images and experiences will generate the next stage of America's moral conversion to a better ideal of racial justice?

We could, I believe, profitably invest some time in considering precisely what kind of experiences, and for whom, will best promote conversion or persuasion. It is certainly not a conventional task for lawyers, however broadly one defines advocacy. Indeed, lawyers are probably part of the problem.

The conventional wisdom, at least among lawyers, is that a great deal of the progress in civil rights has been the result of persuasive arguments about rights. One implication of the argument in this essay, however, is that such rights-based arguments may in the past have been less the persuasive engines of enlightened consensus than merely the language to express a consensus emerging as a result of other means of persuasion and forces of social transformation. As for the future, the role of rights rhetoric is even more problematic.

Without any alternative strategy for argument, and without any other language for expressing means and goals, participants in the civil rights debate will remain stuck. For now, however, the most that seems possible is a heightened awareness of the limits of rights analysis.

It is appropriate for me to conclude on a note of pragmatism, because that hymn has been our reliable bridge from Sabbath inspiration to daily action. The victors in *Brown* v. *Board of Education* knew the Constitution did not require that change occur overnight. When the Supreme Court announced the ill-starred "with all deliberate speed" formula,[29] it was implicitly attempting to reconcile the civil rights of blacks with an interest in the Court's legitimacy, if not an interest in the very stability of society. Now the opponents of effective affirmative action—they would settle for aspirational affirmative action—argue that white rights are at stake and must not be compromised in order to advance the interests of minorities. As I have written elsewhere, this is a straightforward issue, and your position depends on which you care about more: the moral and worldly urgency of black progress, or the moral and other consequences of deviating from the newly embraced principle of a color-blind society. That principle is a convenient invention, and an oppressively ahistorical one. It is both two hundred years late and two generations early.

Of course, some people made up their minds on this question quite awhile ago and refuse to revisit the hard issues. For them, I suppose, low gear is deliberate enough speed even some thirty years after *Brown*.

Justice Harry Blackmun said it well in his opinion in the *Bakke* case: "In order to get beyond racism we must first take race into account . . . and in order to treat some persons equally we must first treat them differently. We cannot—we dare not—let the Equal Protection Clause perpetuate racial supremacy."[30] Indeed, rights rhetoric may be a trap.

Notes

1. I mean "affirmative action" to include "quotas," except where otherwise obvious from the context. There are several reasons, including my sense that most people lump together all remedial racial preferences, whether they favor or oppose them. I do, however, mean to distinguish "equal opportunity," in the narrow sense that is usually intended, namely, absence of overt discrimination against minorities. I suspect that most if not all of what follows is relevant for nonracial groups that have been systematically and pervasively discriminated against and disadvantaged by individual attitudes and state practices. I do not randomly intersperse references to women, Native Americans, or Mexican-Americans, for example, because (a) it would be

stylistically confusing, (b) I am not prepared in this essay to "prove" the similarities I suppose to exist across groups, and (c) I've thought more about the case of blacks because I am one.

2. At the conference for which this essay was initially prepared, I participated on a panel with Wm. Bradford Reynolds, assistant attorney general for civil rights in the Reagan administration; Richard Wasserstrom, a legal philosopher noted for his scholarship supporting affirmative action; and Orlando Patterson, a noted sociologist. Speaking immediately after the diametrically opposed presentations of Wasserstrom and Reynolds, I observed that locking the two of them in a room together from now until the millennium would produce insanity before it produced agreement. Remarkably, scholarship, debate, and conferences continue nevertheless.

3. I mean something distinguishable from "color-blindness," which implies that differences should be ignored or invisible. The difficulty with the color-blindness theme is that to many people this means an extreme kind of assimilationism. *Majority* group members may well find this attractive for a variety of reasons, but *minority* group members may have a strong desire to preserve aspects of groupness, such as their special cultural identity. More abstractly, the reasonable fear is that color-blindness may require that I surrender or deny those parts of my person or self which have to do with my color and subgroup affiliation. This theme of tension between self-liberating and self-disregarding impulses was sounded by W.E.B. Dubois in *The Souls of Black Folks*, 26th edition (New York: Fawcett Publications, 1961), chap. 1.

From a minority perspective, the goal is to reduce the burdens of disadvantage which now flow from different color, without giving up the felt benefits of subgroup affiliation. One must embrace unreservedly the assimilationist ideal only if one supposes some sociological law that group differences *must always* generate costs for the minority, rather than benefits alone. The costs and benefits of heterogeneity to the majority seem even more ambiguous.

See Lloyd Weinreb, "The Complete Idea of Justice," *University of Chicago Law Review* 51 (1984): 797, 800–02. (An extreme conception of "equality" can require extreme homogeneity; but "A harmonious community will subscribe to principles of liberty and equality that are congruent and give a coherent shape to its members' conceptions of self.").

4. There is also the matter of risk-aversion. People differ on what kinds of risks they will take in order to make "progress." Many disputes about remedies, such as thumb-on-the scale affirmative action, are disputes about risk-aversion and, therefore, underlying differences in commitment.

5. And yet we continue trying such arguments. Compare Robert Nozick, *Philosophical Explanations* (Cambridge: Belknap Press/Harvard University Press, 1981), pp. 3–8.

6. The three elements to the core Article III requirement of standing now appear to be: plaintiff has suffered some injury (perhaps negligible), caused by the defendant (perhaps only remotely), which the court has remedial powers to redress. Further prudential standing requirements include that plaintiff's injury be peculiar rather than shared in common with the public at large, the interests sought to be protected are within the zone of interests intended for protection under the statute, and the interests are those of the plaintiff rather than of some third party. See generally Abram Chayes, "Public Law Litigation and the Burger Court," *Harvard Law Review* 96 (1982): 4, 22–23.

7. These conflicts seem most pointed when Native American uses are given preferential status because of treaty provisions; the Anglos are offended and embittered. The comparisons with affirmative action are striking.

8. See, e.g., Roberto Unger, "The Critical Legal Studies Movement," *Harvard Law Review* 95 (1983): 561, 597.

[O]ur dominant conception of right imagines the right as a zone of discretion of the rightholder, a zone whose boundaries are more or less rigidly fixed at the time of the initial definition of the right. The right is a loaded gun that the rightholder may shoot at will in his corner of town. Outside that corner the other licensed gunmen may shoot him down. But the give-and-take of communal life and its characteristic concern for the actual effect of any decision upon the other person are incompatible with this view of right and therefore, if this is the only possible view, with any regime of rights.

See also Charles Fried, *An Anatomy of Values* (Cambridge: Harvard University Press, 1978) (going so far as to define the ordinarily communal notion of equality in alienated terms of self-protection).

9. Charles Fried, *Right and Wrong* (Cambridge: Harvard University Press, 1978), chap. 2. This is, in a sense, Fried's attempt to avoid the slippery slope and subjective, or political, character of liability rules based on causation or foreseeability. Its failings as an overarching theory are, as I argue below more generally for rights and liability schemes, that it forces a destructively alienating emphasis on the individual in opposition to the community, and it actually fails to escape subjectivity. The latter point is clear simply from asking what, in Fried's scheme, would be the method for defining or characterizing the "act" which Fried would make prerequisite to liability, thus limiting the reach of liability? And what, if not some version of reasonableness, will constitute evidence and proof of intent? I can imagine no solution to these definitional issues that avoids the problem of policy- and politics-ridden subjectivity in drawing lines.

10. Common law exceptions to fault-based liability include the doctrines of vicarious liability (blameless employer is liable for the negligence of employee); and strict liability for trespassing animals and abnormally dangerous conditions, substances, or activities (one who brings onto his land a non-natural substance "likely to do mischief" is liable for damages if the substance escapes, regardless of the absence or presence of fault). See generally *Prosser & Keeton Hornbook on Torts* (Minneapolis: West Publishing, 1984), p. 534. Even for these exceptions, however, there is a nexus or attenuated link of causation.

11. See John Hart Ely, *Democracy and Distrust* (Cambridge: Harvard University Press, 1980), chap. 4.

12. See *Firefighters Local Union No. 1784* v. *Stotts*, 104 S. Ct. 2576, 2586 (1984) (majority opinion by Justice White): "Title VII protects bona fide seniority systems, and it is inappropriate to deny an innocent employee the benefits of his seniority in order to provide a remedy in a pattern or practice suit such as this." See also *Stotts* v. *Memphis Fire Dept.*, 679 F. 2d 541 (1981) (decision below).

13. See, e.g., Ronald Dworkin, *Taking Rights Seriously*, rev. ed. (Cambridge: Harvard University Press, 1977), chap. 9 (reverse discrimination). Dworkin's effort to parse the claims of discrimination and reverse discrimination based on a difference between a right to equal treatment and a right to be treated as equals is powerful only if one is already skeptical about the reverse discrimination claim. Like all rights-based arguments for affirmative action, it has something of the quality of preaching to the converted. See also Paul Brest, "The Supreme Court, 1975 Term—Foreword: In Defense of the Antidiscrimination Principle," *Harvard Law Review* 90 (1976): 1, 42–43; John Hart Ely, "The Constitutionality of Reverse Discrimination," *University of Chicago Law Review* 41 (1974): 41.

14. *Fullilove* v. *Klutznick*, 448 U.S. at 484 (1980).

15. Compare Charles Fried's argument that liability should attach only for the intended consequences of a moral actor's choices. Fried, *Right and Wrong*.

16. See Boris Bittker, *The Case for Black Reparations* (New York: Random House, 1973).

17. *Stotts* v. *Memphis Fire Dept.*, 679 F. 2d 579 (6th Cir. 1982), rev'd., *Firefighters Local Union No. 1784* v. *Stotts*, 104 S. Ct. 2576, 2586 (1984); *NAACP* v. *Beecher*, 679 F. 2d 965, 977 (1st Cir. 1982) (Boston police and firefighters).

18. This is an extension of an analogy used by President Lyndon Johnson in his historic commencement address at Howard University in 1965. See "Johnson Pledges to Help Negroes to Full Equality," *New York Times*, June 5, 1965, 1:5 (Tom Wicker): "You do not take a man, who for years, has been hobbled by chains, liberate him, bring him to the starting line of a race, saying, 'you are free to compete with all the others,' and still justly believe you have been completely fair."

19. 401 U.S. 424 (1971). Among recent commentaries on *Griggs*, its significance and its aftermath, are Elizabeth Bartholet, "Application of the VII to Jobs in High Places," *Harvard Law Review* 95 (1982); Robert Belton, "Discrimination and Affirmative Action: An Analysis of Competing Theories of Equality and Weber," *North Carolina Law Review* 59 (1981); and Derrick Bell, *Race, Racism, and American Law*, 2nd ed. (Boston: Little, Brown, 1980), pp. 619–53.

20. This is for suits brought on a disparate impact theory. For suits based on a theory of disparate treatment, the plaintiff must show injury as a result of intentional discrimination. A major consequence of bringing the suit under the disparate treatment theory is that plaintiffs who prove personal injury may recover personal damages and, in some circumstances, compensatory seniority.

21. There is a substantial literature on the problematic public-private distinction in law. See, e.g., Gerald Frug, "The City as a Legal Concept," *Harvard Law Review* 93 (1980): 1057, 1099–1120.

22. See note 6 above.

23. See Bittker, *The Case for Black Reparations*.

24. Drew Days, III, "Turning Back the Clock: The Reagan Administration and Civil Rights," *Harvard Civil Rights—Civil Liberties Law Review* 19 (1984): 309.

25. See, e.g., Weinreb, "The Complete Idea of Justice"; Dworkin, *Taking Rights Seriously*, pp. 150–83 (justice requires rights, with equality the most fundamental among them).

26. The conditions of integration can obviously be negative, too. Prisons are a good example. See also Charles Murray, "Affirmative Racism," *New Republic*, December 31, 1984, pp. 18–23.

27. I discovered support for this contention in a recent conversation with Donald Cunningham, a doctoral candidate in Harvard's sociology department. Cunningham has conducted numerous interviews for his research on liberal white southerners in the 1954–80 period. He reports that, contrary to what he had imagined, whites did not generally abandon their support for segregation or their sympathy with theories of racial superiority as a result of being struck by lightning *or* being persuaded of the correctness of an argument concerning rights. It was, rather, a gradual accretion of experiences, combined with reflection about general moral values, especially what those individuals took to be "Christian values," which finally moved them into the relatively progressive camp.

28. See the discussion of color-blindness as a goal and the potential oppression of assimilation, note 3.

29. 349 U.S. 294, 301 (1955) (remedial decree).

30. *Regents of the University of California* v. *Bakke*, 438 U.S. 265, 407 (1978) (Blackmun, J. concurring).

7

Why Can't We Find Consensus on Affirmative Action?

Orlando Patterson

I DOUBT VERY MUCH whether it will be possible for us to achieve consensus on affirmative action, although I am not necessarily pessimistic about affirmative action itself. The very idea of consensus, however, must be brought into question. A society is not a static entity in which moral and political decisions are best achieved under conditions of general agreement. First, certain issues, by their very nature, involve a fundamental clash of interests among citizens, who always have competing claims. Second, the realization of one goal may conflict with the achievement of another. For example, our reverence for private property must at some point conflict with our desire for some minimum standard of welfare; the ideal of individual liberty presents obstacles to the realization of a crime-free society. Third, societies change, especially modern industrial societies. The pre-conditions of consensus in one period may be the basis of conflict in another. Indeed, our very commitment to a competitive industrial order implies the desirability of not having too much consensus, since this may encourage a deadening complacency.[1]

None of this denies that consensus is important. Rather, I wish to place it within a wider context in which we recognize that its apparent antithesis, conflict, might sometimes be a constructive force. The first problem is to decide just when and under what circumstances consensus is desirable. Assuming that we have decided that it is indeed desirable, the next task is to ascertain why we are not achieving it. I propose three basic reasons why we have failed to achieve consensus on affirmative action.

The first is philosophical and pertains to the fact that the debate over affirmative action is really a practical controversy over the problem of equality. Equality is a difficult concept to pin down. We often argue about it at cross-purposes, largely because we have differing views on it. And even when we agree on a given definition of equality, we vary in our degree of commitment to it as an ideal. Equality usually refers to two things: the properties of persons (or groups), and the treatment of such properties. It is the idea that persons, or rather the properties of persons that are alike, should be treated alike. This immediately presents a host of problems. People are not just different, but different in different ways: they are smart and stupid, motivated and unmotivated, rural-southern in culture or urban-northern, male or female, and so on. Some of these differences we have no problem assessing. Most of them, however, present severe definitional and measurement problems. For example, as the I.Q. controversy indicates, we have failed to define an objective criterion for deciding who is really smart and who is not. We really don't know why the same person is smart at one thing and poor at another, and often being smart at one thing does not mean one is smart at another thing. It was recently revealed, for instance, that doing well on tests for entering medical schools and on examinations during the first year bears no relationship whatsoever to one's ability as a practicing doctor.

But the problems with equality do not end here. Assuming that we know how to define and measure the different properties of persons, the additional problem still remains of deciding which of the properties so defined are to be highly valued or neglected. Not so long ago, in one of Europe's most civilized nations, having a Semitic appearance was a matter of life and death. Now it is irrelevant; at least we hope so. Among the British, the "old school tie" and a classical education, even with "gentleman's C" grades, were more desired than a demonstrated high intelligence or a diploma from a first-rate grammar school. This is changing. The point I am making, which cannot be overemphasized, is that our choice of which properties we make important is a value-laden decision. Nearly all theories of distributive justice may be reduced to a single problem—how we develop objective standards for making such choices. I have been persuaded by none of them. The theory that usually comes to mind when we think of affirmative action is what may be called the meritocratic view of justice and equality. Properties are selected on the basis of their objective structural significance for the society. The problem with this theory is that no one has ever succeeded in coming up with a meaningful measure of functional significance. Are doctors more important than priests? If not, why are doctors paid so much more than priests? Are actors less important than doctors? If yes, why does Richard Chamberlain, playing a doctor on a soap opera or in a TV drama, earn ten times more than the real, lifesaving doctors he impersonates?

The fact that the choices we make are value-laden does not mean that they are arbitrary. Rather, like all value-based decisions, they are the product of struggles over power and authority. Doctors are highly paid in this country not because what they do is so difficult that only a tiny minority of the super-bright can be trusted with this task, but because the medical profession, as my colleague Paul Starr has recently shown, is able to exercise monopolistic control over the recruitment of persons to the profession.[2] At the same time, what could be more important than giving birth to, and raising, children? Certainly it must be true that it is at least as important to create and nourish life as to cure illnesses. Yet, mothers are not paid a penny for what they do. Mothering, for all its obvious functional significance for society, is financially undervalued and socially patronized because women in their role as mothers, as in their many other vital roles, have little or no power.

The relevance of all this to the affirmative action debate should be obvious. As an ideal affirmative action demands equality for excluded groups. Vested interests, however, have defined the properties that we consider important, and our manner of assessing such properties, in ways that make it difficult for outsiders to enter or achieve success with them.

Before leaving the problem of equality I should point out that another, more profound value issue at stake is not addressed in the discussion above. Equality as an ideal may exist even in the face of the above-mentioned problems. While no one can deny that there are differences among persons, it is equally undeniable that there are similarities among them and that these similarities far outweigh the differences. We are a single species. Not even the most extreme racists and sexists deny that anymore. Equality as an ideal has its roots in the inherent unity of the human species. What it proclaims is that the many properties people share as people should be emphasized. Even more nobly, when people differ, they can always be made to become less different, or more equal, and so, be treated more equally. Many persons who advocate affirmative action hold to this view of equality as an ideal. It is possible for supporters of affirmative action not to share this ideal, but it is not possible to hold this ideal and not support affirmative action. It is a curious fact that America, historically, has held more to the ideal than to the reality of the equality concept. The authors of the Declaration of Independence declared boldly that all men are created equal, even though few, perhaps none of them, lived by this creed. And yet they were not being hypocritical. What they saw with extraordinary clarity was that, in most respects, people are equal and that it is possible to choose to emphasize those respects. They were inclined, by their own interests, to emphasize the differences, but with greater insight and sincerity they saw that there was no way in which these differences could be justified objectively. Hence they urged their countrymen, like preachers who knew existentially what sin was all about, to strive for the ideal that was objective in its clarity and its frank statement as a belief. Those who struggle for affirmative action are responding to that historic urging of the Republic's founding fathers. Those who are against it have simply dismissed the ideal as unrealizable.

Now, we either believe in an ideal or we do not. Once a significant segment of a population rejects the ideal, there is no possibility of working out a consensus. We can no more reach a consensus on an ideal than we can reach a consensus on the belief that God exists. You believe or you do not. And you can disagree peacefully, or you can struggle over it. We used to disagree peacefully about the ideal of separation of church and state; we no longer do. The struggle over affirmative action is a reflection of a broader breakdown not so much of consensus, but of the willingness of people to disagree peacefully over ideals. These are quietly frightening times.

The second reason for the failure of consensus is more social-psychological in nature. Over the past quarter of a century we have witnessed a major civil rights movement that had several important consequences. Because of the removal of Jim Crow laws, there has been a significant improvement in the legal status of blacks and a rise in their level of education. These improvements, in turn, have resulted in two contrasting trends. On the one hand, there has been a major increase in the proportion of blacks with middle-class status: approximately 40 percent of blacks are now lower-middle or middle class, compared with no more than 5 percent in 1940. On the other hand, the condition of the bottom third of the black population has worsened in both economic and social terms.

The improved status of the black middle class, as well as the growth of more liberal values, has resulted in changing attitudes and beliefs about black Americans. As Thomas Pettigrew recently observed, "White attitudes on a wide range of racial issues have modified sharply over recent decades, especially in improved stereotypes of blacks and in less support of blatant forms of racial discrimination."[3] Old-fashioned "dominative racism" is out, replaced by what Joel Kovel calls "aversive racism."[4] The institutional basis of discrimination persists in many important areas but is not so perceived by whites. Furthermore, whites have tended to reject most efforts aimed at improving the condition of the black poor. Pettigrew summarizes the present situation as follows: "White Americans increasingly reject racial injustice in principle, but are reluctant to accept the measures necessary to eliminate the injustice."[5]

The perception that racism no longer exists and the refusal to recognize the realities of historically derived and structurally reinforced patterns of exclusion together constitute a major obstacle to the achievement of consensus on affirmative action programs.

The third reason for the failure of consensus has its source in the moral presuppositions of American society. There is a profound reluctance in the Anglo-American moral and legal tradition to accept the principle of group rights and claims. This is due to the deep commitment to individualism and to its supporting ethic of self-determination. To be sure, it is simply not possible for a modern—or indeed any—society to work without some recognition and acceptance of the ideal of group obligations and claims. We accept the reality of states as actors in the international community, and within states we accept the existence of corporate groups such as firms, trade unions, and the like. It may be argued that we hold the individual leaders and managers of such groups legally responsible for their actions, but there are clear limits to their responsibility, as the laws themselves demonstrate. Noncorporate groups, however, have almost never been granted recognition as the holders of claims and obligations. The refusal to do so conflicts with other principles. Thus we accept the right of noncorporate groups to practice their religion. In so doing, we implicitly accept the existence of a noncorporate group as a holder of claims, since it is not possible for a religion to exist except as a set of beliefs and rites shared by a community. When we say that Jews have the right to practice their religion, we recognize the existence of a noncorporate group made up of Jewish people since Judaism, as Jewish religious leaders rightly insist, has no meaning or existence outside the Jewish people.

Now when American Indians, blacks, and women press their case for the recognition of their claims as a group, they are appealing to the same principle which accepts the reality of the noncorporate group of believers. The major difference is, of course, that the claims are secular rather than religious. The objection is really to the extension of group claims to the secular, especially economic, sphere. There is no change in principle.

More problematic is the challenge to the underlying ethic of self-determination implicit in many arguments in favor of affirmative action. The whole weight of the social sciences inclines us to the view that we are overwhelmingly the product of our genetic and socio-economic environment (I leave aside the question of which is more determining—the genetic or the socio-economic). And yet the fundamental moral assumption in our behavior is that individuals are responsible for their actions and for their fate. Blacks, other minorities, and women, in appealing to the conditioning role of their socio-economic environment to explain their disadvantaged situation and the way in which it is generationally reproduced, have the findings of the social sciences on their side. But they run headlong into the indeterministic ethic when they seek to go beyond explanation and demand restitution and meaningful change by insisting on equality of results as the only way of breaking out of the cycle of dependency. The dominant Anglo-American tradition insists on self-improvement even while accepting social determination.

Incidentally, this seemingly contradictory stance runs deep in the western tradition. We find its direct spiritual counterpoint in the Augustinian as well as the Calvinist and Lutheran acceptance of predestination *and* personal salvation at one and the same time. I qualify the contradiction as one that is *seemingly* so because once we understand the reason for it, we are usually obliged to accept it. Speaking personally, the neo-Kantian approach to this dilemma is the only sensible one. That is, there is no gainsaying the fact that in terms of pure reason it is hopelessly contradictory to accept the deterministic precepts of social science (and predestination) and the indeterministic precept of personal responsibility for one's secular (and spiritual) salvation. And yet we have to. Why? Because, in terms of practical reasoning, this is the only way the world can be made to work. A society simply would not function if, every time we confronted disadvantage, failure, or deviance, we excused it in deterministic terms, however scientifically valid such an excuse may be. The idea or myth of autonomy is one of those holy lies that is an imperative of practical judgment. Ironically, the more complex our world, and the more we learn about it from the social sciences, the more we need the idea.[6]

Where does this leave us with regard to the affirmative action controversy? It clearly explains a great deal about the absence of consensus. I think that one may safely make the generalization that all excluded or disadvantaged groups pressing for inclusion are going to challenge the myth of autonomy on the grounds that it blames the victim; whereas all groups already securely "in" are going to defend its sanctity. It seems to me that it is vitally important for minorities and women to recognize that this challenge has got to be carefully handled. The challenge is a necessary part of the struggle to get in, but the members of disadvantaged groups, more than any other, must realize that in the final reckoning they have to assume responsibility for their own fate. The challenge can be only a transitional tactic. Its dangers must be fully realized. It is foolish to expect too much help from those who benefit from one's disadvantaged situation. And too great an assault on the myth of autonomy always runs the dangerous risk of dissipating motivation.

Now, while the myth of autonomy is an imperative of practical reason, it is equally evident from this mode of reasoning that the capacity to act autonomously can be stunted by being disadvantaged and excluded. Behaving autonomously is itself something we learn mainly by doing. This is a classic case of the divine paradox: to him that hath it shall be given; to him that hath not it shall be taken away. Success breeds success; failure, failure. How do the "hath-not" break out of the trap? They do so through struggle. The very act of struggling is itself self-motivating. It is important to understand what is being struggled for, however, as well as the short-term and long-term gains that struggle makes possible.

I want to suggest that there is an overt and essentially short-term agenda in the struggle for affirmative action as well as a covert and long-term agenda. To understand what these agendas are, let me propose a simple model of exclusion drawn from an analogy on game-playing. In society, we may see power and success as a game that certain groups are simply excluded from playing. This is the elementary form of exclusion. Blacks and women, by being confined to what Daniel Bell once called the private household, as opposed to the public household where the game is played, were for long simply excluded from the ballpark. The next step involved an acceptance of the principle that blacks and women may enter the ballpark and play if they can. Here they face the second kind of exclusion: they can't play simply because they do not know how to. The solution offered is equal opportunity to learn the rules of the game. Now they are not only in the ballpark but on the field, and here they face the subtlest, yet most entrenched, form of exclusion: they do not know how to play well. They have learned the rules, but others have been playing ball for so long that there is no way that they are ever going to get to center field. More training, greater equal opportunity, they discover, will never solve this problem because increased training is open to all. Thus, each increment of training they receive is matched by an equal increment among those already way ahead. If they protest and ask, say, two increments of training for each one given those already at center field, the latter cry foul, loud and powerfully. So the skills of everyone improve with equal opportunity, the game gets better, but the newcomers never get closer to the power plays at center field.

Indeed, their relative situation may even worsen with improved educational opportunities, since education and experience operate interactively. Those who are already experienced are able to gain greater benefits from equal inputs of educational opportunity than those with no experience.

And yet another problem may surface at this time. The newcomers may find that they just don't like the game or the way it is played. Even if by some superhuman effort a token few of them make it closer to center field, they may find that they do not particularly enjoy "kicking a little ass" for the hell of it, as our vice president so joyfully expresses it.

It is at this point that the third and most important kind of struggle emerges, and it is here that the hidden and essentially long-term agenda of affirmative action comes into play. The struggle now is not about playing the game, but about the rules of the game itself, about who sets the rules, and about the style and purpose of the game.

A great deal of the heat in the debate over affirmative action, I submit, is generated by the usually unstated recognition that this is really what the struggle is about. Those who control our society like to think there is something eternal and sacred about the rules of the game. Simply to bring them into question excites anxiety and outrage. If comparative and historical sociology teaches us one thing about societies, however, it is the fact that the rules by which we play in our social organizations are not like genetic codes. They can and do change. Furthermore, we also know that the same objective can often be obtained by different means. A good case in point is the current debate about the shortcomings of the American pattern of management when compared with its Japanese counterpart. For decades, many people thought that the rules of management were those encoded in the case studies of the Harvard Business School. It was a real culture shock when corporate America learned that there are radically different ways of maximizing profits. My point is not to idealize the Japanese alternative, which I personally have many reservations about, but rather to illustrate the fact that the rules of the game more often reflect the interests, values, and class of those who are at the center of power than they do any hard-to-grasp essences that only the chosen few can fathom. To put the matter another way, if we insist on running our car factories the way Detroit does, then it follows, as night follows day, that only people who look, think, feel, and behave like Lee Iacocca will ever end up at the top of the executive ladder. No black and no woman could ever exhibit the kind of white male executive macho with which Mr. Iacocca so obligingly regales his TV viewers in his commercial spots for Chrysler. The example of top executive positions in the auto industry represents the most extreme height of power. I should point out that my argument applies to nearly all areas and levels of exclusion, from fire-fighting and police work to law and medicine. We can now understand the true nature of the crisis that affirmative action creates. It is not just the presence of the formerly excluded that presents problems for the establishment, but the fear that they might change the way we run things. These fears are indeed justified, since it is true that if women and minorities are to be included beyond token numbers, the rules will have to change.

Before I am wholly misunderstood by those who wave the banner of high standards (rarely, I might add, are they those who most achieve these standards), let me make it clear that the redefinition of rules in no way entails a lessening of standards, or the abandonment of the merit principle. I am not proposing that we do away with rules and structures, but that we redefine them in a manner that makes it possible for those now excluded to play by them. I am, in short, urging a commitment to the very things that critics of affirmative action insist on, a genuine universalization of the rules of conduct. Such a universalization cannot stop short of the rules by which we change the rules. Affirmative action is the only means by which this last but most critical citadel of exclusion can be invaded. The stakes are high, hence the intensity of the reaction.

To conclude, by way of summary, the lack of consensus on affirmative action may be attributed to deep-seated disagreements over three kinds of rules—what may be called the rules of allocation, of application, and of determination.

It is a struggle, first, over the age-old problem of equality and the difficulty of arriving at some acceptable conception of distributive justice. There is disagreement over what constitutes fair distribution of wealth and power, and even where it is agreed that some effort ought to be made to reduce the gap between the haves and have-nots, there is disagreement over the rules of allocation, the means by which we achieve less inequality. In a nutshell, those who support affirmative action believe that inegalitarian rules of allocation are just where the objective is a more egalitarian distribution of rewards. Those opposed to affirmative action take the opposite view, questioning even the long-established principle of a graduated income tax— the classic example of an inegalitarian rule of allocation aimed at a more egalitarian distribution.

Second, the debate is a conflict over the rules of application, that is, the problem of whether groups, especially noncorporate disadvantaged groups, are entitled to special claims as a result of the special damages they have suffered historically and continue to suffer in institutional terms. Supporters of affirmative action accept the legitimacy of such claims; those opposed insist that only individuals, as individuals rather than as members of victimized groups, can claim damages and are entitled to compensatory treatment.

Finally, the covert agenda of the struggle for affirmative action is that it seeks to change the underlying, axial rules of determination in our society. It seeks to restrain the freedom and power of some people to maintain an order that results in the chronic disadvantage of others. This is clearly a power struggle, and as with all such struggles it may be waged by means of violence—not only political, which is increasingly unlikely, but psychological, cultural, and criminal violence, which we daily witness—or by legislation. The disadvantaged not only need to get the overprivileged off their backs, but to ensure that they stay off. This they accomplish by being positioned to play meaningful roles in our society and, just as important, by having a say in the way the rules by which we live are defined, maintained, and changed.

The struggle is endless, because in our competitive capitalist democracy there will always be inequality. Not only will some justly do better than others, but many will unjustly do so. As Rousseau saw more than two centuries ago, there is an inevitable tendency toward inequality in our society. This, however, is no reason for accepting it. To the contrary: "It is precisely because the force of things always tends to destroy equality that the force of legislation should always tend to maintain it."[7]

Notes

1. The "unsocial sociability" of human beings, as Kant pointed out, is the source of that creative "antagonism" that accounts for all human progress. "All the culture and art which adorn mankind and the finest social order man creates are fruits of his unsociability." Immanuel Kant, "Idea for a Universal History with a Cosmopolitan Purpose," *Kant's Political Writings*, edited by Hans Reiss (Cambridge: Cambridge University Press, 1970), especially pp. 44–46.

2. Paul Starr, *The Social Transformation of American Medicine* (New York: Basic Books, 1983).

3. Thomas Pettigrew, "Race and Class in the 1980's: An Interactive View," *Daedalus* 110 (Spring 1981).

4. Cited in Pettigrew, "Race and Class in the 1980's."

5. Ibid.

6. This argument is merely a sociological extension of Kant's theory of freedom. In the *Groundwork of the Metaphysic of Morals*, he argued that freedom must be presupposed as a property of the will of all rational beings. Such a presupposition, however, stands in stark contradiction to the dictates of pure reason which assert a natural, sensible world subject to the laws of causality, of natural necessity, and therefore

admitting of no freedom. Kant's "practical" solution to the problem was to make a "rough" distinction between the "sensible" and the "intelligible" worlds and to argue that human beings can consider themselves from two points of view, as sensible entities subject to the laws of nature (including society), and as uniquely free creatures acting in an intelligible world independent of nature, one with laws that "are not empirical but have their ground in reason alone." He argues further: "To the Idea of freedom there is inseparably attached the concept of autonomy and to this in turn the universal principle of morality—a principle which in Idea forms the ground for all the actions of rational beings, just as the law of nature does for all appearances." In the final analysis, Kant readily admitted, "we shall never be able to comprehend how freedom is possible," but while logically incomprehensible it is morally and sociologically necessary. Immanuel Kant, *Groundwork of the Metaphysic of Morals*, translated by H. J. Paton (New York: Harper & Row, 1964).

I have elsewhere attempted to apply a sociological version of Kant's theory to the moral dilemmas of black Americans. See "The Moral Crisis of the Black American," *The Public Interest*, Summer 1973.

7. Jean Jacques Rousseau, *The Social Contract*, book 2, chap. 11. Translated by Willmoore Kendall (Chicago: Henry Regency Co., 1954).

8

Questions and Answers

At the conference at which the papers in this volume were first delivered, Reynolds, Wasserstrom, Edley, and Patterson spoke on a panel, which was followed by a question-and-answer period. Since the discussion that ensued permitted the speakers to address each other directly in a way that shed light on many of the points at issue, an edited transcript of it is included here. Questions and comments from the floor are included as well, where they triggered responses from the panelists.

Edley: I feel somewhat remiss in not saying something directly to Brad Reynolds. Here are five brief points.

First, on the *Stotts* case and the interpretation of the significance of that opinion, I think Brad Reynolds is dead wrong. The question of limiting "make whole" relief to individuals seems to me to be fairly restricted to contexts in which, say, an identifiable white worker is being displaced by an identifiable black worker. In general, the discussion in the majority and concurring opinions seems to me to refer to situations in which *compensatory seniority* has been awarded, and in the past it has been only awarded to identified victims.

My second point is that I don't believe that in putting a very broad gloss on the opinion Brad Reynolds is being disingenuous. I think that he believes what he says about the meaning of the opinion—just as I believe what I say about the meaning of the opinion. It is a problem of interpretation. A Supreme Court opinion is not an algebraic proof which can be read and understood in one way. It is more like a sonnet. To some extent what you see—what you read—is what you want.

Which brings me to my third point. I think the problem is one of persuasion. Brad Reynolds will read the opinion one way, I would read it another way, and we don't have effective ways of trying to persuade each other about who is right about what society should be like.

My fourth point is that I didn't mean by my remarks to suggest that I don't think that there is a place for rights rhetoric in our discourse. It seems to me that certainly there is a place for rights rhetoric within the confines of the law. If you hire me in your Title VII litigation, I will go into court and I will rightfully employ rights rhetoric. If you hire Brad Reynolds, he will do the same thing. We both will identify rights and try to construct some calculus using them in different ways. So I do think that there remains some role for rights rhetoric, but we have to appreciate its limits, its manipulability. In addition, I think there is an important role for rights rhetoric in Dick Wasserstrom's sense, a role of providing sustenance to those of us who are already converted. In other words, giving us moral food that enables us to go out and continue to do battle. What I have doubts about is the extent to which a discourse in rights really accomplishes persuasion, accomplishes the conversion that I mentioned.

And that's my last point, number five, which refers to what Bob Fullinwider has said. "Bull" Conner did more to convert than arguments about who has what kind of right. In other words, the explanation of what our rights are or ought to be has persuasive power because of something that has preceded it in terms of persuading the listener about the kind of society he or she wants. I think what we have to figure out if we are interested in persuading each other about affirmative action is exactly what those antecedents to persuasion are and how to go about marshaling them.

Reynolds: Let me just make a few points. I'll start by saying that I personally don't subscribe to the theory of institutional discrimination. I think that institutions are run by individuals, they are shaped by individual actions and behavior, and the institutions are discriminatory as a direct result of the individual's policies and attitudes. And I do think that if you have institutions that are in the hands of individuals who are committed to rid the institutions of discriminatory activities, they will indeed get rid of discriminatory activities. My focus would remain on the individual conduct, where I think the focus of our laws also is.

This is not a debate that can properly be cast as one where one side is saying that white rights are at stake and the other side that black rights are at stake. The debate is more appropriately cast in terms of individual rights vs. group rights.

I would agree with the suggestion that the discourse on rights is perhaps too constraining. I think that one of the real difficulties with this whole discussion is that it narrows the focus of affirmative action and suggests that affirmative action remedies can solve the broad array of problems that exist by reason of discriminatory activities in our society. Congress did not pass Title VII or any of the other civil rights acts with a mind to deal with all those difficulties that are confronting society because of discriminatory behavior. And I think that one of the failings in the past decade has been the requirements of those laws to carry all the baggage of everybody's view of how to address the fact that we have still with us discrimination in this society and we have still with us the effects of past discrimination. There are serious, fundamental problems, some of which we've touched on here, that are not going to be cured, or indeed treated very effectively, when you focus only on affirmative action or on remedial techniques in the jurisprudence that we have under our laws. They were more modest in the way they were framed. The congressmen who were focusing on a discrete problem at the time, the need to ensure protection for individuals from identifiable wrongs, did not take the approach that Congress was going to deal with these systemic problems, requiring systemic relief. It is not to suggest Congress could not undertake to do that, but we do live in a society where we have to go by the laws that Congress has actually passed. I think that the laws are much more modest in their reach than some of the advocates of these other remedial techniques would like to admit, and I think we ought to undertake in these kinds of discussions to broaden our horizons and recognize that affirmative action is not going to solve very much more than the discrete individual discrimination that is targeted by Title VII. There are other more pervasive problems and they require, I think, more thoughtful and more pervasive solutions than we have yet faced up to collectively as well as we should have.

Wasserstrom: I am a romantic. I mean, I think the way to get consensus is to try to think as correctly as you can about the problem and consensus will converge on the most accurate theory. But I would like to sharpen one point of disagreement between Mr. Reynolds and myself in connection with what he was just saying. That is, that one way to think about things is to say that you don't have discriminatory systems, you just have individuals who might be prejudiced and through their actions treat other people unfairly. If you didn't have that you wouldn't have a problem. I'd just like to tell you a little story about how I think that way of thinking does harm. The question is whether a black defendant has anything to complain about in a criminal case, if all the jurors on the case are white. One way to think about it is to say no, not unless the jurors are prejudiced. Not unless they'll vote to convict this person because he is black. I mean, we know that many juries in Alabama used to do stuff like that. But if they don't do that, if they are fair-minded people, then what difference does it make whether the jurors are black or white? And in the same way, there is no reason why a white should worry about blacks being on the jury unless the blacks are prejudiced or angry against whites so that they would disregard the evidence.

In the early 70s I represented a black defendant who had been selling Black Panther newspapers on the corner of 41st and Central in Los Angeles. The cops came by (the Los Angeles Police Department at that time was virtually all white) and they said, "Nigger, if we see you on the street with those papers, we'll kick your ass." He said something equally provocative to them and the next thing he knew he was in jail and charged with throwing a Coke bottle at the police car with intent to do great bodily injury, a felony that carries up to five years in California. Now, the cops made up that story, I suspect, because they had a theory at that time that members of the Black Panther Party were a danger to society, and since the courts couldn't be counted on to put Black Panthers where they ought to be, they tried to make sure the system did things the right way. So at the preliminary hearing each of the four cops in the car said that they were minding their own business and here came this Coke bottle that bounced on the hood of the car and almost caused a serious accident. I asked each of them a batch of questions at the preliminary hearing and they all testified to the same story: he threw the Coke bottle in a line drive with his right hand. Well, it turned out that not only was the defendant left-handed, but his right hand was a little bit withered. So by the time of the trial I was able to get quite good evidence that if somebody had in fact thrown a Coke bottle, it wasn't him. He was acquitted, but it took the all white jury eight hours to bring in an acquittal. I think the reason was simply this. I suspect that it was the same thing that gave me a lot of trouble. I suspect that in the experiences of the white jurors there had been nothing very much that made it easy for them to believe that four cops would get on the stand, one right after the other, and deliberately tell a lie in order to put somebody in jail. I think that the best explanation of why it took this jury eight hours to acquit a man who couldn't have thrown this bottle, unless you make the most improbable assumption about what left-handed people do with their withered right hands when they're under conditions of stress, was the problem they had trying to figure out what could have been going on here. How would it have been different if there had been, say, five or six blacks from South Central, L.A., the community where this event had happened, on the jury? My conjecture is that given the way black life was lived then, and still is now, in that community, they wouldn't have had anywhere near the same intellectual difficulty in entertaining the possibility of cops fudging if not totally distorting the facts when they were making a bust of blacks whom they didn't like, because they were apt to have had a friend or a relative who had had such an experience, or they themselves had had one of this sort. If I'm more or less right about that, then it does seem to me that there's a sharpness to the issue that divides Reynolds and me. The most fair-minded whites in the world would not do a good job in all cases in figuring out who was guilty and who was innocent, even though they weren't prejudiced.

I think there is a more general point that this story illustrates. For in the same way, I think the university would be a different place in the way it thought about all social problems, if all the views about the problems were, say, not the views of persons who were both white and male. That is, there are other points of view, other ways in which people think about our society, and these are points of view shaped in part by their experiences as blacks or women living in our society. Unless these points of view are represented in the way the problems are thought about, pursued, defined, and constructed, a distortion results that has nothing to do with prejudice, nothing to do with persons not trying to be fair-minded or anything else. It has to do with all of the unnoticed ways in which we count on things and suppose that everybody else, if they were only like us, in our ability to look at things clearly, would see everything exactly the same way we do.

Question: First of all, I'm enjoying this tremendously. I'm trained as a therapist and so I'm interested in games. I wrote here an African proverb: By the time the fool learns the rules of the game, the players have moved on. I indeed believe that that's what's happening with all of this. I should tell you also that I was an orphan in the ghetto of Pittsburgh at age six; I've done everything that I wanted to do here; I don't want any white people to give me anything, but I think that merit is a lot of garbage. Let me tell you why. Part of the obfuscation that we see happening here is that we don't even know what racism is. Let me give you a brief four-part definition. Number one, it's a delusion of superiority based on race, color. Two, it is an expectation of rights and privileges just because of skin color. Three, a subordinate group is arbitrarily defined as *inferior*, and it is decided that they must be kept in their place. And fourth, and most important, the people who make that arbitrary decision have the power to control the institutions to see that those subordinate people are kept in an inferior place. Whites have always in this country expected jobs, promotions, etc., just because they were white. So I think it is crazy when intelligent blacks and whites sit here and have people say we choose on merit. We've never done it on merit, and I think we ought to stop playing that game because it's a lie.

Question: The question continues to be how can we find consensus regarding affirmative action. This is the wrong question. I'd like to suggest why. I don't find affirmative action inspirational; I don't find it transformational. I find its rhetoric not only not religious, but not poetic. It is very difficult to see how we're going to inspire people with that kind of approach. This administration has broken with past programs on the rights of blacks and women. From abortion to civil rights we have an administration now that feeds off the wreckage of consensus. Can we really talk about how to find consensus on affirmative action?

Wasserstrom: I don't believe that there is *a* right policy. I think there are lots of right policies. Again in respect to my view of the systemic nature of the problem, preferential treatment is useful, but obviously it is not by itself going to transform society. Neither are voting rights. Neither is education. But every single one of them is worth doing, because what they all do is help in all sorts of expected and unexpected ways to change the system. They make changes in conditions that tend to perpetuate injustice. So, as I say, my general strategy is connected with a theory about the systemic nature of the problem, about how society works, and how social change comes about.

Edley: I have a couple of different reactions. I think there's an extremely valid point suggested by the last two comments. I reject a flat statement that all forms of preferential treatment are to be required *or* rejected. We have to recognize that different kinds of preferential treatment have produced different moral costs and benefits. There are bad ways to define affirmative action and there are good ways to define affirmative action. Some turn me off. We have to keep our eye on what might be the moral costs. This doesn't mean we should shy away altogether from preferences because of the moral costs or the risks to consensus. We have to ask if there is a way to change public perception of what the moral costs are.

Patterson: There is no doubt that every job involves certain skills. Some are more demanding of certain kinds of qualities than others.

But we should note several things. First of all, for the vast majority of occupations, all the skills are acquired on the job. The problem then is that being on the job has a reinforcement effect and being excluded from the job has the opposite effect. The second thing to note about meritocracy is that, ironically, the most conservative elements in society have always been uncomfortable with it. There is a sense in which our more conservative leaders have always favored a certain form of affirmative action. It is not only expected but it's considered good to promote the interests of our children. It is good to promote the interests of your family members even though you may recognize that they are not very smart. We expect a parent to apply affirmative action. The same holds regarding community, friends. For some, it is good to help members of your ethnic group.

Another important point. There is little if any relationship between academic preparation and end results. Studies of medical students show little correlation between performance on entrance exams and performance later on as doctors. We have to consider whether we want a pure meritocracy, and we have to keep in mind that 90 percent of the skills to do a job are acquired after being on the job. Access is crucial. This is what affirmative action addresses.

Reynolds: I think that the topic for this panel discussion is appropriate, but a focus on affirmative action need not exclude concern with other issues. What the administration has done in other areas we can discuss at an appropriate time.

I do want to make a point on meritocracy: it is a fact that there are any number of compromises to the merit system—family, friends, veterans' preferences. The fundamental opposition to preferential treatment is that we have embedded in our Constitution and in our laws a mandate not to exclude anyone because of race. There is as a corollary the view that people's qualifications should be uppermost in decision-making, but what is at the heart of opposition to preferential treatment is not, for many, a principle of merit and whether that is sacrosanct but rather the principle that one should not be disadvantaged on account of race.

Question: The problem is that the narrow policy of remedies followed by the Justice Department applies to only a very small number of individuals. This doesn't touch the effects on the black community of segregation and discrimination. The black community is affected in various ways: through the underfunding of education, through lack of public transportation to jobs, through employment practices that disseminate job information through contacts, and so on.

Reynolds: You are right. "Rightful place" cannot cope with the kind of community discrimination you outlined. I don't think that affirmative action and preferential treatment cope with it any better. We have a host of problems, and to suggest that affirmative action can carry all of that baggage and remove the kind of community discrimination you describe is asking too much of the law and certainly going well beyond what the law was intended to do. School and employment law was designed to desegregate, but to do so through outreach and recruitment programs, by bringing to the school and workplace members of previously neglected communities. But I don't think that if we were to embrace wholeheartedly preferential treatment we would make any kind of dent in the problems you were talking about.

Wasserstrom: Well, it would change the character of the individuals serving in the community, working in business and institutions; it would change how folks thought about those places. Preferential affirmative action might not do the whole thing, but I don't see how you can expect any of these things to happen without preferential treatment.

Reynolds: That assumes that the affirmative action remedies we are following do not bring into the work force or to elected offices or into the school yards increased numbers of minorities. That just isn't so. There's no resistance to the idea that we ought to open doors and bring into business, schools, etc., increased numbers of minorities. My point is you shouldn't do this with racial preferences.

Wasserstrom: If you think that it's a fundamental moral principle that one should never advantage or disadvantage any person on the grounds of race, then you are precluded on moral grounds from seeing the desirability of getting blacks more fully represented in these institutions because of what happens when they are. That is, it seems to be inconsistent to hold to that principle and yet applaud the fact that the society would be a better one in all sorts of ways if only blacks and other minorities were more fully present in the institutions than they are now. There are a lot more blacks in law school now than there were when I went to law school because there were none in either of the law schools I attended and there were none when I started teaching at UCLA in 1967. There are now a lot of blacks in the law school and a lot on the faculty, and the reason why is because we had a policy that said it was relevant in deciding whom to admit to law school and to appoint to the faculty that somebody was non-white. The stupidity of the reasoning in some of the opinions of the

Supreme Court in the *Bakke* case is reflected in the fact that most of the justices couldn't see the point of these preferences, so now everyone has to engage in a subterfuge to do what nobody has disagreed is a good thing.

Question: Let's take the administration policy on its own terms. You are concerned that innocent third parties, white workers, are disadvantaged by preferences. And you don't really believe in institutional discrimination; for you, discrimination rests in the hearts and acts of individuals. Take this last point. If we seriously believe that discrimination rests in the acts of individuals, then wouldn't we want to take strong measures to discourage those kinds of acts? My question is: what action has the administration taken to increase the penalties for individuals discriminating? For example, have you proposed amending the Civil Rights Act of 1964 so that someone found guilty of discrimination goes to jail?

Reynolds: We haven't proposed any legislation along those lines. The way current legislation is framed, it is designed to effectively remove discrimination and repair the wrong that's done. I don't know offhand what additional punitive measures would be appropriate, in the context of statutes that have been on the books for twenty years. Of course there are some criminal civil rights laws for special circumstances.

I think the political impetus in this country is toward eliminating discrimination and I think there can be no slackening of effort. There are a host of problems in education that deserve attention in their own right. There are family problems, the question of discipline in schools, problems of how we can better deal with school desegregation. We have for too long proceeded on the assumption that the existing body of civil rights statutes is adequate to the task of dealing with the many societal problems.

Question: I want to return to the question of consensus. How can we recapture a sense of common purpose? In the 1960s, witnessing the actions of the Bull Connors and the George Wallaces, watching the assaults on civil rights workers, produced a fervor to act. We don't have that fervor now. Preferential programs, though necessary, are deeply flawed because they don't make anybody happy. Consensus requires our recapturing that lost fervor.

Patterson: We assume that consensus is a good thing. It isn't always a good thing. It may even be that for a vibrant society to maintain its vibrancy, too much consensus is a bad thing. Conflict is inherent in life, and it is not always without value. Conflict arises when we don't agree about the values we hold—equality, freedom, etc.

So-called agreement comes about in two ways. You can demonstrate we ought to do something because it promotes certain values we share. In many aspects I think we may have exhausted that avenue, exhausted the moral reservoir of shared values. What happens then? Weak societies fall apart under conflict, but strong societies, muscular, vibrant societies, resolve their problems through conflict. It becomes a matter of power, a matter of struggle. One group can force agreement from another by making it in the interest of the latter to come around to its point of view. It is not in the interest of the larger society to have a large black underclass. We all pay a price. Such an underclass, or any outcast group, asserts a negative power. We shouldn't make consensus sacred. Struggle and self-interest may have to suffice.

Reynolds: I think it is well not to lose sight of what this discussion is focusing on. There is, I am convinced, a consensus in this country that it is committed to act against discrimination. There is no disagreement about this goal or end. What we have as the point of discussion today is one means that has been tried. It is suggested that there are better means to get us to that end and that is what has caused this debate to accelerate. I'm not sure whether we will reach a consensus on affirmative action. I am sure that the fact that we have focused this much attention on it is a healthy thing; as long as we continue to search for the best method of getting to the goal we are going to be on solid ground; and it is probably very well that we not become complacent with any remedy. And the search for consensus should not stop our stretching our minds to find ways to solve virtually intractable problems. It's well to keep in sight that we are talking about means to get to a common objective.

Edley: I don't believe that fervor is as important as we sometimes think it is. I believe it is necessary but it's far from sufficient. Consensus can be dangerous, because a stable consensus can be oppressive. So my emphasis would be not so much on striving for consensus because that can mean that we limit ourselves to progress of the least common denominator sort, but rather that our focus be on how to persuade. There is a failure on the part of those engaged in the debate to listen carefully to each other. The image comes to mind of an umpire and a baseball manager, standing toe to toe screaming at each other, waving their hands, carefully trying not to strike each other, but not persuading each other of anything despite their fervor. On the other hand, I don't believe that even a rational discourse in our intellectual sense, certainly not one built around our familiar shibboleths of Anglo-American jurisprudence, is likely to result in the kind of persuasion that seems necessary to move beyond the truly difficult moral and socioeconomic problems that face us. Indeed, I think we're far more likely to find the means of persuasion from the wizards on Madison Avenue or from inspiring oratory, because the answer has got to be to describe not some empirical means-end connection that everyone can agree upon, but rather a vision about a kind of community that people will want to be members of. That's not the tone of our discussions, and I'm afraid that until that becomes the case, until we change the character of our discussions and the character of our arguments, we'll continue to come to meetings in which people's views don't really change.

Wasserstrom: I'm still an optimist. I still think if people will think together about these things carefully, we can get answers. I'm not sure that the ideas of liberalism and rights are all that impoverished, but that is another story. So what do I think? I think that the preferential treatment programs are temporary by design, that they're designed to do something and when they've done it there's no point in having them anymore. I'm not sure that they're any more or less deeply problematic than lots of other strategies pursued in the past for dealing with important issues.

I think the problem that we still have is in part an intellectual one of not having thought carefully enough. Mr. Reynolds and I agree there's an intractable problem. What *is* the problem? It seems to me it's the perpetuation in more subtle, less visible ways of the kind of oppression that blacks have been subjected to for as long as we've had a country. If that's the problem, it has nothing to do with a kind of abstract intellectual prohibition of taking race into account arbitrarily, for no reason. The point of all of those civil rights statutes was not to prohibit just some *arbitrary* behavior, it was to try to stop people from beating blacks over the head, both physically and economically. That's the problem we still have to deal with, and if we see that's still the problem, it seems to me there should be much less that's deeply problematic or controversial about the policies we are discussing here today.

9

Achieving Equal Opportunity

Robert K. Fullinwider

THE CONTROVERSY ABOUT AFFIRMATIVE ACTION continues to dominate public debate on civil rights. The nub of the controversy is the use of racial and sexual preferences. It is not uncommon for an affirmative action plan enforced by a court or a government consent decree to require a firm or institution to hire, select, or promote a certain number or ratio of minorities and women. The acceptability of such preferential treatment is the question that strongly divides people.

Anyone who has followed closely the two-decade public debate on "goals and quotas," "reverse discrimination," and race-conscious remedies" cannot fail to have been struck by its sterility. The debate never gets anywhere; the arguments of today are little different from the arguments of fifteen years ago. The only progress is in the increased rigidity of the opposing positions.

Why is the issue so intransigent? One answer is that people are divided at the level of fundamental principle. Consequently, reconciling differences will be next to impossible. There remains no common ground upon which to stand.

Wm. Bradford Reynolds, in his contribution to this volume, and elsewhere, subscribes to a version of this answer. The debate about preferential treatment, he says, is between those who, like himself, favor "equality of opportunity" and those who favor "equality of results."[1] If this characterization of the debate is correct, then we confront a hard-core disagreement deriving from two fundamentally opposed ways of looking at justice.

However, in the question-and-answer section, Reynolds offers a quite different characterization of the situation. "There is," he says, "a consensus in this country that it is committed to act against discrimination. *There is no disagreement about this goal or end.* What we have as the point of discussion today is one *means.* . . ." We are all committed to the "search for the best method of getting to the goal"; some persons believe, however, that "there are better means to get us to that end" than preferential treatment.[2]

Now, a disagreement about ends is one thing, a dispute about means to a common end quite another. Which is it? If there is to be any progress in the affirmative action debate, we need the best possible understanding of what divides us. Even when we identify precise points of disagreement, we may not be able to overcome or circumvent them; but we clearly cannot hope for progress if in fact we persistently misidentify our differences. In the latter case we will simply continue talking past one another.

Is it fruitful to understand differences on affirmative action as differences about ends or differences about means? I think the debate in this book between Wm. Bradford Reynolds and Richard Wasserstrom is instructive on this question. Wasserstrom argues for occasional and selective uses of preferential treatment. It is plain that his endorsement is conditional. He sees racial preferences as potentially effective levers against the inertial weight of a system of racial oppression that diminishes the opportunities afforded to blacks.

Racial discrimination is "systematic in nature"; "things are linked together" so that even where the "intentions and motivations of those occupying positions of relative power are wholly benign and proper . . . it is likely that the system will perpetuate itself unless blacks come to occupy substantially more of the positions . . . of power."[3] Getting blacks into such positions is "*a* way of weakening the interlocking system of social practices, structures, and ideology." Preferential programs are justified to the extent "that they are designed specifically to accomplish this end" and to the extent that they "do accomplish it."[4]

Wasserstrom's defense of preferential treatment does not fit into the initial equal-opportunity-versus-equal-results mold offered by Reynolds. He favors preferential programs not in order to establish some pattern of proportional representation ("equal results") but to undermine a social system that still denies equality of opportunity. Reynolds and Wasserstrom do not differ in wanting to achieve a color-blind society.[5] Where, then, *does* their disagreement lie?

It appears to derive, in part, from differing views about the nature and extent of discrimination. Wasserstrom speaks of the systemic, institutional nature of discrimination. Discrimination works not just through the specific, ill-motivated acts of individuals but through "social practices, structures, and ideology" which support and reinforce certain ways of perceiving and acting by individuals (and the organizations in which they act).[6] Reynolds, in contrast, says in the question-and-answer section: "I personally don't subscribe to the theory of institutional discrimination. I think that institutions are run by individuals, they are shaped by individual actions and behavior, and institutions are discriminatory as a direct result of the individual's policies and attitudes. And I do think that if you have institutions that are in the hands of individuals who are committed to rid the institutions of discriminatory activities, they will indeed get rid of discriminatory activities."[7]

Reynolds does not amplify these remarks on discrimination, but it is apparent that he makes them in order to distance himself from what he takes to be Wasserstrom's position. Wasserstrom, in response, takes notice of these remarks to "sharpen" the disagreement between himself and Reynolds.[8] The details of the disagreement remain obscure, but it seems to me clear enough that it is on this terrain, and not within some controversy about ends, that we are most likely to clarify the distance between Reynolds and Wasserstrom, and most likely to move forward the affirmative action controversy. Consequently, I want to dwell further on what divides, or might divide, Reynolds and Wasserstrom on the nature of discrimination and how best to act against it.

I

To limit the boundaries of examination, I plan to focus on employment discrimination. The initial bases of employment antidiscrimination policy—Title VII of the Civil Rights Act of 1964 and Executive Order 11246 of 1965—forbid discrimination but do not define it. Nevertheless, the general aim in each case is clear enough: to ensure that a person's race or gender is not a special burden in getting a job, a promotion, a raise, and so on.

Reynolds's remarks about discrimination actually address two distinct questions, one of *agency* and one of *eradication*. Individuals rather than institutions are the agents of discrimination, he says, and we may expect, when institutions are in the "hands of individuals who are committed to rid institutions of discriminatory activities, that they will get rid of discriminatory activities." The two issues, of agency and eradication, are in fact interrelated because it is our interest in the second which shapes our conclusions about the first.

What is the point of saying that individuals rather than institutions discriminate? It is clear enough that the acts of institutions are constituted out of the acts of individuals, but this is not disputed by anybody. To sift out what is at stake here, consider four examples:

(a) The president of a firm explicitly orders subordinates to follow a policy of excluding women from executive jobs.

(b) Company policy requires racially neutral selections but a biased personnel officer covertly subverts the policy by ranking blacks lowest.

(c) A company, all white because of past practices, eliminates explicit racial exclusion but retains its traditional policy of requiring new applicants to be recommended by a current or former employee.

(d) A foreman rates workers on his assembly line. He finds that women workers are away from their stations for longer periods than male workers and transfers many of the women to other departments with less remunerative jobs. (The reason women are tardy: the factory was formerly segregated by sex and female assemblers have to walk three floors to the restroom.)

I suggest that what governs our attention in each of these examples is the feature of the institution that needs to be changed in order to eradicate discrimination.[9] In the first two cases, our concern focuses on specific individuals because their intentions to exclude blacks and women seem most salient. To get at discrimination in (a) and (b) we can change the hearts of the relevant individuals or substitute different individuals with better intentions. But a similar focus in (c) and (d) would not be productive. Changing foremen in (d) would accomplish nothing. The culprit in this instance is the actual physical layout of the factory, which reflects a past reality of sex segregation and now creates a special burden for female assemblers. The problem in case (c) is similar: a nominally neutral policy of requiring recommendations from present or past employees, although not designed to exclude blacks and not the handiwork of any current officers of the company, works dramatically to hinder the prospects of black employment at the company.

The first pair of cases seems to fit Reynolds's description of discrimination "as a direct result of the individual's policies and attitudes," but the second pair does not. Because what needs altering in the latter cases are features of the institutions, not the people in them, it seems perfectly reasonable to speak here of "institutional discrimination." Of course, any changes we desire in the institutions will have to be effectuated by one or more individuals (acting on their own volition or under orders); but this shows only that the distinction between individual and institutional discrimination is a pragmatic, not a metaphysical, one.

It is also true that in (a), as in (c) and (d), what needs changing is a feature of the institution, namely the company policy instituted by the president. What distinguishes this case from the other two is the connection between the policy and the intention and desire of the president. The latter pair of cases, on the other hand, exemplifies Wasserstrom's contention that even where no one in power has a bad motive—i.e., an active design to exclude or burden blacks or women—discrimination can persist nevertheless.

Persistence without plan—this seems to be what especially motivates talk about institutional discrimination, although it, in fact, cuts across the individual/institutional dichotomy. The matter of persistence is central because of its connection with the aim of eradication. The question is how discrimination can persist and whether preferential treatment can be an antidote.

Start with individuals. They may want to act fairly but be unable to. One study describes the case of

> a small southern manufacturing company where the personnel execu-tive reports his most difficult problem is that of "overcoming southern prejudice in old line managers in the 55 to 65 age bracket." It is not an easy task to ask these managers to hire people they always have believed are inferior. . . . Even where prejudice is not overt, there are many managers who think both women and minority-group members lack the capability to perform certain kinds of work. In many cases, these managers have had very little experience working closely with women and minorities.[10]

Deeply rooted habits of perception and belief can make an individual incapable of assessing fairly the capabilities of blacks and women. Although the "southern manager" may sincerely agree to hire quali-fied blacks without bias, we will not be surprised that he finds few qualified applicants who are not white.

Habits of perception and judgment can be so deeply rooted, in fact, that they work directly counter to one's conscious intentions.

> Sometimes, managers who pride themselves on being free of preju-dice, liberal, open-minded, and so forth still make their selection decisions consistently in favor of majority candidates. . . . Studies involving hiring or promotion decisions for management jobs have been conducted using applications or work histories that are identical except for the fact that one bears a man's name and the other a woman's. The results typically indicate the existence of anti-female biases with regard to the ability to handle higher level responsibilities.[11]

Thus, conscious desire to not discriminate, to judge fairly, may be ineffective. What is lacking is not good will but knowledge or capabil-ity. The individual doesn't realize his habits of judgment and percep-tion are unreliable or he is unable in the circumstances to modify and control his judgment and perception to make them reliable.

Now add to this picture an institutional background that reinforces the very perceptions and judgments that need changing. In a firm with a one-hundred-year history of sex segregation, say, everything about the organizational setup is going to reflect that history, from physical layout, job classification, and equipment design to work rules, assignment policies, and operating schedules. All of this provides a background that nourishes and supports the expectations and perceptions of those who make decisions within the firm, and likewise a background tailored to the productive capacities of male workers. We would reasonably expect such an institution to have a difficult time now integrating all of its operations, even assuming good will, although it might quickly eliminate some of the more egregious manifestations of discrimination.

Taking account of how discrimination may be more or less deeply rooted should affect our responses to it, in particular, which of two basic strategies we think appropriate. One way to alter reality is to alter behavior. A court may order an offending firm to dismantle its formal edifice of discrimination and replace it with policies that are neutral on their face: transfer and assignment rules are to apply uniformly to men and women, blacks and whites; selection, evaluation, and promotion are to be gender- and race-neutral. The court may further anticipate the hidden biases that can creep into judgments and require the adoption of mechanical and objective procedures wherever possible. For example, employees are no longer to be promoted on a supervisor's recommendation but on the basis of time-in-grade and performance of certain objectively measurable tasks. By thus altering the firm's "habits," the court seeks to change the underlying reality of sex and race segregation. By behaving according to the mandated changes, the firm will, it is hoped, begin giving substantially equal opportunity to its women and black employees.

Frequently, such altered behavior is enough to bring about change. However, sometimes significant barriers to opportunity can remain in place because the changed behavior does not go deep enough. The simplistic example of restroom location, used earlier, can illustrate this point. The foreman transfers out women not because of his subjective (and biased) judgment that they don't perform well on the assembly line but because they really are away from their stations longer than men. He is scrupulous in using an objective measure. And this is how matters are likely to remain without further intervention.

We know *why* the women are away; but does the foreman (or any of his superiors)? If he *starts* with the assumption that women workers ought to be as good assemblers as men, he will cast about for some further explanation of their greater absences and will eventually come upon the problem of the distant restroom. But if he *starts* with the assumption that women are not suited for this kind of work, their disproportionate absences only confirm what he already believes, and he will have no motive to look elsewhere for an explanation.

In the latter case, although the foreman follows the mandated rules of nondiscriminatory evaluation, institutional setup and automatic expectations interact to maintain a special burden for women workers. If it believes that this phenomenon pervades all the firm's operations, a court might opt for an alternative approach to eradicating discrimination. Instead of hoping to *change reality by changing habits*—a hope futile because the habits are so deeply entrenched—it aims to *change the habits by changing the reality*. It orders that a fixed number of women occupy the assembly jobs and other positions in the firm.

The court's order works dramatically to alter the reality upon which old habits and expectations feed. Now the firm has to maintain a certain number of women at the assembly stations even if they seem to be performing less effectively than men. Under the circumstances, it must either tolerate lowered productivity or find out how to reduce time away from station. Soon enough the foreman will be led to the restroom problem and solve it.

The same will be true about other aspects of the firm that invisibly work a hardship on women. No longer can the firm be content to find women "unqualified" (even offering objective evidence!); it is stuck with them and will have to find ways to make their presence productive. It discovers, for example, that one problem is solved by redesigning a machine so that its fifty-pound removable generator is slipped in at the bottom rather than lifted in at the top. This and other discoveries and adjustments would not have occurred—or would have occurred only at a snail's pace—but for the presence of women ordered by the court. After a few years, the firm has squeezed out many or most of the subtle and invisible barriers that especially hindered the opportunities of women.

If a court reasons correctly that only a scheme of preferential hiring or promotions will break up an entrenched pattern of discrimination, its ordering of the use of quotas promotes equality of opportunity. Opposition to the court order might rest on the belief that the court hasn't reasoned correctly. The court's reasoning might fail in one of two ways. It might have reasoned incorrectly in the particular case, failing to see less radical changes that would have been equally effective. Or its general premise might be incorrect, namely that discrimination can be subtle and deep and beyond the reach of good will.

Where are we to fit the disagreement between Reynolds and

Wasserstrom? They see themselves differing at a fairly general level. Does Reynolds believe that *as a matter of fact* discrimination is never so subtle and intransigent as Wasserstrom believes it sometimes is, or does he believe that the *very idea* of such discrimination is incoherent? Does he believe that discrimination is always transparent, that it is easy to uproot, or that we have at hand tools effective in all cases of discrimination, tools that don't involve preferences? Does he believe that there are cases of discrimination intractable to ordinary measures, but that preferential treatment never works in those cases either? Reynolds's own comments on discrimination, here and elsewhere, are too undeveloped for us to answer these questions with any confidence. Yet, if the affirmative action controversy is to be measured against the goal of equal opportunity, answers to these questions are indispensable.

II

In the simplified examples above, the sort of reasoning I attributed to a court is not fanciful or purely imaginary. In fact, much of the apparatus of affirmative action, including racial and sexual quotas, evolved from the efforts of courts to grapple with the complexities they faced in trying to apply Title VII of the Civil Rights Act. Very early on it became clear to them that much besides nominally discriminatory practices would have to be changed if blacks and women were not to continue to face diminished opportunities because of their race or gender. Consider a manufacturer that had always placed blacks in the lower-paying labor department and whites in the operations and technical departments. If the manufacturer also uses a departmental seniority system rather than a plant seniority system, then little has been done for long-term black employees in forcing the company to open entry into the operations and technical departments to all workers. Such blacks would have to yield all their accumulated seniority and layoff protection to make the move.[12] In cases like this courts began ordering the alteration of employment policies that had the effect of locking into place the disadvantages already visited on blacks by their initial segregation.

In attacking the persisting effects of past discrimination, courts began to use "numerical remedies"—orders to hire specific numbers or ratios of minorities or women. In the late 1960s and early 1970s scores of unions, fire departments, police departments, and business firms were subjected to such orders. Courts tied the orders to the aim of securing nondiscrimination and equal opportunity (hiring goals "as a means to achieving equal opportunity,"[13] "to prevent future discrimination,"[14] "to assure nonexistence of future barriers to equal opportunity,"[15] "to counteract the detrimental effects . . . discrimination has had upon the prospects of achieving . . . distribution of jobs . . . not affected by discrimination,"[16] "to break down traditional patterns which foreclose opportunities to blacks and women"[17]), where alternative measures seemed insufficient ("no other method was available,"[18] goals are "essential to make meaningful progress,"[19] and "necessary to insure prior and present practices of discrimination would be eliminated"[20]).

Courts were impressed by the difficulty of altering the habits of institutions. One court observed: "After centuries of viewing through colored lenses, eyes do not quickly adjust when the lenses are removed. Discrimination has a way of perpetuating itself, albeit unintentionally, because the resulting inequalities make new opportunities less accessible. Preferential treatment is one partial prescription. . . ."[21] Old habits die hard, especially when much of the reality that spawned them remains in place to sustain them. The last resort is directly to alter the reality itself—the absence of blacks and women—by means of "numerical remedies."

In 1974 the Court of Appeals of the Fifth Circuit reviewed several years of litigation aimed at integrating the Mississippi and Alabama state police. In Mississippi, a federal district court had ordered the highway patrol to stop discriminating and to engage in affirmative action. But the court imposed no quotas. In a state with more than 30 percent blacks, the highway patrol subsequently managed to find only 6 black troopers in the next 91 troopers it hired. Surveying this result, the circuit court instructed the lower court to impose quotas.[22] Over the next decade the level of black participation in the force was raised from 1 percent to 15 percent.[23]

In Alabama in 1972 the Department of Public Safety was composed thus: 650 white state troopers; 26 white trooper cadets; 279 white support personnel; 500 white auxiliary troopers; 5 black menial laborers.[24] Although the state had been ordered in 1970 to stop discriminating in its selection of support personnel, by 1972 it had yet to find any blacks. In that year, a federal district court imposed quotas on the Department of Public Safety. In two years it managed to add 8 black support personnel and to hire 25 black state troopers in its next 50 selections where for the preceding 37 years it had hired none.[25]

The circuit court upheld the lower court's "numerical remedy" and offered this equal opportunity theory:

> By mandating the hiring of those who have been the object of discrimination, quota relief promptly operates to change the outward and visible signs of yesterday's racial distinctions and thus, to provide an

impetus to the process of dismantling the barriers, psychological or otherwise, erected by past practices. It is a temporary remedy that seeks to spend itself as promptly as it can by creating a climate in which objective, neutral employment critieria can successfully operate to select public employees solely on the basis of job-related merit. For once an environment where merit can prevail exists, equality of access satisfies the demand of the Constitution.[26]

III

Reynolds makes a legal as well as moral case against preferential policies. He bases his opposition on an interpretation of section 706(g) of Title VII of the Civil Rights Act. This section comes into play when a violation of the title's prohibition of discrimination has been established: "The court may then enjoin the respondent from engaging in such unlawful employment practice, and *order such affirmative action as may be appropriate,* which may include, but is not limited to, reinstatement or hiring of employees, with or without backpay . . . or any other equitable relief as the court deems appropriate."[27] It is upon this section that courts base their orders, including those that mandate preferential treatment.

When an individual has been wrongfully denied a job or promotion, we believe it a matter of justice that the offending firm be ordered to take him on. The idea of such remedial orders is "to make persons whole for injuries suffered on account of employment discrimination."[28] The "make whole" theory underlies countless court orders. But, according to Reynolds, when a court orders a "class-based remedy," i.e., orders selection according to a quota, it is no longer "making whole" the victims of an institution's discrimination.

When we restore someone to a position he would have had but for a wrong done him, we put him in his rightful place. But to order the selection of someone who merely happens to be the same race or gender of the victim is not to put *him* (the selectee) in *his* rightful place; *he* has suffered no loss which must be made whole. A defense of affirmative action rooted in compensatory justice would not support preferences, implies Reynolds. In order to fit "class-based remedies" under the compensation rubric, it would be necessary to appeal to some sort of group-theory of justice. The numerical remedies would have to be defended as putting groups in *their* rightful places. It is to such defenses that Reynolds directs his objections about "group rights."

It is not difficult to find in the judicial record and in the legal literature defenses of preferences that have this flavor. The Court of Appeals of the Second Circuit upheld a 30 percent nonwhite goal imposed on union admissions by saying: "The remedial quota is a limited one. It seeks to place eligible *minority members* in the position which the *minority* would have enjoyed if *it* had not been the victim of discrimination."[29] The minority members are not placed in positions *they* would have had; rather, minority members are to be chosen in sufficient numbers to bring minority representation to the level *it* would have been had there been no discrimination. That level is assumed to be one of proportional representation.

Such a conception of "numerical remedies" is open to the complaints Reynolds makes about "group rights theories" and "equal results." To the extent that remedial orders are *backward-looking*, that is, seek to right past wrongs, they seem less secured in justice when they are class-based than when they are directed toward the amelioration of identifiable individual losses. They may be less secured in the law as well: Justice White's majority opinion in the recent *Stotts* decision declared that make-whole relief is available "only to those who have been actual victims of illegal discrimination."[30]

However the legal and philosophical arguments go on this matter, they do not touch the wholly independent *forward-looking* remedial orders, such as those upheld by the circuit court in the Mississippi and Alabama highway patrol cases. Preferences were argued there to be "essential to prevent future discrimination."[31] This is a defense rooted squarely in the purpose of the Civil Rights Act, not in some controversial theory of group rights.

Reynolds concludes his essay in this book by saying that the "overriding objective" is to provide "all citizens with a truly equal opportunity to compete on merit for the benefits our society has to offer." It was, in fact, fear that orders short of "class-based remedies" would leave countless blacks and women in institutions unwilling or unable to give them "truly equal opportunity" that prompted most courts to require preferential treatment. They, too, share Reynolds's overriding objective.

So, we come back to the central question: are there cases where the use of preferences is the only, or the most effective, tool for dislodging discrimination? That this *is* the central question is apparent if we suppose an affirmative answer. Committed as he is to the "overriding objective" of equality of opportunity, what would Reynolds say were he to confront a situation where discrimination was so built into the system, such a virtual "way of life,"[32] that only superficial improvements could be expected using nonpreferential tools? If it were also reasonable in the situation to believe that introducing substantial numbers of blacks or women into the system would greatly accelerate the process of transformation, would he forgo this means?

The objection to the use of racial and sexual preferences is that they are unfair to the white males who lose out under them. The unfairness of quotas ought not, I believe, be dismissed. But in the situation just described, we no longer have a choice between being fair and being unfair. We have only the choice between greater and lesser unfairness, now and in the future. In the circumstances described, we can reduce the amount of future discrimination overall by utilizing selective discrimination now; or we can refrain from deliberate unfairness now at the cost of permitting greater unfairness in the future than there otherwise would have been. There may be decisive reasons for refusing to adopt preferential measures in this situation, but it should be evident that those reasons must have to do with something besides the "overriding objective" of equal opportunity.

The central question, then, is one of efficacy. Are preferential policies sometimes needed to overcome discrimination? Can preferences effectively speed up the process of integration and nondiscrimination? If they are never needed, or are never effective, then they can never be defended in the name of equal opportunity. If they sometimes are needed, sometimes are effective, then they can sometimes be defended in the name of equal opportunity.

IV

In the question-and-answer section, Wasserstrom emphasizes how preferences can change the character of institutions by integrating blacks and women into them. Reynolds responds that the nonpreferential policies followed during his tenure in the Justice Department have continued to increase integration.[33] Here the details of current civil rights settlements would be instructive. How rapidly are women and blacks being integrated into the workplace? Is the rate faster or slower than in earlier settlements that relied on preferences? If current policies vigorously push women and blacks into skilled jobs, decision-making roles, and positions of authority, then the case for preferences is undermined: they are simply unnecessary. By contrast, if the rate of integration is falling off significantly, the case for preferences may be strengthened.

Since 1965, hundreds of public agencies, unions, and businesses have temporarily utilized preferences. What happened in those cases? Is the Minneapolis fire department a better or worse department than it was in 1970? Are its race relations improving or deteriorating? Would it have achieved its current level of integration in the absence of the preferential hiring it was ordered to undertake? Is the department freer of discrimination than it otherwise would have been?[34]

What about the construction industry in Philadelphia? The U. S. steel industry? The Bridgeport police department? The Alabama Highway Patrol? Kaiser Aluminum? AT & T?[35] Is there more or less equality of opportunity in these places today than there would have been had preferential programs not been put in place?

These questions direct our attention away from abstract principles down to the concrete details of specific cases and specific policies. Answers to these questions, to the extent we can get them, lie in thorough factual inquiry.

Does this mean that the affirmative action debate ought to be conducted as a "technical" issue, in the sense used by Christopher Edley in his contribution to this book? I think the debate would be more fruitful if it were.

Edley is dubious that we can reduce our disagreements about affirmative action to "technical" questions involving factual calculations and estimates about effective instrumentalities. Such a reduction can hide the deeper "subjective" (value) differences that divide us.[36] Now, Edley may be right that we are divided at the level of values, but I think nevertheless the affirmative action debate is best carried on as a "technical" one. There are two reasons why.

First, what divides some of us may be no more than factual differences. The effect of being immersed in the details of a case like Lee Way Motors, described by one judge as "the most sorry case he'd ever heard of,"[37] may jar some opponents of preferences to the conclusion that sometimes there is no other recourse than a hard remedy. Edley suggests that what we may need most is conversion. There is often no better converter than brute fact, so brute it doesn't let us take refuge in complacent generalities. Thus, some opponents to preferences may change their minds if confronted with the right sort of factual description.

On the other side, the commitments of those who believe preferences indispensable may yield under the sharp light of current empirical inquiry. Twenty, even ten, years ago so many institutions were so deeply mired in the past that there seemed little hope of eliminating their discrimination without the shocks and prods of harsh measures imposed on them. Today new generations lead institutions, generations not nearly so habituated to the realities we want to alter. Consequently, nondiscrimination efforts that dispense with preferences may be sufficient to secure a climate of equal opportunity. A detailed look at the effects of alternative antidiscrimination measures may change the minds of those who support preferences.

There is a second reason why conducting the affirmative action debate on the "technical" level is salutary. Suppose a factual inquiry persuades an opponent of preferences who is committed to equality of opportunity that we are faced with a situation where failure now to impose preferential hiring on a company will leave some discriminatory features unchallenged. Must he then support preferences? Not necessarily. Although brought to factual agreement, he may dissent on value grounds. But where *is* the value disagreement, since commitment to equal opportunity is common to both opponent and proponent?

There may be any number of reasons why agreement is not generated by convergence on the facts. For example, the opponent might feel that deliberately imposing preferences on the company involves *our* doing wrong (though to bring about right), whereas the company's discrimination, despite our best (nonpreferential) efforts at eradication, is *its* wrong; and that it is worse to do wrong than to allow it. It is on this judgment that the opponent and proponent may be at odds.

The point here is that we would not have identified *this* value difference had it not been forced out into the open by our arriving first at agreement on the facts. Both sides may or may not now be able to work through their differences about the strength and applicability of the doing/allowing distinction, but at least they can talk to, not past, each other. Thus, carrying on the affirmative action debate as a "technical" issue can yield valuable results even when "nontechnical" reasons are what divide us.[38]

Notes

1. Wm. Bradford Reynolds, *"Stotts:* Equal Opportunity, Not Equal Results," this volume, chapter 4, p. 39. See also Wm. Bradford Reynolds, "Individualism v. Group Rights: the Legacy of *Brown,"* *Yale Law Journal* 93 (May 1984): 995–1005.

2. In "Questions and Answers," this volume, chapter 8, p. 97. Emphasis added.

3. Richard Wasserstrom, "One Way to Understand and Defend Programs of Preferential Treatment," this volume, chapter 5, p. 47. Wasserstrom restricts his comments to race but means for his arguments to apply generally to gender as well.

4. Ibid., p. 48.

5. On Wasserstrom's racial ideals, see Richard Wasserstrom, "Racism, Sexism, and Preferential Treatment: An Approach to the Topics," *UCLA Law Review* 24 (February 1977): 581–622; and "Racism and Sexism" and "Preferential Treatment" in Richard Wasserstrom, *Philosophy and Social Issues: Five Studies* (Notre Dame, Ind.: University of Notre Dame Press, 1980), pp. 11–50, 51–82.

6. Wasserstrom, this volume, chapter 5, p. 47.

7. "Questions and Answers," this volume, chapter 8, p. 89.

8. Ibid., p. 90.

9. Here we touch up against the problem briefly discussed in Chapter One about the meaning of discrimination. Does example *d* reflect discrimination at or by the foreman's company? Under current law, some hindrances to successful performance by minorities and women count as discriminatory, some not. Example *d* is meant to represent a range of hindrances that share three features: 1. they bear heavily against a particular group; 2. that they exist is a function of the way the world was previously arranged to accommodate the fact of segregation; 3. they require some effort to identify and may not be immediately seen as connected with poor performance by the relevant group. Many instances in this range will qualify as discrimination under current law. Because the restroom situation in *d* is, first, a legacy of past discrimination and, second, easily remediable by the company, I take the company's failure to make changes to constitute discrimination.

10. Mary Green Miner and John B. Miner, *Employee Selection Within the Law* (Washington, D.C.: Bureau of National Affairs, 1978), p. 360.

11. Ibid., p. 361.

12. See, e.g., *Papermakers, Local 189* v. *United States*, 416 F.2d 980 (1969).

13. *Associated General Contractors of Mass., Inc.* v. *Altschuler*, 490 F.2d 9 (1973), at 14.

14. *Asbestos Workers, Local 53* v. *Vogler*, 407 F.2d 1047 (1969), at 1053.

15. *United States* v. *Ironworkers Local 86*, 443 F.2d 544 (1970), at 545 and 553.

16. *EEOC* v. *American Tel. & Tel. Co.*, 556 F.2d 167 (1977), at 169.

17. *United States* v. *City of Alexandria*, 614 F.2d 1358 (1980), at 1366.

18. *Vulcan Society* v. *Civil Service Commission*, 490 F.2d 387 (1973).

19. *NAACP* v. *Allen*, 493 F.2d 614 (1974), at 620–21.

20. *Chisholm* v. *United Postal Service*, 665 F.2d 482 (1981), at 485.

21. *Associated General Contractors* v. *Altschuler*, at 16.

22. *Morrow* v. *Crisler*, 491 F.2d 1053 (1974).

23. *New York Times*, April 20, 1985, p. A22.

24. *NAACP* v. *Allen*, at 616.

25. Ibid., at 620–21.

26. Ibid., at 621. The failure of the lower court in the Mississippi case to order quotas "had the effect of prolonging the pre-existing discriminatory environment." Ibid., at 618.

27. 42 U.S.C. 2000e–5(g). Emphasis added.

28. *Albemarle Paper Company* v. *Moody*, 442 U.S. 405 (1974), at 418.

29. *Rios* v. *Enterprise Association Steamfitters Local 638*, 501 F.2d 622 (1974), at 632. Emphasis added.

30. *Firefighters Local Union No. 1784* v. *Stotts*, 104 S. Ct. 2576 (1984), at 2588–2589.

31. Toward the end of his essay Reynolds does take cognizance of the forward-looking defense: "proponents of . . . preferences also argue that they are necessary to ensure that the employer does not return to his discriminatory ways. The fallacy in this reasoning is self-evident. Far from *preventing* future discrimination, imposition of such remedial devices *guarantees* future discrimination." (Chapter 4, this volume, p. 44) This dismissive response does not even take the defense seriously. Of course preferences guarantee some future discrimination against whites or males, but with the aim and expectation that this will produce less future discrimination against blacks and women and less future discrimination overall.

32. As one court characterized the pattern of discrimination in a trucking company. *United States* v. *Lee Way Motor Freight, Inc.* 625 F.2d 918 (1979), at 943. Lee Way Motors persisted in a decade of obstructionist litigation despite a history of flagrant discrimination and despite the fact that the legal sanctions levied against it were mild and unburdensome. The company, a very large freight carrier with depots throughout the Southwest, never employed a black over-the-road driver until 1968, after it was already in litigation. Even thereafter its employment of black over-the-road drivers, mechanics, and clerical workers was desultory. It resisted for ten years yielding on its no-transfer policy, which locked black city drivers out of the lucrative over-the-road jobs; and

when required to make transfers and provide back pay to those it discriminated against, it raised a host of petty, technical, frivilous objections keeping the litigation going for years. The company was still re-raising the validity of its no-transfer rule in 1979 when the matter had already been settled against it in earlier court proceedings and after seven years of Supreme Court rulings made it plain such a rule could not stand under the circumstances; it was arguing that the court should only consider its hiring practices after 1968, when it dropped its blanket exclusion of blacks (even though the Civil Rights Act had been in effect since 1965!); and it was offering specious and unreliable evidence to show it was nondiscriminating after 1968; and much more. What makes the company's obduracy especially amazing was that it was only required to give up its explicit segregative hiring, to relax the no-transfer rule, and to pay modest compensation to the victims of its discrimination. No affirmative action plan and no wholesale revision of its employment practices was imposed on it.

33. "Questions and Answers," this volume, chapter 8, p. 95.

34. See *Carter* v. *Gallagher*, 452 F.2d 315 (1971).

35. See *Contractors Association of Eastern Pennsylvania* v. *Secretary of Labor*, 442 F.2d 159 (1971); *United States* v. *Allegheny-Ludlum Industries*, 11 FEP Cases 167 (1975); *Bridgeport Guardians, Inc.* v. *Bridgeport Civil Service Commission*, 354 F. Supp. 778 (1973); *NAACP* v. *Allen*, 493 F.2d 614 (1974); *Weber* v. *Kaiser Aluminum & Chemical Corp*, 563 F.2d 216 (1977); *EEOC* v. *AT&T*, 365 F. Supp. 1105 (1973).

36. Christopher Edley, Jr., "Affirmative Action and the Rights Rhetoric Trap," this volume, chapter 6, p. 57.

37. *United States* v. *Lee Way Motor Freight, Inc.* at 944.

38. This essay was written during a period of support by the National Endowment for the Humanities to work on equality of opportunity in American social policy.

SECTION II

Gender

10

Gender and Equality: Introduction
Robert K. Fullinwider and Claudia Mills

THE SURFACE SIMPLICITY of the Civil Rights Act masked a shallow consensus about the meaning of racial discrimination and its appropriate remedies, a consensus that gave way under subsequent application and interpretation of the law. The lack of consensus is even more acute when we turn from race to gender, for here there was never even a superficial consensus to start with. Gender was added to the Civil Rights Act by its congressional opponents as a device to weaken support for the bill; liberal supporters of the act voted against the addition but lost.[1] Whereas most people give at least lip service to color-blindness as the ideal posture of law, however distant its actual attainment, there is no similar shared recognition of gender-blindness as a desirable ideal—neither in 1964 nor twenty years later.

Gender was tacked on to Lyndon Johnson's executive order two years after it was issued.[2] The Civil Rights Act itself allows gender on occasion to count as a "bonafide occupational qualification"; it does not similarly allow race.[3] Nor has the Supreme Court assimilated gender to race in its interpretation of Fifth and Fourteenth Amendment protections. The Court has not been able to make up its mind on what legal and constitutional equality of the sexes entails. It has upheld some gender classifications that favor women[4] and invalidated others.[5] It has overturned single-sex education programs[6] and allowed single-sex education programs.[7] It has struck down some gender classifications that burden women[8] and refused to strike down others.[9] In a Title VII case, it declared that men and women could not be treated differently in a municipal retirement annuity program, even if the different treatment was based on "true generalizations" about the lifespans of the sexes,[10] while in a constitutional case it upheld a state sex-specific statutory rape law on the grounds that "the sexes are not similarly situated in certain circumstances."[11]

117

In general, the Court's decisions are hazy, unclear, and imprecise—
but certainty, clarity, and precision are not in any case easy to come
by here. Public understanding of gender equality is divided and
public debate inchoate and inconclusive. Part of the problem inheres
in the notion of equality itself and the uses we make of it. Important
political contests about the shape and direction of society, law, and
economic life are carried on in the name of equality, as if equality itself
were a substantive notion whose proper understanding would guide
us to a more just policy. But the concept of equality is too thin to bear
the weight placed on it, and to carry on substantive debate about the
political and legal implications of "equality" *unqualified* is to obscure
the real values upon which our differences turn.

Equality is a relation: X and Y are equal *with respect to quality Q*, or *by
reference to standard S*. Two individuals are equal in height, unequal in
weight, or two objects are equal in value but unequal in age, and so
on. Any proposition to the effect that two things are equal is elliptical,
containing a suppressed reference to some standard or other. Even
the simplest equalities, such as mathematical equalities, presuppose a
particular standard. For example, the formula $1 + 5 = 2 \times 3$ is true in
virtue of the arithmetical properties of its terms. But for a numerolo-
gist, 3 and 2 may have magical powers quite different from those of 1
and 5, and from this point of view the formula above does *not* state an
equality.

Sometimes the standard taken to be appropriate as the basis of
comparison is so common that we fail to realize its presence in the
background. Failure to attend to the background standard can produce confusion and inconclusiveness in arguments about equality
since, almost always, what is really at issue is the appropriateness or
suitability of the standard of comparison. This is a particularly acute
problem when we turn from judgments of descriptive equality to
judgments of prescriptive equality. Aristotle's injunction to treat likes
alike is indeterminate because everything is like and unlike everything else (this essay is like every other in this volume in being in
English; it is unlike every other in order of composition, being written
last).[12] The injunction gets content when we understand it to require
equal treatment of those *relevantly* equal, with the measure of relevance provided by some background standard, either assumed or
stipulated. If a prize is offered for the best essay in English in this
volume, this essay should be considered equally a candidate with the
others; if a prize is offered for the best essay in the first fifty pages,
this essay is not in the running.

Every argument about equality has two parts: the equality axiom (treat likes alike) *plus* the standard of comparison. Our contention is that framing debates in the name of equality pushes the focus to the left side of the plus rather than the right side, thus pushing it away from what is actually central to the argument.

This point cannot be stressed too much, since innumerable legal and political debates about equality simply beg the central question by failing to address head on the justifiability of the standards of comparison they presuppose. An argument by Justice Stewart in a recent case upholding a sex-specific statutory rape law illustrates the point.

> The Constitution is violated when government . . . invidiously classi-
> fies similarly situated people on the basis of the immutable characteris-
> tics with which they are born. Thus, detrimental racial classifications
> by government always violate the Constitution, for the simple reason
> that, so far as the Constitution is concerned, people of different races
> are always similarly situated. . . . By contrast, while detrimental gender
> classifications by government often violate the Constitution, they do
> not always do so, for the reason that there are differences between
> males and females that the Constitution necessarily recognizes.[13]

Justice Stewart believes that he has offered an argument, in terms of the axiom of treating likes alike, for not assimilating race to sex, and for permitting a sex-specific gender classification (based on the "dif-ference" that women run the risk of pregnancy while men do not); but he has offered no argument at all. The conclusions have been begged entirely since they are generated *not* by the axiom of equality but by *unstated* standards of comparison Justice Stewart accepts.

Consider the contention that as far as the Constitution is concerned blacks and whites are similarly situated. This cannot mean that the Constitution just tracks the fact that there are no differences between blacks and whites. There are innumerable differences between blacks and whites. It means that the Constitution refuses to take these differences into account. Yet, on the matter of gender, the Constitu-tion is pictured by Stewart as the helpless recorder of facts: it "necessarily" recognizes differences between men and women. But the differences between men and women are no more dispositive than the differences between blacks and whites.[14] If the Constitution can refuse to recognize the latter, it can likewise refuse to recognize the former. The real axis upon which Justice Stewart's view turns is not the axiom of equality but some unstated conception of human dignity and flourishing which accepts as appropriate certain social arrangements built upon gender. The point is not that Justice Stewart has a faulty or inadequate conception of human dignity or human flourishing; it is, rather, that since the conception remains unstated but actually drives his conclusions, we cannot assess the conception for its adequacy nor his conclusions for their cogency.

The lesson to be drawn from this example, and from arguments about equality generally, is to recognize the role played in equality statements by the background standard of comparison and to make plain to ourselves and to others what background standard (social arrangements, moral ideals, historical benchmarks) we presuppose in our own equality claims. Equality arguments whose background standards are unstated and cannot be reconstructed are too indeterminate to come to grips with. We can't know what claim they are actually making.

In this volume Catharine MacKinnon directly challenges certain legal doctrines about equality, especially those that implicitly presuppose the male as the standard of comparison for distributing legal rights and powers. She objects that deference to the Aristotelian maxim has wrongly focused debate on determining whether women are like men or unlike men. Some feminists are bent on proving the former, that women are "as good as" men and so are entitled to access to male powers and privileges. Other feminists have insisted that this approach merely perpetuates a male-based standard and that instead women should value themselves and be valued by society for the ways in which they are distinctive from men. MacKinnon rejects both approaches. For her, the key issue is not sameness or difference, but the wrongness of oppressing *any* group: "No amount of difference justifies treating women as subhuman, and eliminating that is what equality law is for."

Susan Okin's chapter, "Are Our Theories of Justice Gender-Neutral?," takes up a broader topic in which equality is implicit. Her survey of theories of justice in the western philosophical tradition finds, not surprisingly, bias in their treatment of women. The basic terms of the theories of Aristotle, Hume, Kant, Hegel, and others make no essential reference to gender, yet the application of the theories produced gender-biased outcomes.

The theorists either took for granted the institutions of marriage and the family (and the attendant sexual division of labor) and didn't extend the terms of their theories to them, or they had supplementary views about male and female nature that led them to exclude marriage and the family from the scope of their theories. Okin leaves open the possibility that the terms of these theories could be extended in consistent and nonbiased ways to gender and the family (with perhaps radical implications for the justice of contemporary institutions).

In a series of earlier works on sexual harassment and feminist jurisprudence,[15] Catharine MacKinnon has forcefully challenged the possibility of the kind of extension Okin leaves open. There is no such thing as a neutral, objective theory of justice that can be extended undistortedly to women. All theories are "gendered."[16]

The controverted issue here raises profound questions about our ability to use received theories of justice to understand and advance equality for women. To oversimplify, there are three possibilities. First, it might be true of some received theories that they have ample resources for imaginative and undistorted extensions to questions of gender, but past theorists couldn't break free from the grip of sexism to make the extensions possible on their own terms. (A crude analogy: a pair of glasses allows the observer to perceive accurately anything he looks at; he fails or refuses to focus on or attend carefully to certain objects.)

Second, it might be true of the best received theories that they have resources for extension to gender questions, but nevertheless the very terms or structures of the theories themselves make it easy and natural to neglect gender issues or to fail to accord them the same priority or concern as other issues. Although they do not dictate particular conclusions about gender, the theories nevertheless make nonneutral (male-biased) conclusions easier to come by than neutral conclusions. (To carry further the spectacles analogy: a person wearing tinted glasses may have greater difficulty in distinguishing some colors on the spectrum. The world too easily seems green. He *could* accurately distinguish colors but it would require special efforts and perhaps indirect tests. So the glasses don't dictate false conclusions, but do make them easy to reach.)

The third possibility is this: the goal of gender-neutrality is a chimera. There is no such thing. Thus, nonfeminist theories of justice, no matter how neutral and pliable they seem, will never allow adequate appreciation of women's situation. (Perhaps the analogy is like this: it is a mistake to think there is a world out there beyond the glasses against which to judge the accuracy of our perceptions. Perception, understanding, point of view is wholly a function of the lenses. How you make the lenses is how you will see "the world.")

In a very rough way, we can situate Okin in possibility two and MacKinnon in possibility three. For MacKinnon, a feminist theory of justice (and corresponding jurisprudence) would be a "theory of women's point of view."[17] Illustrative, for her, of how law might develop in line with such a theory is the case *State* v. *Wanrow* in which the Washington Supreme Court overturned the murder conviction of Yvonne Wanrow, who had claimed self-defense in the killing of a man who menaced first a child, then her.[18] The trial court erred, according to the supreme court's judgment, not only by instructing the jury to apply an objective standard of self-defense, but also by leaving the jury with the impression that

> the objective standard to be applied is that applicable in an altercation between two men. The impression created—that a 5' 4" woman with a cast on her leg and using a crutch must . . . somehow repel an assault by a 6' 2" intoxicated man without employing weapons in her defense, unless the jury finds her determination of the degree of danger to be objectively reasonable . . . violates the respondent's right to equal protection of the law. The respondent was entitled to have the jury consider her actions in light of her own perceptions of the situation, *including those perceptions which were the product of our nation's "long and unfortunate history of sex discrimination."* Until such time as the effects of that history are eradicated, care must be taken to assure that our self-defense instructions afford women the right to have their conduct judged in light of the individual physical handicaps which are the product of sex discrimination.[19]

MacKinnon sees the *Wanrow* decision as pointing to a feminist perspective. Under such an interpretation, she says,

> Subjectivity, as construed in *Wanrow*, does not turn on the psychology of the self-defendant's individual feelings at the time, or particularly weight, in detail, her personal background or cognitions. Rather, subjectivity is interpreted as the point of view of *her situation as a woman* under these particular conditions, in which the meaning such a woman would give what Yvonne saw and knew is defined as reasonable. . . . The inquiry into Yvonne's subjectivity . . . [becomes] an inquiry into the *substantive history of a group standpoint*. 'What she did feel' is presumed the same as 'what is the point of view of women's situation.'[20]

Rachel Flick, in her contribution to this volume, responds to MacKinnon's claim that the law cannot be neutral and objective. According to Flick, "objectivity is the essence of law" and the modification of law to accommodate multiple, incommensurable points of view "is antithetical to the rule of law itself." Likewise, Flick raises objections to MacKinnon's project of rendering "women's subjective experience" as reflecting a "group standpoint." She worries that such a collectivist viewpoint will in fact turn out to be "the perspective of the collectivity according to some one person or some group of people who will claim to speak for it," and this, she claims, leads to the tyranny of the few over the many. Finally, she takes issue with MacKinnon's assessment of the extent to which women are oppressed in our society, arguing that male-female relations are more complex than the "brute exploitation" MacKinnon assumes. Readers are invited to examine for themselves MacKinnon's essays as well as Flick's criticism in this volume to judge the merits of this important controversy.

The final two essays differ from the others in this section in that they do not discuss foundational issues about gender and equality. Instead they debate what has been dubbed "the civil rights issue of the decade": comparable worth. Advocates of "comparable worth" argue that "equal pay for equal work" does not go far enough in targeting and eliminating sex discrimination in the workplace; even where men and women do substantially different work, discrimination can still be evident if women are systematically paid less than men for doing work of equal or comparable value.

Heidi Hartmann defends a comparable worth approach for addressing deep-seated inequities in a workplace still very much segregated by gender. She argues that opponents who raise the specter of government-wide setting of wage rates have a false picture of how comparable worth in fact operates. It is designed to be implemented gradually on an employer-by-employer basis, not through a sweeping judicial overturning of supply and demand. Far from wreaking havoc with the "free market," she claims, it will help the market to function better. Discrimination, according to Hartmann, is not an efficient use of human resources.

Mark Killingsworth counters that comparable worth strategies will only end up worsening the situation of working women. By making female labor more expensive, they will have the effect of reducing rather than enhancing women's employment opportunities. In Killingsworth's view, "Comparable worth amounts to putting a tax on labor in predominantly female jobs and distributing the revenues to the workers in those jobs who are fortunate enough to remain employed after the tax is imposed!" To Hartmann, of course, that comparable worth might lead to some female unemployment is irrelevant if the issue is one of fairness. After all, arguments could be made that equal pay for blacks and whites amounts to a tax on the labor of blacks, who otherwise could underbid white workers. In any case, the debate over comparable worth will doubtless be with us for many years to come.

Notes

1. Congressional Record, February 8, 1964, p. 2577; Gary Orfield, *Congressional Power: Congress and Social Change* (New York: Harcourt Brace Jovanovich, 1975), pp. 299–300; Gilbert Y. Steiner, *Constitutional Inequality* (Washington, D.C.: Brookings Institution, 1985), pp. 11–12.

2. Executive Order 11375 (1967).

3. 42 U.S.C. 2000e—2c.
4. *Schlesinger* v. *Ballard*, 419 U.S. 498 (1975).
5. *Craig* v. *Boren*, 429 U.S. 190 (1976).
6. *Mississippi University for Women* v. *Hogan*, 458 U.S. 718 (1982).
7. *Williams* v. *McNair*, 401 U.S. 951 (1971); *Vorcheimer* v. *School District*, 97 S. Ct 1671 (1978).
8. *Frontiero* v. *Richardson*, 411 U.S. 677 (1973); *Reed* v. *Reed*, 404 U.S. 71 (1971).
9. *Dothard* v. *Rawlinson*, 433 U.S. 321 (1977).
10. *Los Angeles Department of Water and Power* v. *Manhart*, 435 U.S. 702, 708 (1978).
11. *Michael M.* v. *Superior Court of Sonoma County*, 450 U.S. 464, 469 (1981).
12. Aristotle, *Nichomachean Ethics*, Book V, III, 1131a–1131b.
13. 450 U.S. at 477–78.
14. This point is illustrated in the Court's disposition of a Title VII case, *Dothard* v. *Rawlinson*, 433 U.S. 321 (1977), upholding an Alabama prohibition of women guards in certain male prisons. The Court found the prohibition to be reasonably based on the greater liability of female guards to sexual assault by male inmates. In parallel circumstances, however, we can imagine prisons where, because of racially hostile white inmate populations, black guards would be more liable to physical assault than white guards. Yet the Court would not have been persuaded by this genuine difference between white and black guards to have sustained any prohibition of black guards.
15. *Sexual Harassment of Working Women* (New Haven: Yale University Press, 1979); "Toward Feminist Jurisprudence," *Stanford Law Review* 34 (February 1982): 703–737; "Feminism, Marxism, Method, and the State: An Agenda for Theory," *Signs* 7 (1982): 515–44; "Feminism, Marxism, Method, and the State: Toward Feminist Jurisprudence," *Signs* 8 (1983): 635–58.
16. "Feminism, Marxism, Method, and the State: An Agenda for Theory," pp. 536–38; "Feminism, Marxism, Method, and the State: Toward Feminist Jurisprudence," pp. 636, 638, 658.
17. "Feminism, Marxism, Method, and the State: An Agenda for Theory," p. 535.
18. 558 P. 2d 548 (1977)
19. 558 P. 2d at 558–59. Emphasis added.
20. "Toward Feminist Jurisprudence," pp. 733–34. Emphasis added.

11

Are Our Theories of Justice Gender-Neutral?

Susan Moller Okin

MY ANSWER TO THE QUESTION posed is, not surprisingly, "no." The
more interesting parts of the answer—necessary in any case to justify
the negative response—are about *how* and *why* our traditional theories of justice are gender-biased. In my attempt to answer these
questions, I will reach far back in the western tradition, in order to
examine theories of justice that still influence the ways in which we
think about it. I will trace a chronological, though broken, path from
Aristotle to Hume, Rousseau, Kant, Hegel, Mill, and thence to
contemporary theories of justice. My focus, however, is not historical, but conceptual; I attempt to characterize conceptions of justice
and corresponding ways of thinking about women into four identifiable though overlapping types.

Theories of justice have to do with the distribution by societies of
benefits and burdens. Concerned with political rights, with legal
equality or differentiation, with the assignment of property, positions, or roles to some and not to others, these theories attempt to
show why things should be distributed in one way rather than
another, and why some differences among human beings justify
unequal treatment, while others do not. One might think that the fact
that humanity is comprised of two different sexes would provide a
fundamental part of the subject matter of theories of justice. To the
contrary, most of the theories of justice central to the western
tradition of political thought have either not attempted to justify the
very different treatment of men and women by society at all, or have
argued about the different treatment of the sexes in ways that
contrast, and often conflict with, their discussions of inequalities
among men. There is, then, a strong strain in our political tradition

that regards only men as the appropriate subjects for a theory of social and political justice.

I will take Aristotle as the exemplar of the first type of reasoning leading to this conclusion; as we shall see later, there is much unacknowledged Aristotelianism prevalent in contemporary thinking about justice. In Aristotle's political theory, the treatment of women is consistent with his generally hierarchical understanding of both nature and society. Women, like the majority of men, are viewed not as separate human individuals with ends of their own, but as inferior and necessarily subordinate members of society whose function is to serve the ends of the free, leisured men who alone can live "the good life." That Aristotle's instrumental treatment of slaves and laborers has received considerably more attention until very recently than his very similar disposition of women itself constitutes evidence that the functionalist mode of thinking about women has survived unexamined in spite of the supposedly individualistic premises of modern liberalism.

The essential foundations of Aristotle's exclusion of woman from the realm of political justice are to be found in his theory of reproductive biology. This theory, which reigned unchallenged until recent centuries, is founded on the assumption that the male is the generic type of the human species, and that the only reason for the existence of the female is that the male distinction of form (soul) from matter (body) requires sexual reproduction. Thus, he says, "we should look on the female as being as it were a deformity, though one which occurs in the ordinary course of nature."[1] Even with respect to reproduction, the only reason that she exists at all, the female is characterized as inferior and disabled. Since she provides only the matter out of which the male semen forms the new human being, she is "as it were an infertile male"; she is "female in virtue of a particular inability."[2] This perception of women as instruments needed for the proper reproduction of men underlies the discussion of them in Aristotle's ethical and political writings.

Distributive justice, in Aristotle's discussion, is essentially meritocratic. A distribution, to be just, must reflect the equality or inequality of merit of the persons to whom it is to apply: "the ratio between the shares will be the same as that between the persons. If the persons are not equal, their [just] shares will not be equal."[3] By the same reasoning, Aristotle concludes that among persons who are *essentially* unequal, issues of political justice do not even arise; "there is only something which bears a resemblance to what is just."[4] Between a free man and his slaves, or his children, there can be no such thing as justice or injustice, just as there can be no such thing as injustice toward the self. Justice between husband and wife *is* somewhat more complicated. Although it is different from what is just in social and political matters, it *is* a form of justice, which Aristotle calls "household justice." Household justice, he explains, is analogous to the relationship between the different parts of the soul, where the more rational should rule over the less rational.[5] While women should regulate those domestic matters in which they have more expertise, men rightly control relations between the household and the outside world and are the only adult members of the household who emerge from the household into that outside world to become participating citizens of the polis, ruling and being ruled in turn. Women are totally excluded from the realm of political justice.

As I among others have pointed out, Aristotle's conclusions about women and justice, from which in its fullest meaning they are completely excluded, follow logically from his reproductive biology, but the latter is founded upon the totally unargued assumption that men are the biological norm of the human species and that women exist only in order for men to be reproduced in a way appropriate to their high status.[6] This assumption is consistent with Aristotle's hierarchical vision of nature, in which those forms of life he adjudges to be lower serve functions benefiting those above them, while those at the top, though emulating the Gods, serve purposes of their own in the context of a just community of peers.

As interpretations of society and theories of justice based on assumptions of natural or God-given hierarchy were questioned more frequently, especially in the seventeenth century, a new intellectual problem arose for those who were still intent on preserving and justifying the unequal treatment of women. Hobbes, as feminist political theorists have pointed out in recent years, was completely unable to reconcile familial patriarchy with his radically contractual vision of a politics which—although it led to absolute sovereignty— was centrally founded on the natural freedom and equality of human beings, including women.[7] His only solution was to "lose" women completely, defining a family as comprised of "a man, and his children, and servants together: wherein the Father or Master is the Sovereign."[8] This was hardly a solution that could withstand much scrutiny. Locke's solution, which exemplifies the second of my four types of reasoning about women and justice, was little better.

The second mode of thinking that has served to exclude women from equal consideration in theories of justice and political rights is the notion that men's superior physical strength legitimates their rule over women both within and outside the family. Both Locke and Rousseau, in spite of their general rejection of "might is right" principles, resorted to them in the context of relations between the sexes. Since I will discuss Rousseau in the context of the third mode of reasoning, I will use Locke as my example here. Locke was somewhat pushed into a corner on the subject of family patriarchalism by the fact that the primary purpose of his writing about government was to refute *political* patriarchalism. Having claimed, in the course of destroying the patriarchal argument for absolute monarchy, that mothers share parental authority with fathers, Locke was then faced with the problem of how to preserve the essentials of patriarchy within the family. He justifies the subjection of wives to their husbands' authority on matters that are "of their Common Interest and Property" by invoking the notion that men are "the abler and stronger." He does not spell out *how* men are abler; he does not deny, as Aristotle had, that women's part in reproduction is indeed greater than men's. And he takes no account at all of the very different degrees and types of education afforded to the sexes at the time. But, quite apart from such problems of evidence about women's lesser abilities, Locke's justification of paternal authority within the family seriously conflicts with his own rejection of the rule of the stronger, as characteristic of relations among beasts, not human beings, and with his explicit argument that "Excellency of Parts and Merit" cannot justify the subjection of any man to the will or authority of any other.[9] The subordinate status of women was clearly in tension with the fundamentals of liberalism. Indeed, Locke's difficulty in maintaining patriarchal relations between the sexes while rejecting political patriarchalism illustrates clearly that new arguments were going to be needed to justify the subordination of women and their exclusion from the realm of political justice.

I come now to the third and fourth types of reasoning about gender and justice, which together constitute a set of assumptions and arguments that have been remarkably prevalent in the continued justification of women's political, economic, and social subordination. These assumptions and arguments have appeared in the works of political theorists from at least the eighteenth century until the present. (In some respects they can be seen in embryo as far back as Plato.) But they also appear in political and judicial reasoning, in discussions about women and property, women and professional life, women and politics. First, I will summarize them, then I will illustrate them in more detail, by referring to the works of major political theorists.

By the late seventeenth and early eighteenth centuries, it is clear that a new conception of the nuclear family had begun to appear. Some family historians have recently argued that *actual* family life, at least among the upper social strata, was changing with the new perceptions of it. About this, I think, the evidence is decidedly ambiguous. But there is far less ambiguity in the claim that the family, as depicted and idealized by political theorists, was a very different family from that to be found in the works of Hobbes or even Locke.

What is this new idealized family like? First, it is founded upon love and personal choice, rather than upon practical considerations such as property. Intimacy and psychological commitment are more important, both between spouses and between parents and children. Companionship is stressed. The new family is depicted as cherishing its private and intimate sphere of domesticity.

Family historians have argued in recent years that the new family type, both in theory and in practice, was considerably less patriarchal, and more egalitarian, than its predecessor. Companionship between husband and wife, the implication goes, requires equality. But with the help of illustrations taken from some of the most influential of eighteenth- and nineteenth-century political theorists— Rousseau, Hume, Kant, and Hegel—I will argue that, far from extending the modern ideal of social and political equality to women, the idealized conception of what I have termed the "sentimental family" in fact served to *reinforce* unequal relations between men and women, and the exclusion of women from the realm of political and social justice.[10]

First, families came to be seen as characterized by relations in contrast with those of the outside world. Although the family comprises two adult members, the likelihood of any conflict of interest between the two (such as would be taken for granted in other contexts) is denied on the grounds that the family is founded on love, altruism, and self-sacrifice. Since the family therefore has only one interest, it can without injustice be both ruled internally and represented in the public realm by its male head. No injustice can be claimed by wives, because one cannot do injustice where only a single interest is involved, and because justice is an inappropriate moral virtue to apply within families, where the higher moral virtues of love and generosity prevail. Thus women do not *need* either familial equality or the equality of citizenship, and no injustice is done them by the denial of these things.

Second, women become characterized by the moral virtues that are regarded as essential for their role in the newly idealized family: sentiment, love, being rooted in particularity, preference for those close to them. But, significantly, these same virtues and emotions are regarded as *dis*qualifying women from citizenship, which requires rationality, powers of abstraction, and dedication to the impartial rule of justice. So if women are to be as the theorists insist they ought to be as family members, wives and mothers, they must be excluded from the world of politics, where they can only constitute a force subversive of the public good.

These two modes of argument, which frequently occur in combination, constitute the third and fourth modes of reasoning that, I claim, make our traditional theories of justice far from gender-neutral. One mode is most evident in the works of Rousseau and Hume, the other in the works of Kant and Hegel.

In Rousseau's political theory, and particularly in *Émile*, far more attention is paid both to sexuality and to relations between the sexes than is typically found in such works. These ideas have been much discussed in recent years; here, we can focus on only the two elements most pertinent to Rousseau's conclusions about the necessity for male governance of and female seclusion within the family. First, Rousseau thought that women wielded a potentially vast power over men through their capacity to arouse them sexually, and he was clearly concerned with counteracting this potential power through social and political means. Second, Rousseau was well-nigh obsessed with the uncertainty of paternity. Again and again in his works, he maintains, as the reason a husband must control his wife, even to the extent of keeping her totally secluded from other men, that "it is essential for him to be certain that the children, whom he is compelled to recognize and maintain, belong to no one but himself."[11] Without this assurance, which must be based not only on the actual absolute fidelity of married women, but also on their flawless reputations, Rousseau considers that a man will have no incentive to provide for the children his wife bears. Thus, he argues, it is a dictate of nature that *women's* lives must be controlled to a very large extent by *men's* need to compensate for this biological difference between the sexes. Rousseau gives no sign of recognition that it was at least as much the structure of society as it was the different biological role of the sexes in reproduction that rendered contemporary women and children economically dependent upon men.

Thus the *reasons* stressed by Rousseau for the necessity of the patriarchal rule of husbands over wives and the exclusion of women from all but domestic life follow from his views about sexuality and reproduction. But the *justification* that this otherwise egalitarian and democratic philosopher provides for the subordination of women is that the family, unlike the wider society, is founded upon love. Thus, unlike a government, which must be strictly accountable to its people, the father of a family "in order to act aright, . . . has only to consult his heart."[12] The loving husband and father, apparently, can always be trusted to foster the united interests of those he loves. Thus women can, without prejudice to their well-being, be both ruled within the family and excluded from the political realm, in which their husbands will represent the interests of each family unit.

David Hume, Rousseau's English contemporary, made very similar arguments, both for the necessity of preserving female chastity and modesty of reputation and about the family as a place where the need for justice was precluded by the rule of love. Though his case about the necessity of ensuring paternity seems far less impassioned than Rousseau's, it is otherwise parallel. From the "trivial and anatomical observation" that only a woman can know infallibly that she is a child's parent "is derived that vast difference between the education and duties of the two sexes."[13] And in parallel manner, too, Hume argued about relations within the family.

Hume begins his discussion of justice by pointing out the circumstances in which justice is *not* the appropriate or expedient moral virtue. In situations of profuse abundance of resources, or in situations of extreme deprivation, he claims that distributive justice would be unnecessary or inappropriate. Likewise, he supposes that in circumstances of "enlarged affections," in which every man "feels no more concern for his own interest than for that of his fellows," justice would be useless. Hume regards the family as one of the most complete instances of such enlarged affections, in which justice is inappropriate because "all distinction of property be, in a great measure, lost and confounded." He writes: "Between married persons, the cement of friendship is by the laws supposed so strong as to abolish all division of possessions; and has often, in reality, the force ascribed to it."[14] The impression given by Hume here of the common law's disposition of property within marriage is highly misleading. For the law did not institute the communal ownership of the husband's and wife's property. Rather, it automatically transferred all of the wife's personal property, as well as control over and the income from her real property, into the hands of her husband. Both what she had before marriage and what she earned or inherited within it became, by the common law, his. But nothing of what was his became hers. As Mill was later to put it, "the two are called 'one person in law,' for the purpose of inferring that whatever is hers is his, but the parallel inference is never drawn that whatever is his is hers."[15] What Hume's fictional account of the unified family serves to justify is the completely one-sided dependence of wives upon husbands.

There are at least two problems involved in the arguments summarized above. There is both a type of circularity and a clear inconsis-

tency about a theory that adheres to an idealized vision of family life
in order to justify male supremacy both within the family and in the
wider society, and that also insists that women live chaste and
secluded lives or else they and their children will be in danger of
abandonment and destitution. First, the circularity: without the male
supremacy and control of property, there would be far less need for
women to be able to assure their husbands that they were indeed
their children's fathers. If the women of the propertied classes in
Hume's England, for example, had not been deprived of their property by marriage and denied access to paid employment, they would
have been far more capable of supporting their children unaided.
Second, the inconsistency: if the family is characterized by unity,
generosity, and love, to a degree sufficient to ensure women's welfare
even though they are deprived of the legal and political rights that
men are regarded as needing for their self-protection, then why in
such a benign relationship should husbands have reason to be
suspicious about their children's biological paternity? There seem to
be two very different pictures of family life here. The woman is
supposed to rely on love and trust, but the man apparently has such
serious reason for *mistrust*, even on the most intimate of issues, that
the violation of his wife's liberties, even her freedom of movement,
are held to be justified by it. The problems involved in such a mixture
of arguments are obvious. In his fictional depictions of family life,
Rousseau himself indicates that he was aware of them; the husbands
and fathers he invents are far from ideal. But in spite of his own
recognition of the fragility of the myth on which it was based, he
could see no alternative to the position of women that he regarded as
dictated by nature.

The fourth mode of reasoning about women and justice is closely
related to the third. It is best exemplified in the works of Kant and,
drawn at greater length, Hegel. Both theorists, in Kant's case influ-
enced by Rousseau and in Hegel's case probably by Rousseau and
Kant, also adhere to the notion that the family is such a united place
that women *need* no separate rights, whether within or outside the
household. In Kant's case, this means that all his most cherished
human ideals are violated so far as married women are concerned.
The unity of the family justifies the denial to any married woman of
the right of equal freedom, it places her under the paternalistic rule of
her husband, it validates a legal contract in which a person becomes
permanently subject to the authority of a master—all of these things
constituting clear violations of Kant's universally binding moral principles. Even if we do not question his idealization of the family, the
subordinate position of wives, which Kant explicitly endorses, is

exactly analogous to that of the subjects of a benevolent despot, which he argues is incompatible with human freedom and dignity.

In addition to that mode of reasoning clearly enunciated by Rousseau and Hume, Kant and Hegel employ another type of reasoning to argue that women's nature, which fits them admirably for family life, renders them equally *unsuited* to life outside the family. In an early essay, Kant contrasts the complementary natures of men and women. Men, the sublime, are characterized by depth of understanding and reflection; women, the beautiful, by fineness of understanding, sentiment, and sympathy. Echoing Rousseau to some extent, Kant claims that these differences are partly innate, but insists that they must be fostered by the modes of socialization of the two sexes. Moreover, the further Kant enters into discussion of what a woman suited for life within the sentimental family should be like, the clearer it becomes that she does not belong within the category of "all rational beings as such" to whom his moral theory is applicable. Women's "philosophy is not to reason, but to feel"; their virtue, unlike men's, is to be inspired by the desire to please; for women, Kant asserts, there is to be "nothing of *ought,* nothing of *must,* nothing of *due.*"[16] Clearly, the characteristics required by their role within the family are such as to disqualify them from participation as moral subjects in any other aspect of human life.

Hegel develops the same ideas, though more systematically and in considerably more detail. He provides the most striking example among political theorists of the notion that, while the family dictates what women must be like, the characteristics it requires of them are fundamentally opposed to those required of a good citizen. Thus women are necessarily excluded from the sphere of political justice.

Hegel talks of the family, in contrast to the state, as "a *natural* ethical community." He continues: "as the *element* of the nation's actual existence, it stands opposed to the nation itself; as the immediate being of the ethical order, it stands over against that order which shapes and maintains itself by working for the universal; the Penates stand opposed to the universal Spirit."[17] The family, according to Hegel, is necessarily characterized by feeling, altruism, and particularity, with woman as its natural guardian. The state, by contrast, while also demanding a wider altruism, is built on reason and universality; thus man must be its guardian. While neither the family nor the state is complete without the other, only the man has the capacity to inhabit both realms. He can both live "a subjective ethical life on the plane of feeling" within his family, and also go out, as the family's representative, into the community, in which "he finds his self-conscious being."[18] Women, having no control over property or rights to active citizenship in the state, cannot have complete ethical personalities, by Hegel's criteria. Rather, "to be imbued with family piety is [their] ethical frame of mind."[19]

In both the *Phenomenology* and *The Philosophy of Right*, Hegel spells out at some length the representation by women of only one side of the tension between the particular interests of members of individual families and the needs of the state. "Womankind in general," Hegel states, is the "internal enemy" of the community, its "everlasting irony. Womankind changes by intrigue the universal end of the government into a private end, transforms its universal activity into a work of some particular individual, and perverts the universal property of the State into a possession and ornament of the Family."[20] Even confined within the household and deprived of political rights, Hegel regards women as enemies of the state. They will "ridicule" the needs of the universal and encourage their children to do likewise; in particular, they will attempt to subvert the state's need for their sons' lives in war. It is above all as mothers of potential soldiers—"the brave youth in whom woman finds her pleasure"—that women even as family members come into conflict with the needs of Hegel's state.

If women should come to hold political power, however, Hegel considers the problem would be greatly exacerbated. In unusually straightforward language, he states, "When women hold the helm of government, the state is at once in jeopardy, because women regulate their actions not by the demands of universality but by arbitrary inclinations and opinions."[21] The best solution, then, is at least to ensure that women do not have access to political power. For the very qualities that Hegel regards as fitting them best for their important role within the family—particularistic altruism and guidance by feelings—make them a threat to the larger community. Rather than even considering whether active citizenship might enlarge women's horizons and encourage them to value more universal interests, he regarded them as a source of potential subversion. His conclusions, then, parallel to Kant's, are that women are less than complete ethical beings, incapacitated for public life and properly devoid of civil and political rights, because of those very qualities that render them the natural guardians of family life.

Not long after Hegel contributed to the long tradition that confirmed and attempted to justify women's exclusion from the rights and principles of justice that were considered essential for men, John Stuart Mill confronted this tradition. The only mainstream liberal theorist to have explicitly applied his arguments about justice to women, Mill argued against the second, third, and fourth modes of reasoning outlined above—all of which were still clearly influential in the theoretical foundations of patriarchy.

Mill was well aware of the tensions that the continued subordination of women caused within the liberal tradition, though he was not surprised by its persistence in societies that had in most respects eschewed the rule of the stronger as a principle of justice. Speaking of "this one case of a social relation grounded on force," he says, "So long as it does not proclaim its own origin, and as discussion has not brought out its true character, [it] is not felt to jar with modern civilization, any more than domestic slavery among the Greeks jarred with their notion of themselves as a free people."[22] Mill attacks head-on justifications of patriarchy that claim that, unlike other forms of domination, the authority of men over women is "natural." All forms of domination have been regarded as natural as long as they have been regarded as legitimate, Mill asserts, for "unnatural generally means only uncustomary, and . . . everything which is usual appears natural."[23] Theories such as Locke's, which grounded political and legal rights in the natural equality of human beings, and then tried to retain the inequalities of women's rights on which familial patriarchy was based by appeal to the natural differences between the sexes, were examples of selective uses of "nature" that Mill refused to allow.

He also confronts the highly idealized perceptions of family life that previous defenders of patriarchy had used in order to argue that women did not need equality because their interests would always be protected by the love and altruism characteristic of family relations. (Indeed, his own father had made exactly this claim, in his *Essay on Government* (1820).[24] Arguing that the type of power given to husbands and fathers encourages human tendencies to selfishness, he writes:

> If the family in its best forms is, as it is often said to be, a school of sympathy, tenderness, and loving forgetfulness of self, it is still oftener, as respects its chief, a school of wilfulness, overbearingness, unbounded self-indulgence, and a double-dyed and idealized selfishness, of which sacrifice itself is only a particular form: the care for the wife and children being only care for them as parts of the man's own interests and belongings, and their individual happiness being immolated in every shape to his smallest preferences.[25]

Recognizing that the interests of family members were by no means always united or compatible with each other, he stressed that the only just form of decision making within marriage was shared authority and compromise between men and women who had equal rights both within and outside the family.

As for the notion that woman's moral nature, while rendering her suited for wifehood and motherhood, made her careless of the general good, unable to reason impartially, and therefore unsuited to citizenship, Mill holds it up to ridicule, together with all other arguments based on women's alleged "nature." "I deny," Mill asserts, "that anyone knows, or can know, the nature of the two sexes, as long as they have only been seen in their present relation to one another. . . . What is now called the nature of women is an eminently artificial thing—the result of forced repression in some directions, unnatural stimulation in others."[26] If women are at present narrow-minded and partial to their families, Mill asserts, how could one expect anything else, so long as they are cut off from participation in public life. Give women the vote, and the same right as men to enter the realm of life outside the home in various capacities, and their moral "natures" will change accordingly.

In spite of his bold confrontation of these influential claims of antifeminist theories of justice, however, Mill's feminist reasoning stopped short of challenging the traditional division of labor between the sexes within the family. Partly, no doubt, because the circumstances of reproduction when he wrote were in most respects closer to those of Aristotle's day than to those of the present—high infant mortality, lack of reliable contraception, unsatisfactory alternatives to breast-feeding—Mill clearly regards the lives of married women as necessarily constrained to a very large extent by their reproductive and domestic roles. Thus while married women should have the right and the necessary education to enable them to work outside of the home, Mill clearly argues that it is better for them in practice not to do so. In spite of his bold challenge to traditional theories of justice on the issue of women's *rights*, Mill accepts as just very much the same division of labor that the other theorists had defended.

Even within the context of his own feminist arguments, however, this assumption of the sexual division of labor and endorsement of the gendered structure of the family causes problems. For one thing, Mill was clearly aware of the effect of economic dependence on power relations;[27] thus, by not questioning women's responsibility for the unpaid labor of the family, he in effect condones the relative powerlessness of wives. Again, though he was aware that women's creativity and intellectual productivity had been very much constrained by the continual interruptions that resulted from their domestic duties,[28] he proposes no sharing of even those responsibilities that could readily have been shared at the time. And finally, although he argued that participation in the wider world of the community was necessary for the enlargement of moral reasoning and sympathy, he *practically* interdicts such participation for married women with children. One is impelled to ask how the family could become, as Mill said it might, "a school of sympathy in equality" if in practice the sex roles of its adult members perpetuated the same power imbalance, unequal opportunity to develop one's talents, and unequal access to the outside world that had characterized it in the past.

Mill addressed the injustice of women's legal and political subordination to men as had no other traditional theorist of justice. He did not address the injustice of the sexual division of labor, except to argue for women's legal right to compete for paid jobs from which they were excluded on the grounds of sex. But as we turn to look briefly at twentieth-century theories of justice, we shall see that, despite the technological changes regarding reproduction that might lead one to expect such questioning of the justice of traditional sex roles, most modern theorists of justice have ignored them.

Much of the legal discrimination against women that Mill claimed was so grossly inconsistent with the central tenets of liberalism has been rectified during the century since he wrote. A considerable amount of this change has been accomplished in the United States only within the last fifteen years. Formal legal equality, however, does not by any means guarantee justice for actual *men* living in society; still less does it for *women*. The heavy weight of sexist tradition, combined with the effects of socialization broadly defined, still work powerfully to reinforce roles for the two sexes that are commonly regarded as of unequal prestige and worth. To a large extent, this division of roles is still rooted within the family, where it influences us in our most formative years, and from where it extends its repercussions into every other social sphere.

This gender system has not been much subjected to the general tests of justice employed by contemporary political theorists and moral philosophers. Even in a recent book entitled *Justice, Equal Opportunity and the Family*, the constraints on women's equality of opportunity that result from the gender structure of the family are ignored.[29] Though Fishkin addresses the issue of sex as well as race discrimination in employment practices, he does not even mention the effects of the internal gender structure of contemporary families, including the extent of unpaid and largely unrecognized labor that is done by women. Though this structure clearly affects power relations within the family, the practices of the workplace (where it is still assumed that the worker has a wife at home, although in most cases he or she does not), and the roles into which children are socialized, Fishkin apparently does not consider it relevant to his discussion of justice and equal opportuinty.

The weight of a tradition of theories of justice that assume, for the various reasons discussed above, that their subjects are male heads of households rather than all human individuals, is also clearly evident in John Rawls's *A Theory of Justice*.[30] An ambiguity runs throughout Rawls's book that is continually noticeable to anyone reading it from a feminist perspective. The book is written using individual terms of reference. The supposedly generic terms "men," "he," and "his" are interspersed with nonsexist terms of reference such as "individual" and "moral person." Sometimes we think, despite the male terms of reference, that the argument is about all of us, women as well as men. But in fact, Rawls says that, though it is not necessary for him to do so, he will generally think of the subjects of his theory as "heads of families." Though the head of a family need not necessarily be a man, Rawls does nothing to dispel the impression, confirmed by common usage, that any adult male in a household takes precedence over a female as its "head." He words his discussion about justice between generations in terms of "fathers" and "sons" and likens the difference principle to "the principle of fraternity."

The significance of Rawls's head of household assumption is that, in effect, it traps him into the traditional mode of thinking that life within the family and relations between the sexes are not properly to be regarded as part of the subject matter of a theory of justice. Interestingly, he falls into this mode of thinking in spite of the fact that he both indicates on several occasions that a person's sex, like his or her race, is a morally arbitrary and contingent characteristic and also states explicitly that the family is one of those basic social institutions to which the principles of justice must apply.

Rawls includes "the monogamous family" in his initial list of major social institutions that must conform to the principles of justice since it, like the others (the constitution, the legal protection of essential freedoms, property arrangements, and so on), has such profound effects on people's lives. He then develops his two principles of justice, the first of which institutes equal basic liberty and the second of which requires that inequalities benefit the least advantaged and that positions of inequality be open to all. He then proceeds to apply them to almost all of the major social institutions that he has identified as basic at the outset of the theory. But throughout the discussions of the legal protection of liberties, of democratic constitutional procedures, of markets and property ownership, the question of whether the monogamous family, in either its traditional or any other form, is a just social institution is never raised. Instead, when Rawls at length mentions the family "in some form" as a just institution, he does so not to *consider* whether or not, or in what form, it might be just, but to *assume* it.[31] Moreover, when he writes about the family that he is assuming to be just, his uncharacteristic references to the virtues of wives as well as those of husbands, of daughters as well as sons, suggest that he is thinking in terms of traditional, gendered family structure.[32]

However, the implication that such a family is a just institution is completely unfounded, by Rawls's own criteria. The central argument of his theory is that the two principles of justice characterize institutions whose members could hypothetically have agreed to their structure and rules without knowing which position in the institution they were to occupy. But since those in the original position are the heads of families, they are not in a position to determine what structure and practices are just *within* those families, for wives (or whichever members of each family are not its "head") are absent from the deliberations. If families are just, then they must *become* just in some different way (unspecified by Rawls) than do other institutions, for it is impossible to see how the viewpoint of their less advantaged members ever gets to be heard. The only reason that Rawls is able to ignore the difficult question of whether the gender structure of the family is just is because he makes the assumption made by almost the entire liberal tradition—that issues of justice concern only heads of families. But this assumption is clearly indefensible in the light of the fact that his theory of justice purports to be based on the principle of all human beings as free and equal moral persons.

If we take the individualistic premises of Rawls's theory more seriously than he does himself, there seems to be no reason why the family and the gender system—as basic social institutions—should not be subject to the principles of justice. We must take the relevant positions of both sexes into account in both formulating and applying the principles of justice. Moreover, it seems inescapable that this will lead to the rejection of a gender-structured society. For the second of Rawls's two principles requires both that inequalities be "reasonably expected to be to everyone's advantage" and that they be "attached to positions and offices open to all."[33] If any roles analogous to our current sex roles, including those of husband and wife, mother and father, were to survive the demands of the first requirement, the second requirement would reject any linkage between these roles and the innate characteristic of sex. No roles or positions except those involved in parts of the reproductive process that are biologically sex-linked would be socially assignable by sex.

What is perhaps more significant than the fact that the gender system fails the test of a thoroughly applied Rawlsian theory of justice is that if women were to share equally with men in being parties to the original position, the whole theory of justice might well

turn out to look very different. While Rawls and most other philosophers have assumed that human ways of thinking about moral issues
are completely represented by the males of the species, recent feminist research and theory have been increasingly unmasking this
assumption as itself part of the male-dominated ideology of a gendered society. It seems increasingly clear that a theory of justice that
takes full account of women's standpoint, and does not exclude from
its concerns that whole realm of nurturance and relationship that has
been excluded, along with women, from previous theories of justice,
will be different in significant respects from traditional theories. The
exclusion of women from considerations about justice has carried
with it the exclusion of much that is necessarily and significantly part
of human life.

I will conclude with a few words about the connections between
what I have said and the history of legal sex discrimination in the
United States. Other contributors to this volume are far better ac-
quainted than I am with the contemporary legal aspects of patriarchy
and address the question of what the law can and cannot do to
accomplish justice between the sexes. I will go no further, therefore,
than to suggest briefly some of the ways in which the modes of
thinking about women and gender that appear within our traditional
theories of justice have affected us through the law and its constitutional foundation.

The Constitution of the United States is worded in terms of
"persons," but there is little doubt that its framers, in the tradition of
Aristotle and Locke, intended that word to mean "male heads of
families." The state and federal constitutions were written with the
understanding that, in many important respects, women were not
legally persons, but subordinate members of patriarchal households.
The second section of the Fourteenth Amendment reinforced this
assumption by introducing the word "male" into the Constitution for
the first time, suggesting that the first section's guarantees of equal
protection of the laws "would have, at best, qualified application to
women."[34] Indeed, the history of legal sex discrimination throughout
the past century suggests that, until very recently, women have only
in a qualified sense been adjudged to be persons.

In some cases, and as recently as 1931, courts argued that women
could be legitimately excluded from rights and principles that statutes
explicitly guaranteed to "all persons." As the Massachusetts Supreme
Court asserted in 1931, for example, in reference to a statutory
reference to "every person qualified to vote": "No intention to
include women can be deduced from the omission of the word
male."[35] Just as the theorists discussed above, with the exception of

Mill, assumed, justice was a matter of relations among male heads of households.

The notion that women are not always, legally, persons has been supplemented by other ways of upholding the constitutionality of statutes that discriminate between the sexes. Often referring to "nature" and the "natural," justices have employed several of the other modes of reasoning examined above, in justifying the differential treatment of women and men.[36] First, for many years following *Muller* v. *Oregon* (1908), a circular type of judicial reasoning took as a given the social significance of men's superior physical strength and women's economic dependence and used these supposedly unalterable "facts" to justify not only the paternalistic "protection" of women in the labor force, but the exclusion of women from educational institutions, occupations to which physical strength is totally irrelevant, and civil rights such as jury service. Second, this tendency to abuse the precedent of *Muller* was reinforced by the explicit assumption that women's primary function is reproduction and the maintenance of family life—that women are, as the Supreme Court stated in 1961, "the center of the home and family life" and therefore legitimately excluded or automatically exempt from civil duties or equal treatment in the labor market. To this day, women candidates for office are likely to be castigated for not being at home taking care of their families. The Aristotelian type of functionalist reasoning about women's role is still with us in the antiabortion movement, and the presumption that women are, above all, naturally and normally reproducers seems to be the only way to explain the Supreme Court's extraordinary claim that the exclusion of pregnancy-related disabilities from a generally all-inclusive disability insurance program was not sex-based discrimination. Finally, the unity of an idealized family, as "the entity on which our civilization is built," has been frequently used, earlier to uphold laws barring women from independent careers and, more recently, to deny women's equality in making decisions within the family.

During the 1970s, at least partly in response to the changing facts of women's lives, these modes of reasoning finally began to be less easily accepted. The Supreme Court began to apply stricter standards to statutes discriminating between the sexes, with some of its members declaring sex, like race and national origin, an "inherently suspect" legal classification that must meet the test of "strict scrutiny." But despite the considerable advances of the 1970s, we still do not have an E.R.A., and many forms of legal and de facto sex discrimination still remind us of the fact that women, though now citizens, are not equal ones.

Understanding the ways in which traditional theories of justice are essentially gender-biased can help us to think and act more clearly as we try to develop a more just alternative. One thing we are learning along the way is never to be surprised when we find in past or present theories the modes of thinking I have discussed above. For, after all, theories reflect at the same time as they reinforce practices, and the theories of justice that I have addressed are those that have accompanied the slow progression from the patriarchal past into the not much less patriarchal present.

Notes

1. Aristotle, *The Generation of Animals*, trans. A. L. Peck (Cambridge: Loeb Classical Library, 1943), IV, 775a.
2. Ibid., I, 728a; IV, 766a.
3. Aristotle, *The Nicomachean Ethics*, trans. David Ross (London: Oxford University Press, 1954), V, 3.
4. Ibid., V, 6.
5. Ibid., V, 11.
6. Susan Moller Okin, *Women in Western Political Thought* (Princeton: Princeton University Press, 1979), chap. 4; Elizabeth V. Spelman, "Aristotle and the Politicization of the Soul," in *Discovering Reality: Feminist Perspectives on Epistemology, Metaphysics, Methodology, and Philosophy of Science*, edited by Sandra Harding and Merrill B. Hintikka (Dordrecht: Reidel, 1983).
7. Teresa Brennan and Carole Pateman, " 'Mere Auxiliaries to the Commonwealth': Women and the Origins of Liberalism," *Political Studies* 27, no. 2 (June 1979): 183–200.
8. Thomas Hobbes, *Leviathan*, XX, par. 15.
9. John Locke, *Second Treatise*, in *Two Treatises of Government*, edited by Peter Laslett (Cambridge: Cambridge University Press, 1969), par. 1, 54; see also Brennan and Pateman, " 'Mere Auxiliaries.' "
10. See Susan Moller Okin, "Women and the Making of the Sentimental Family," *Philosophy & Public Affairs* 11, no. 1 (Winter 1982): 65–88, for a longer version of part of the argument that follows.
11. Jean-Jacques Rousseau, *Third Discourse on Political Economy, Oeuvres Complètes*, edited by B. Gagnebin and M. Raymond (Paris: Pléiade, 1959–1969), vol. 3, pp. 241–42; *Politics and the Arts: Letter to M. d'Alembert on the Theatre*, trans. Allan Bloom (Ithaca: Cornell University Press, 1960), pp. 83–85.
12. Rousseau, *Third Discourse*, pp. 241–42.
13. David Hume, *A Treatise on Human Nature*, introduced by A. D. Lindsay (London: J. M. Dent and Sons, 1911), XII, "Of Chastity and Modesty," p. 268.
14. David Hume, *An Enquiry Concerning the Principles of Morals*, in *Enquiries Concerning the Human Understanding and Concerning the Principles of Morals*, edited by L.A. Selby-Bigge, second edition (Oxford: Clarendon Press, 1902), Sec. III, "Of Justice," p. 185.
15. John Stuart Mill, *The Subjection of Women*, in *Essays on Sex Equality* by J. S. Mill and Harriet Taylor, edited by Alice S. Rossi (Chicago: University of Chicago Press, 1970), p. 159.
16. Immanuel Kant, "Observations on the Feeling of the Beautiful and Sublime," 1799 translation, reprinted in *Women in Western Thought*, edited by Martha Lee Osborne (New York: Random House, 1979), Section III, p. 157.
17. G.W.F. Hegel, *The Phenomenology of Spirit*, trans. A. V. Miller (Oxford: Clarendon Press, 1977), p. 268.
18. Ibid., p. 276.

19. G.W.F. Hegel, *The Philosophy of Right*, trans. T. M. Knox (Oxford: Clarendon Press, 1957), p. 114.

20. Hegel, *Phenomenology*, p. 288.

21. Hegel, *Philosophy of Right*, pp. 263–64.

22. Mill, *The Subjection of Women*, p. 132.

23. Ibid., p. 138.

24. James Mill, *Essays on Government* (Indianapolis: Bobbs-Merrill, 1955).

25. Mill, *The Subjection of Women*, pp. 165–66.

26. Ibid., p. 148. See also pp. 149–50.

27. Ibid., p. 170.

28. Ibid., pp. 209–10.

29. James S. Fishkin, *Justice, Equal Opportunity, and the Family* (New Haven: Yale University Press, 1983).

30. John Rawls, *A Theory of Justice* (Cambridge: Harvard University Press, 1971). The discussion that follows is summarized from a longer discussion of contemporary theories of justice in Susan Moller Okin, "Justice and Gender," *Philosophy & Public Affairs* (forthcoming).

31. Rawls, *A Theory of Justice*, p. 490.

32. Ibid., pp. 467–68.

33. Ibid., p. 60.

34. Ruth B. Ginsberg, *Constitutional Aspects of Sex-Based Discrimination* (St. Paul: West Publishing Company, 1974), p. 3.

35. See Okin, *Women in Western Political Thought*, p. 251 and references.

36. For an enlargement of the following points, see ibid., pp. 253–73 and references.

12

Difference and Dominance: On Sex Discrimination

Catharine A. MacKinnon

TWO QUESTIONS that are seldom confronted underlie applications of the equality principle to issues of gender. One is, what is a gender question a question of? The other is, what is an inequality question a question of? I think it speaks to the way gender structures thought and perception that most legal and moral theory tacitly proceed from one answer: both are questions of sameness and difference. The mainstream doctrine of sex discrimination law that results is, in my view, largely responsible for the fact that sex equality law has been so utterly ineffective at getting women what we need and are socially prevented from having on the basis of a condition of birth: a chance at productive lives of reasonable physical security, self-expression, individuation, and minimal respect and dignity. Here, I expose and analyze the sameness/difference theory of sex equality, briefly show how it dominates sex discrimination law and policy, and underlies its discontents, and propose an alternative that may do something.

I.

Equality is an equivalence and sex is a distinction, according to the approach to sex equality that has dominated politics, law, and social perception. The legal mandate of equal treatment, which is both a systemic norm and a specific legal doctrine, is, then, a matter of treating likes alike and unlikes unlike, and the sexes are defined as such by their mutual unlikeness. Put another way, gender is socially constructed as difference epistemologically, and sex discrimination law bounds gender equality by difference doctrinally. A built-in tension exists between this concept of equality, which presupposes sameness, and this concept of sex, which presupposes difference. Sex

144

equality thus becomes a contradiction in terms, something of an oxymoron, which may suggest why we are having such a difficult time getting it.

Upon further scrutiny, two alternate paths to equality for women emerge within this dominant approach, paths that roughly correspond to the poles of this tension. The leading one is: be the same as men. This standard is termed gender-neutrality doctrinally and the single standard philosophically. It is testimony to how substance becomes form in law that this rule is considered formal equality. Because it mirrors the ideology of the social world, it is considered abstract, meaning transparent of substance; also for this reason, it is considered not only to be *the* standard, but *a* standard at all. It is so far the leading rule that the words "equal to" are code for, equivalent to, the words "the same as"—referent for both unspecified.

To women who want equality yet find they are different, the doctrine provides an alternate route: be different from men. This equal recognition of difference is termed the special benefit rule or special protection rule legally, the double standard philosophically. It is in rather bad odor. Like pregnancy, which always brings it up, it is a bit disreputable, a doctrinal embarrassment. Considered an exception to true equality and not really a rule of law at all, it is the one place where the law of sex discrimination admits it is recognizing substance. With the Bona Fide Occupational Qualification, the unique physical characteristic exception under ERA policy,[1] compensatory legislation, and sex-conscious relief in particular litigation, affirmative action is thought to live here.

The philosophy underlying this approach is that sex *is* a difference, a division, a distinction, beneath which lies a stratum of human commonality, sameness. The moral thrust of the sameness standard is to grant women access to what men have access to: to the extent that women are no different from men, we deserve what they have. The differences standard, which is generally seen as patronizing but necessary to avoid absurdity, exists to value or compensate women for what we are or have become distinctively as women (by which is meant, unlike men) under existing conditions.

My concern is not with which of these paths to sex equality is preferable in the long run or more appropriate to any particular issue, although most discourse on sex discrimination revolves about these concerns as if they are all there is. My point is logically prior: to treat issues of sex equality as issues of sameness and difference *is to take a particular approach.* I call it the difference approach because it is obsessed with the sex difference. The dialogue it has scripted for us contains a main theme, "we're the same, we're the same, we're the same," and a counterpoint theme (in a higher register), "But we're different, but we're different, but we're different." Its underlying story is: on the first day, difference was; on the second day, a division was created upon it; on the third day, occasional dominance arose. Division may be rational or irrational. Dominance either seems or is justified. Difference *is*.

There is a politics to this. Concealed is the substantive way in which man has become the measure of all things. Under the sameness standard, women are measured according to our correspondence with man, our equality judged by our proximity to his measure. Under the difference standard, we are measured according to our lack of correspondence from him, our womanhood judged by our distance from his measure. Gender-neutrality is thus simply the male standard, and the special protection rule is simply the female standard, but do not be deceived: manhood is the referent for both. Think about it like those anatomy models in medical school. The male body is the human body; all those extra things women have are studied in ob/gyn. It truly is a situation in which more is less. Approaching sex discrimination in this way, as if sex questions are difference questions and equality questions are sameness questions, merely provides two ways for the law to hold women to a male standard and call that sex equality.

II.

Having been very hard on the difference answer to sex equality questions, I should say that it takes up a very important problem: how to get women access to everything we have been excluded from, while also valuing everything that women are or have been allowed to become or have developed as a consequence of our struggle either not to be excluded from most of life's pursuits or to be taken seriously under the terms that have been permitted to be our terms. It negotiates what we have managed in relation to men. Legally articulated as the need to conform normative standards to existing reality, the strongest doctrinal expression of its sameness idea would prohibit taking gender into account in any way.

The guiding impulse is: we're as good as you. Anything you can do, we can do. Just get out of the way. I have to confess a sincere affection for this approach. It has gotten women some access to employment,[2] education,[3] the public pursuits including academia,[4] the professions,[5] blue collar[6] work, to the military,[7] and more than nominal access to athletics.[8] It has moved to alter the dead ends that were all we were seen as good for, and what passed for women's lack of physical training, which was really serious training in passivity and enforced weakness. It makes you want to cry sometimes to realize how much women just want to do the work of this society, things other people don't even want to do, that it has to be a mission just to get to do it.

The issue of the military draft[9] has presented the sameness answer to the sex equality question in all its simplicity and equivocality. As a citizen, I should have to risk being killed just like you. The consequences of my resistance to this risk should count like yours count. The undercurrent is, what's the matter, don't you want me to learn to kill . . . just like you? Sometimes I imagine this as a dialogue between women in the afterlife. The feminist says to the soldier, we fought for your equality. The soldier says to the feminist, oh, no, *we* fought for *your* equality.

Feminists have this nasty habit of counting bodies and refusing not to notice their gender. So we notice that, as applied, the sameness standard has mostly gotten men the benefit of those few things women have historically had—for all the good they did us. Almost every sex discrimination case that has been won at the Supreme Court level has been brought by a man.[10] Under gender-neutrality, the law of custody and divorce has been transformed, giving men an equal chance at custody of children and at alimony.[11] Men often look like better "parents" under gender-neutral rules like level of income and presence of nuclear family, because men make more money and (as they say) initiate the building of family units.[12] In effect, they get preferred because society advantages them before they get into court, and law is prohibited from taking that preference into account because that would mean taking gender into account. The group realities that make women more in need of alimony are not permitted to matter, because only individual factors, gender-neutrally considered, may matter. So the fact that women will live their lives, as individuals, as members of the group, women, with women's chances in a sex discriminatory society, may not count, or it is sex discrimination. The equality principle in this guise has come to mobilize the idea that the way to get things for women is to get them for men. Admittedly, men have gotten them. But have women? We still have not gotten even equal pay,[13] or equal work,[14] far less equal pay for equal work,[15] and are close to losing separate enclaves like women's schools through this approach.[16]

Here is why. In reality, which this approach is not long on, virtually every quality that distinguishes men from women is already affirmatively compensated in this society. Men's physiology defines most sports, their health needs define insurance coverage, their socially designed biographies define workplace expectations and successful career patterns, their perspectives and concerns define quality in scholarship, their experiences and obsessions define merit, their military service defines citizenship, their presence defines family, their inability to get along with each other—their wars and ruler-ships—defines history, their image defines god, and their genitals define sex. For each of their differences from women, what amounts to an affirmative action plan is in effect, otherwise known as the structure and values of American society. But whenever women are different from men and insist on just not having it held against us, every time a difference is used to keep us second class and we refuse to smile about it, equality law has a paradigm trauma and it's crisis time for the doctrine.

The problem is, what this doctrine has apparently meant by sex inequality is not what happens to us. The law of sex discrimination seems to be looking for only those ways women are kept down that have *not* wrapped themselves up as a difference, whether original, imposed, or imagined. Start with original: what to do about the fact that women actually have an ability men still lack, gestating children in utero. Pregnancy is therefore a difference. Difference doctrine says it is sex discrimination to give women what they need because only women need it. It is not sex discrimination not to give them what they need because then only women will not get what we need.[17] Move into imposed: what to do about the fact that most women are segregated into low-paying jobs where there are no men. Suspecting that the structure of the marketplace will be entirely subverted if comparable worth is put into effect, difference doctrine says that because there is no man to set a standard as against which women's treatment is a deviation, there may be no sex discrimination here, only sex difference. Never mind that there is no man to compare with because no man would do that job if he had a choice, and because he is a man, he does, so he doesn't.[18]

Now move into the so-called subtle reaches of the imposed category, the *de facto* area. Most jobs, in fact, require that the person gender-neutral that is qualified for these jobs will not be the primary caretaker of a preschool child.[19] Pointing out that this raises a concern of sex in a society in which it is women who are expected to care for the children is taken as day one of taking gender into account in the structuring of jobs. To do that would violate the rule against not noticing situated differences based on gender, so it is never noticed that day one of taking gender into account was the day the job was structured with that expectation. Imaginary sex differences I will concede the doctrine can handle.[20]

Clearly, there are many differences between women and men. I mean, can you imagine elevating one half of a population and denigrating the other half and producing a population in which everyone is the same? What the sameness standard fails to notice is that men's differences from women are equal to women's differences from men. There is an equality there. Yet the sexes are not socially equal. What is missing in the difference approach is what Aristotle missed in his empiricist notion that equality means treating likes alike and unlikes unlike and nobody has questioned it since. Why should you have to be the same as a man to get what a man gets simply because he is one? Why does maleness provide an original entitlement, not questioned on the basis of *its* gender, so that it is women who want to make a case of unequal treatment in a world men have made in their image (this is really the part Aristotle missed) who have to show in effect that they are a man in every relevant respect, unfortunately mistaken for a woman on the basis of an accident of birth?

This method shows in highest relief through the women gender-neutrality benefits, and there are some. Mostly they are women who have already been able to construct a biography that approximates the male norm, at least on paper. They are the qualified, the least of sex discrimination's victims. When they are denied a man's chance, it looks the most like sex bias. The more unequal society gets, the fewer such women are permitted to exist. The more unequal society gets, the *less* likely this doctrine is able to do anything about it, because unequal power creates both the appearance and the reality of sex differences along the same lines as it creates its sex inequalities.

Nor has the special benefits side of the difference approach compensated for the differential of being second class, like it is supposed to. The special benefits rule is the only place in mainstream doctrine where you get to identify as a woman and not have that mean giving up all claim to equal treatment—but it comes close. Under its double standard, women who stand to inherit something when their husbands die have gotten the exclusion of a small percentage of inheritance tax, to the tune of Justice Douglas waxing eloquent about the difficulties of all women's economic situation.[21] If we're going to be stigmatized as different, it would be nice to have the compensation fit the disparity. Similarly, women have gotten three more years than men before being advanced or kicked out of the military hierarchy as compensation for being precluded from combat, the usual way to advance.[22] Women have also gotten excluded from contact jobs in male-only prisons because we might be raped, the Court taking the viewpoint of the reasonable rapist on women's employment opportunities.[23] We are also protected out of jobs because of our fertility. The reason is that the job has health hazards, and somebody who might be a real person some day and, therefore, could sue (a fetus) might be hurt if women, who apparently are not real persons and therefore can't sue either for the hazard to our health or for the lost employment opportunity, are given jobs which subject our bodies to possible harm.[24] Excluding women is always an option if equality feels in tension with the pursuit itself. (They never seem to think of redefining the pursuit or excluding the men.) Take combat.[25] Somehow, it takes the glory out of the foxhole, the buddiness out of the trenches, to imagine us out there. You get the feeling they might rather end the draft, they might even rather not fight wars at all, than to have to do it with us.

The double standard of these results does not give women the dignity the single standard does, which is the dignity of corresponding to the male. Nor does it suppress the gender of its referent—which is, of course, the female gender. I must also confess some affection for this standard. The work of Carol Gilligan on gender differences in moral reasoning[26] gives it a lot of dignity, more than it has ever had; more, frankly, than I thought it ever could have. But in the end, the work achieves for moral reasoning what the special protection rule achieves in law: the affirmative rather than negative valuation of that which has accurately distinguished women from men by making it seem as though those attributes, with their consequences, really are somehow ours, rather than what male supremacy has attributed to us for its own use.

Women have been and done good things, and it is a good thing to affirm them. I think quilts are art. I think women have a history. I think we create culture. I also think that we have not only been excluded from making what has been considered art, our artifacts have been excluded from setting the standards by which art is art. Women have a history all right, but it is both a history of what was and of what was not allowed to be. So I am critical of affirming what we have been, which necessarily is what we have been permitted, as if it is women's, ours in the possessive, as if equality, in spite of everything, already ineluctably exists.

I am getting hard on this and am about to get harder on it. I do not think the way women reason morally is morality "in a different voice."[27] I think it is morality in a higher register, in the feminine voice. Women value care because men have valued us according to the care we give them, and we could probably use some. Women think in relational terms because our existence is defined in relation to men. I think further that when you are powerless, you don't just speak differently. A lot, you don't speak. Your speech is not just differently articulated, it is silenced. Eliminated. Gone. You aren't just deprived of a language with which to articulate your distinctiveness, although you are; you are deprived of a life out of which articulation might come. Not being heard is not just a function of lack of recognition, not just that no one knows how to listen to you, although it is that. It is also silence of the deep kind, the silence of being prevented from having anything to say. Sometimes it is permanent. All I am saying is that the damage of sexism is real, and reifying that into differences is an insult to our possibilities.

So long as this is the way these issues are framed, demands for equality will always appear to be asking to have it both ways: the same when we are the same, different when we are different. But the fact of the matter is that this is the way men have it: equal and different too. They have it the same as woman when they are the same and want it, and different from women when they are different or want to be, which usually they do. Equal and different too would only be parity.[28] But under male supremacy, while being told we get it both ways, both the specialness of the pedestal and an even chance at the race, the ability to be a woman and a person, too, few women get much benefit of either.

III.

There is an alternative approach, one which threads its way through existing law and is, I think, the reason equality law exists in the first place. It provides a second answer, a dissident answer in law and philosophy, to both the equality question and the gender question. An equality question is a question of the distribution of power. A gender question is also a question of power, specifically of male supremacy and female subordination. Equality, in terms of what it is going to take to get it, is the antithesis of hierarchy. As hierarchy of power succeeds in constructing social reality and social perception, it produces categorical distinctions, differences. I term this the dominance approach.

On the first day that matters, dominance was achieved, probably by force. By the second day, division along the same lines was firmly, if imperfectly, in place. On the third day if not sooner, differences were demarcated, together with social systems to exaggerate them in perception and in fact, *because* the systematically differential delivery of benefits and deprivations required making no mistake about who is who. Comparatively speaking, man has been resting ever since. Gender might not even code as difference, might not mean distinction epistemologically, were it not for its consequences for social power. The sameness standard under the difference approach misses what this gets: the fact that hierarchy of power produces real as well as fantasied differences, differences that are also inequalities. The differences standard under the difference approach also misses what this gets: that for women to affirm difference, when difference means dominance as it does with gender, is to affirm the qualities and characteristics of powerlessness.

This is the ground I have been standing on to criticize mainstream sex discrimination law. The goal is not to make legal categories to trace and trap the way things are. It is not to make rules that fit reality. It is critical of reality. The task is not to formulate abstract standards that will produce determinate outcomes in particular cases. Its project is more substantive, more jurisprudential than formulaic, which is why it is difficult for the dominant discourse to dignify it as an approach to doctrine or to imagine it as a rule of law at all. It proposes to expose that to which women have had little choice but to be confined, in order to change it.

The dominance approach centers on the most sex-differential abuses of women as a gender, abuses which sex equality law in its difference mode could not confront. It is based on a reality about which little systematic was known before 1970, a reality that calls for a new conception of the problem of sex inequality. This new information includes not only the extent and intractability of sex segregation into poverty, which has been known before, but the range of issues termed violence against women, which has not been. It combines women's material desperation through the relegation to categories of work that pay little to nothing, with the massive amount of rape and attempted rape—44 percent of all women, about which virtually nothing is done[29]; the sexual assault of children, 38 percent of girls and 10 percent of boys, which is apparently endemic to the patriarchal family[30]; the battery of women, systematic in our homes, one third to one quarter of them[31]; prostitution, women's fundamental economic option, what we do when all else fails, and for a good fifth of all women in this country that we know of, all else has failed at some point[32]; and pornography, an industry which traffics in female flesh, making inequality into sex to the tune of $8 billion dollars a year in profits largely to organized crime.[33]

These experiences have been silenced out of the difference doctrine of sex equality largely because they happen almost exclusively to women. Understand: for this reason, they are considered *not* to raise sex equality issues. Because this treatment is almost uniquely done to women, it is implicitly treated as a difference, the sex difference.

What it is, is the socially situated subjection of women. The whole point of women's social relegation to inferiority as a gender is that these abuses do not customarily happen to men. Men are not paid half of what women are paid for doing the same things on the basis of their equal difference. Everything they touch does not turn valueless because they touched it. When they are hit, a person has been assaulted. When they are sexually violated, it is not either simply tolerated or found entertaining or defended as a constitutional right, the necessary structure of the family, or the price of civilization.

Does this differential describe the sex difference? Maybe so. It does describe the systematic relegation of an entire half of the population to a condition of inferiority and attribute it to their nature. If it were biological, maybe biological intervention should be considered. But there are men who do not rape women who have nothing wrong with their hormones. If it were evolutionary, men would have to evolve differently. But there are men who are made sick by pornography and do not eroticize their revulsion who are not underevolved. I think it is political, and its politics construct the deep structure of society. This social status, in which we can be used and abused and trivialized and humiliated and bought and sold and passed around and patted on the head and put in place and told to smile so that we look as though we're enjoying it all, is not what some of us have in mind as the limits of sex equality.

This second approach—which is not abstract, which is at odds with socially imposed reality, and therefore does not look like a standard according to the standard for standards—became the implicit model for racial justice applied by the courts during the sixties. It has since eroded with the erosion of judicial commitment to racial equality. It was based on the realization that the condition of Blacks in particular was not fundamentally a matter of rational or irrational differentiation on the basis of race, but was fundamentally a matter of white supremacy[34], under which racial differences became invidious as a consequence. To consider gender in this way, observe again that men are as different from women as women are from men, but the sexes are not equally socially powerful. To be on the top of a hierarchy is certainly different from being on the bottom, but that is an obfuscatingly neutralized way of putting it, as a hierarchy is a great deal more than that. If gender were merely a question of difference, sex inequality would be a problem of mere sexism, of mistaken differentiation, of inaccurate categorization of individuals. This is what the difference approach thinks it is, and is therefore sensitive to. But if gender is an inequality first, constructed as a socially relevant differentiation in order to keep that inequality in place, sex inequality questions are questions of systematic dominance, of male supremacy, which is not at all abstract and is anything but a mistake.

Looking at the difference approach and the dominance approach in light of each other clarifies some otherwise confusing tensions in sex equality debates. If you look at the world of the difference approach from the point of view of the dominance approach, it becomes clear that the difference approach adopts the point of view of male supremacy on the status of the sexes. Simply by treating the status quo as "the standard," it invisibly and uncritically accepts as its norm the arrangements under male supremacy. In this sense, the difference approach is masculinist, although it can be expressed in a female voice, and the dominance approach is feminist, in that it sees and criticizes the inequalities of the social world from the standpoint of the subordination of women to men.

If you look at the world as the dominance approach imagines it, through the lens of the difference approach, that is, if you try to see real inequality through a lens that has difficulty seeing an inequality as an inequality if it also appears as a difference, demands for change in the distribution of power appear as demands for special protection. This is because the only tools that the difference paradigm offers to comprehend disparity equate the recognition of a gender line with an admission of lack of entitlement to equality under law. Since it confronts equality questions primarily as matters of empirical fit,[35] i.e., as matters of accurately shaping legal rules (implicitly modeled on the standard men set) to the way the world is (also implicitly modeled on the standard men set), any existing differences must be negated to merit equal treatment. As much for ethnicity as for gender, it is basic to mainstream discrimination doctrine to preclude true diversity among equals or true equality within diversity.

It further follows that, to the difference approach, any attempt to change the way the world actually is looks like a moral question requiring a separate judgment of how things ought to be. It imagines that civil rights poses the following disinterested question that can be resolved neutrally with regard to groups: against the weight of empirical difference, should we treat some as the equals of others, even when they may not be entitled to it because they are not up to standard? The dominance approach unmasks this construction of the problem as part of the problem of social inequality itself. To the dominance approach, the foundation of civil rights is not moral. If sex inequalities are approached as matters of imposed status, which are in need of change if a legal mandate of equality means anything at all, whether women should be treated unequally means simply whether women should be treated as less. Once exposed as a naked power question, there is no question as to whether it might be a good idea to treat women as less. There is, therefore, no separable question of what ought to be. The only question is what is and is not a gender question. Once no amount of difference justifies treating women as subhuman, eliminating that is what equality law is for. In this shift of paradigms, equality propositions become no longer propositions of good and evil, but of power and powerlessness, no more disinterested in their origins or neutral in their arrival at conclusions than are the problems they address.

There came a time in Black people's movement for equality in this country when slavery stopped being a question of how it could be justified and became a question of how it could be be ended. Racial disparities surely existed or racism would have been harmless, but at that point—a point not yet reached for issues of sex—no amount of group difference mattered any more. This is the same point at which a group's characteristics, including empirical attributes, become constitutive of the fully human, rather than being defined, as before, as exceptions to or by distinction from the fully human. It incarnates partial standards to one-sidedly measure one group's differences against a standard set by the other. The point at which one's particular qualities become part of the standard by which humanity is measured is a millennial moment.

To summarize the argument: seeing sex equality questions as matters of reasonable or unreasonable classification is part of the way male dominance is expressed in law. If you follow my shift in perspective from gender as difference to gender as dominance, gender changes from a distinction that is presumptively valid to a detriment that is presumptively suspect. The difference approach tries to map reality where the dominance approach tries to challenge and change it. In the dominance approach, sex discrimination stops being a question of morality and starts being a question of politics.

You can tell if sameness is your standard for equality if my critique of hierarchy looks like a request for special protection in disguise. It is not. It envisions a change that would make possible a simple equal chance for the first time. To define the reality of sex as difference and the warrant of equality as sameness not only guarantees that sex equality will never be achieved, it is wrong on both counts. Doctrinally speaking, the deepest problems of sex inequality do not find women "similarly situated"[36] to men, far less do they require intentionally discriminatory acts.[37] They merely require the status quo to be maintained. As a strategy for maintaining social power, first arrange social life unequally. Then permit only those who are already situated as equals to complain about it. Structure perception so that different means inferior. Then require that the only one who illegally discriminates is the one who, when he disadvantages someone different, *knows* he is treating a true equal as less.

Give women equal power in social life. Let what we say matter; then we will discourse on questions of morality. Take your foot off our necks; then we will see in what tongue women speak. So long as sex equality is limited by sex difference, whether you like it or don't like it, whether you choose to value it or to ignore it, whether you stake it out as a grounds for feminism or occupy it as the terrain of misogyny, women will be born, degraded, and die. We would settle for that equal protection of the laws under which one could be born, live, and die, without protection being a dirty word and equality being a special privilege.

Notes

1. The Bona Fide Occupational Qualification (BFOQ) exception to Title VII of the Civil Rights Act of 1964, 29 C.F.R. 1604, permits sex to be a job qualification when it is a valid one. The leading interpretation of the proposed federal Equal Rights Amendment would, pursuing a similar analytic structure, permit a "unique physical characteristic" exception to its otherwise absolute embargo on taking sex into account. Brown, Emerson, Falk, Freedman, "The Equal Rights Amendment: A Constitutional Basis for Equal Rights for Women," *Yale Law Journal* 80 (1971): 893.

2. Title VII of the Civil Rights Law of 1964; *Phillips* v. *Martin-Marietta*, 400 U.S. 542 (1971); *Frontiero* v. *Richardson*, 411 U.S. 484 (1974) is the high water mark. See also *Los Angeles* v. *Manhart*, 435 U.S. 702 (1978); *Newport News Shipbuilding and Dry Dock Co.* v. *EEOC*, 462 U.S. 669 (1983).

3. Title IX of the Education Amendments of 1972; *Cannon* v. *University of Chicago*, 441 U.S. 677 (1981); *Mississippi University for Women* v. *Hogan*, 458 U.S. 718 (1982); see also *De La Cruz* v. *Tormey*, 582 F.2d 45 (1978).

4. Actually, women appear to lose most academic sex discrimination cases that go to trial, although I do not know of a statistical study on the subject. A case that won eventually, elevating the standard of proof in the process, is *Sweeney* v. *Board of Trustees of Keene State College*, 439 U.S. 29 (1979). The ruling for the plaintiff on remand was affirmed at 604 F.2d 106 (1979).

5. *Hishon* v. *King & Spaulding*, 467 U.S. 69 (1984).

6. See *Vanguard Justice* v. *Hughes*, 471 F. Supp. 670 (D. Md. 1979); *Meyer* v. *Missouri State Highway Commission*, 567 F. 2d 804, 891 (8th Cir. 1977); *Payne* v. *Travenol Laboratories Inc.*, 416 F. Supp. 248 (N.D. Miss., 1976). See also *Dothard* v. *Rawlinson*, 433 U.S. 321 (1977) (height and weight requirements for prison guard jobs invalidated as sex discrimination).

7. *Frontiero* v. *Richardson*, 411 U.S. 484 (1974); *Schlesinger* v. *Ballard*, 419 U.S. 498 (1975).

8. This situation is relatively complex. See *Gomes* v. *R.I. Interscholastic League*, 469 F. Supp. 659 (D. Rhode Island, 1979); *Brenden* v. *Independent School District*, 477 F.2d 1292 (8th Cir. 1973); *Hollander* v. *Connecticut Interscholastic Athletic Conference* (Conn. Sup. Ct. 1971); *O'Connor* v. *Board of Education of School District No. 23*, 645 F.2d 578 (7th Cir. 1981); *Cape* v. *Tennessee Secondary School Athletic Association*, 424 F. Supp. 732 (E.D. Tenn. 1976), rev'd. 563 F.2d 793 (6th Cir. 1977); *Yellow Spring Exempted Village School District Board of Education* v. *Ohio High School Athletic Association*, 443 F. Supp. 753 (S.D. Ohio 1978); *Aiken* v. *Lieuallen*, 593 P.2d 1243 (Or. App. 1979).

9. *Rostker* v. *Goldberg*, 453 U.S. 57 (1981). See also L. Kornblum, "Women Warriors

in a Men's World: The Combat Exclusion," *Law & Inequality: A Journal of Theory and Practice* 2 (1984).

10. D. Cole, "Strategies of Difference: Litigating for Women's Rights in a Man's World," *Law & Inequality: A Journal of Theory and Practice* 2 (1984): 34 n. 4 (collecting cases).

11. *Devine v. Devine*, 398 So. 2d 686 (Ala. Sup. Ct. 1981); *Danielson v. Board of Higher Education*, 358 F. Supp. 22 (S.D.N.Y. 1972); *Weinberger v. Wiesenfeld*, 420 U.S. 636 (1975); *Stanley v. Illinois*, 405 U.S. 645 (1971); *Caban v. Mohammed*, 441 U.S. 380 (1979); *Orr v. Orr*, 440 U.S. 268 (1979).

12. L. Weitzman, "The Economics of Divorce: Social and Economic Consequences of Property, Alimony and Child Support Awards," *U.C.L.A. Law Review* 28 (1982): 1181, 1251, documents a decline in women's standard of living of 73 percent and an increase in men's of 42 percent within a year after divorce.

13. Equal Pay Act, 29 U.S.C. 206 (d) (1) (1976). See generally *Schultz v. Wheaton Glass Co.*, 421 F.2d 259 (1970); *Corning Glass Works v. Brennan*, 417 U.S. 18 (1974); *I.U.E. v. Westinghouse*, 631 F.2d 1094 (1980), cert. denied 452 F.2d 353 (3 Cir. 1981).

14. Examples include *Christenson v. State of Iowa*, 563 F.2d 353 (8th Cir. 1977); *Gerlach v. Michigan Bell Tel. Co.*, 501 F. Supp. 1300 (E.D. Mich. 1980); *Odomes v. Nucare, Inc.*, 653 F.2d 246 (6th Cir. 1981) (female nurse's aide denied Title VII remedy because her job duties were not substantially similar to those of better paid male orderly); *Power v. Barry County, Michigan*, 539 F. Supp. 721 (W.D. Mich. 1982).

15. *County of Washington v. Gunther*, 452 U.S. 161 (1981), permits a comparable worth-type challenge where pay inequality can be proven to be a correlate of intentional job segregation. See also *Lemons v. City and County of Denver*, 17 FEP 910 (D. Colo. 1978), 620 F.2d 228 (10 Cir. 1977), cert. denied, 449 U.S. 888 (1980); *AFSCME v. State of Washington*, 770 F.2d 1401 (9th Cir. 1985). See generally C. Pint, "Value, Work and Women," *Law & Inequality: A Journal of Theory and Practice* 1 (1983).

16. Combine *Bob Jones University v. United States*, 461 U.S. 547 (1983) with *Vorcheimer v. School District of Philadelphia*, 532 F.2d 880 (1976).

17. *Miller-Wohl v. Commissioner of Labor*, 515 F. Supp. 1264 (D. Mon. 1981), vacated and dismissed, 685 F.2d 1088 (9 Cir. 1982). *California Federal Savings and Loan Assn. v. Guerra*, 758 F.2d 390 (9th Cir. 1985), cert. granted 54 U.S.L.W. 3460.

18. Most women work at jobs mostly women do, and most of those jobs are paid less than jobs that mostly men do. See, e.g., Pint, "Value, Work and Women," pp. 162–63, notes 19 and 20 (collecting studies).

19. *Phillips v. Martin-Marietta*, 400 U.S. 542 (1971).

20. *Reed v. Reed*, 404 U.S. 71 (1971) (statute barring women from administering estates is sex discrimination). If no women were taught to read and write, as used to be the case, the gender difference would not be imaginary in this case, yet the social situation would be even more sex-discriminatory than it is now.

21. *Kahn v. Shevin*, 416 U.S. 351, 353 (1974).

22. *Schlesinger v. Ballard*, 419 U.S. 498 (1975).

23. *Dothard v. Rawlinson*, 433 U.S. 321 (1977); see also *Michael M. v. Sonoma County Superior Court*, 450 U.S. 464 (1981).

24. *Doerr v. B. F. Goodrich*, 484 F. Supp. 320 (N.D. Ohio 1979). W. Williams, "Firing the Woman to Protect the Fetus: The Reconciliation of Fetal Protection with Employment Opportunity Goals Under Title VII," *Georgetown Law Journal* 69 (1981).

25. Congress requires the Air Force (10 U.S.C. Section 8549 (1983)) and the Navy (10 U.S.C. Section 6015 (1983)) to exclude women from combat, with some exceptions. *Owens v. Brown*, 455 F. Supp. 291 (D.D.C. 1978) had previously invalidated the prior Navy combat exclusion because it prohibited women from filling jobs they could perform and inhibited Navy's discretion to assign women on combat ships. The Army excludes women from combat based upon its own policies under congressional authorization to determine assignment policies (10 U.S.C. Section 3012 (e) (1983)).

26. C. Gilligan, *In a Different Voice* (Cambridge: Harvard University Press, 1982).

27. Ibid.

28. I argued this in Appendix A of *Sexual Harassment of Working Women: A Case of Sex*

Discrimination (New Haven: Yale University Press, 1979). That book ends with "Women want to be equal and different, too." I could have added "Men are." As a standard, this would have reduced women's aspirations for equality to some corresponding version of men's actualities. But as an observation, it would have been true.

29. D. Russell and N. Howell, "The Prevalence of Rape in the United States Revisited," *Signs: Journal of Women in Culture and Society 8* (1983) (44 percent of women in 930 households were victims of rape or attempted rape at some time in their life).

30. D. Russell, "The Incidence and Prevalence of Intrafamilial and Extrafamilial Sexual Abuse of Female Children," *Child Abuse and Neglect: The International Journal 7* (1983).

31. R. Emerson Dobash and Russell Dobash, *Violence Against Wives: A Case Against the Patriarchy* (New York: Free Press, 1979); *Bruno v. Codd*, 396 N.Y.S. 2d 974 (Sup. Ct. 1977).

32. K. Barry, *Female Sexual Slavery* (Englewood Cliffs, N.J.: Prentice-Hall, 1979); Griffin, "Wives, Hookers and the Law: The Case for Decriminalizing Prostitution," *Student Lawyer* 10 (1982); Report of Jean Fernand-Laurent, Special Rapporteur on the Suppression of the Traffic in Persons and the Exploitation of the Prostitution of Others (a United Nations report), in *International Feminism: Networking Against Female Sexual Slavery* 130 (K. Barry, C. Bunch, S. Castley, eds., 1984) (Report of the Global Feminist Workshop to Organize Against Traffic in Women, Rotterdam, Netherlands, April 6–15, 1983).

33. Galloway and Thornton, "Crackdown on Pornography–A No-Win Battle," *U.S. News and World Report*, June 4, 1984, p. 84. See also "The Place of Pornography," *Harper's*, November 1984, p. 31 (citing $7 billion per year).

34. *Loving v. Virginia*, 388 U.S. 1 (1967) first used the term "white supremacy" in invalidating an antimiscegenation law as a violation of equal protection. The law equally forbade whites and Blacks to intermarry.

35. The scholars Tussman and tenBroek first used the term "fit" to characterize the necessary relation between a valid equality rule and the world to which it refers. Tussman and tenBroek, "The Equal Protection of the Laws," *California Law Review* 37 (1949).

36. *Royster Guano Co. v. Virginia*, 253 U.S. 412, 415 (1920): "[A classification] must be reasonable, not arbitrary, and must rest upon some ground of difference having a fair and substantial relation to the object of the legislation, so that all persons similarly circumstanced shall be treated alike." *Reed v. Reed*, 404 U.S. 71 (1971): "Regardless of their sex, persons within any one of the enumerated classes . . . are similarly situated . . . By providing dissimilar treatment for men and women who are thus similarly situated, the challenged section violates the Equal Protection Clause."

37. *Washington v. Davis*, 426 U.S. 229 (1976); *Personnel Administrator of Massachusetts v. Feeney*, 442 U.S. 256 (1979).

13

The Failure of Radical Feminism

Rachel Flick

CATHARINE MACKINNON is a celebrated writer on feminism and the law. She explicates a kind of feminism that she designates "radical." Much of her work is directed toward the development of what she calls "a feminist jurisprudence," which is a jurisprudence that accepts her radicalism as truth and responds to the injustices it purports to identify.

Two things are wrong with "feminist jurisprudence," as MacKinnon understands it. First, it is a contradiction in terms. If MacKinnon succeeded in changing our jurisprudential standards as she wants to, she would not have reformed the law, she would have ended the rule of law as we know it. Second—and more to the point—the jurisprudential change MacKinnon proposes is as fundamental as it is because the kind of feminism that directs it is totalitarian. Radical feminism is based on the dictum "the personal is political," which is a totalitarian concept. You have only to hear this dictum to understand why this is so—it clearly repudiates individuality in favor of collectivity—but I will try to demonstrate how this dictum becomes totalitarian when it takes hold of the law.

I will begin, though, by describing radical feminism as MacKinnon represents it.

MacKinnon thinks that what is called the objective truth about things is not objective but is, in fact, the point of view of men. So great and pervasive is male control over the way we speak, what we think, and the way we live, that the very notion of objectivity is chimerical.

---

*Editors' note—This essay comments on some earlier essays by Catharine MacKinnon outlining the foundations of a "feminist jurisprudence." The articles discussed are: "Feminism, Marxism, Method, and the State: An Agenda for Theory," *Signs* 7 (1982); "Feminism, Marxism, Method and the State: Toward Feminist Jurisprudence," *Signs* 8 (1983); and "Toward Feminist Jurisprudence," *Stanford Law Review* 34 (February 1982).

Of male dominance she writes:

> Its point of view is the standard for point-of-viewlessness, its particu-
> larity the means of universality. Its force is exercised as consent, its
> authority as participation, its supremacy as the paradigm of order, its
> control the definition of legitimacy.[1]

Although she believes that men have defined everything, she is
especially concerned that they have defined the two sexes—what
men are and what women are and how they should live and what
should be the relations between them. MacKinnon thinks that gender
as we know it is not natural but social in origin; it is a made thing and
it was made, as was everything else, by men.

Moreover, MacKinnon thinks that men defined the sexes in men's
own interests. Gender is "a division of power," and the way it divides
power is to give it to men.

In her scheme, then, women are utterly, essentially oppressed.
From the most profound level, from their very definition as women,
women are the creatures of men and the servants of male power.
They are true slaves, enslaved not only materially but also in spirit.
Most women do not even know that they are not free. Women are not
subjects; they are objects. They have been objectified.

It is a wretched position that MacKinnon describes, and she writes
eloquently about it. Women's situation, she says, "offers no outside
to stand on or gaze at, no inside to escape to, too much urgency to
wait, no place else to go, and nothing to use but the twisted tools that
have been shoved down our throats."[2]

Now, all of this begs the question: as what have men defined
women? They have defined women so as to secure male power, but
what does that mean? MacKinnon's answer to this is simple. The
social meaning of gender (and she thinks gender is all social) is
"forced sex as sexuality." Forced sex is obviously rape. "To be rapable," says MacKinnon, "a position which is social, not biological,
defines what a woman is."[3]

So to the question, "What is woman in our world?" MacKinnon
answers that woman is what man has determined she will be, and
what he has determined is that she is rapable. Not just biologically
rapable (though there is that), but more broadly, "socially rapable."

It is worth noting, on the subject of rape, that in MacKinnon's
opinion there appears not to be much difference, if there is any at all,
between rape and ordinary heterosexual activity. This is because the
difference between the two would have to do with a woman's
consent, and she does not believe female consent is a meaningful
concept, because women are essentially enslaved.

These perceptions, then—that what we call objectivity is really the point of view of men; that men have defined the sexes to secure male power; that men have defined women as rapable; that heterosexuality is rape—all of these perceptions are the *raison d'être* of MacKinnon's feminism.

Her feminism explains and justifies itself by declaring that the personal is political. This dictum is absolutely central to her point of view. It is the notion that one's political stature is so much a part of what one is that it defines one's personal stature, too. Political stature is power; it might include such things as physical strength, wealth, and standing in the state. "The personal is political" is the notion that power relations are acted out on the personal plane, and indeed define the personal plane. And ultimately, "the personal is political" is a justification for political intervention in the personal, if either is thought to need correction. It renders intervention acceptable because the political is thought to determine the personal anyway, already.

For the most part, MacKinnon understands American political relations as the products of a crude kind of power, so that she sees their personal expression largely in games of sadism, masochism, and fear. To say that the personal is political, she explains, means that you can discover and verify that gender is in fact a division of power through, as she puts it, "women's intimate experience of sexual objectification, which is definitive of and synonymous with women's lives as gender female."[4] Sexual objectification *defines* and *is* life as a woman. These are her own words. That is what "the personal is political" means. And that is what defines and directs her feminism.

At this point the reader should ask himself: Do I agree with that? Does sexual objectification define femininity? Is that really all that men think of women? And is my personal life really all that political? Very few people will answer that these things are true, a fact which is in itself revealing and important.

It is equally important, though, to look at where these theses actually take the law, when MacKinnon tries to apply them. MacKinnon believes that the law suffers from the same basic problems as the rest of the establishment. It is another of the "twisted tools" that are all women have at their disposal. The law is twisted because: "The law sees and treats women the way men see and treat women."[5] Just as objectivity in the rest of our lives is really the point of view of men, objectivity in law, too, is the point of view of men.

What legal objectivity is supposed to mean is that the law judges any situation on facts and events, not on the persons involved. The law applies the same rules and precedents equally to all people, no matter who they are. By so doing, it is hoped that the law will protect all equally. As MacKinnon herself writes, the idea is that "government of laws not men limits partiality with written constraints."[6]

She believes, though, that while this legal objectivity is supposed to protect everyone, in fact, it institutionalizes the rule of men. The law, which is supposed to judge by standard rules according to "the facts" of the situation, instead of judging according to who the players are, has inevitably served not objectivity but men. This is because our construction of the rules and our perception of the facts is dictated by the male perspective. Therefore, the legal objectivity to which we now aspire, and the pursuit of equal protection by means of this objectivity, must be modified to accommodate the perspective of women. The law must be replaced by a tool that "recognizes women's voice."

As MacKinnon must know, though, such a replacement is antithetical to the rule of law itself. There is arguably no such thing as a law that rejects objectivity and is still *law*. Objectivity is the essence of law. Moreover, the alternative to law is either anarchy or (more relevant here) tyranny. For either guilt and innocence are determined by detached standards, or they are determined by somebody's subjective opinion of truth and falsity, of right and wrong. That somebody who is making a decision of that magnitude is a tyrant.

But what tyrant, if any, emerges from MacKinnon's new jurisprudence? She wants to replace objectivity with "the feminine experience," but the feminine experience as understood by whom? She says "women," but what women? Two legal examples begin to expose her meaning.

The first of these examples is the law against rape. MacKinnon tells us that the legal definition of rape now hinges on two points: the use of force by the rapist, and the lack of consent by the victim. She rejects this because force and consent are meaningless concepts, things between men and women being what they are. The feminist definition of rape, she offers, "lies instead in the meaning of the act from women's point of view."[7]

What is interesting about this change is that the existing law does account for the point of view of at least some women, insofar as it assumes women have a worthwhile opinion concerning whether they were forced and whether they consented. On some level, then, MacKinnon rejects the point of view of women who claim such opinions. By "the meaning of the act from women's point of view" she does not mean "the meaning of the act" according to these women.

The second example is a case called *Wanrow* v. *Washington*. MacKinnon does not unequivocally endorse the feminist position in *Wanrow*, but she takes its novel premises seriously and her discussion of it is revealing.

Wanrow was the trial of a woman who shot a man who had threatened her and abused and threatened her children. The disputed point was whether the shooting was in self-defense. Self-defense was claimed on unusual grounds. It was argued that the defendant was entitled to have her actions considered "in the light of her own perceptions of the situation, including those perceptions which were the products of our nation's long and unfortunate history of sex discrimination."[8]

That we have such a history, and that its discriminatoriness had discernible effects on the female point of view, was taken as given by this defense. Thus, the feminine perspective relevant to this case is drawn from someone's assumptions about our nation's history and the effect that history has had upon a woman's perceptions and capabilities, moreover, upon any woman's perceptions and capabilities. This judgment of the effects of discrimination was not particular to the *Wanrow* defendant (although it was thought to apply to her, as to everyone else). The principles guiding this defense are thus arbitrarily determined, subjective, and generic. The premise is that what some people have determined to be the lifetime experience of all women, in general, should be a factor in the defense of one woman's actions in a particular case. It is a peculiar basis for a determination of guilt or innocence in a criminal case distinguished—as are all criminal cases—by particular people and events.

We see much the same thing in *Wanrow*, then, that we saw in the proposed rape law. In both cases, we see an interest in codifying "women's point of view." And in both cases, we see that the "women's point of view" espoused by the new feminist jurisprudence does not necessarily mean the point of view of the individual woman involved. It is more likely to mean an allegedly collective perspective intended to apply to all women, as simply determined by some unnamed party.

This arbitrary and collective determination is not surprising. Throughout MacKinnon's work, it is clear that for "women's subjective experience" she is prepared to plug in her own opinion of their subjective experience. If women claim an experience different from what she thinks they're having, she tunes them out. If a woman claims, for example, not to be objectified by men, MacKinnon assumes that that woman is wrong about her own experience, and that she, MacKinnon, is right. She has one of those maddening systems that essentially asserts: "Health is seeing things this way and disease is seeing them any other way," so that she can dismiss all disputants as just particularly sick cases.

Thus the feminine point of view that MacKinnon hopes to impose upon legal judgment is a collectivist point of view. And like all points of view that call themselves collectivist, this one is really the perspective of the collectivity according to some one person or some group of people who will claim to speak for it. Like most collectivities, this one is a tyrant. It is the tyranny of the few over many individuals. MacKinnon's feminist jurisprudence—the jurisprudence based on "the personal is political"—is tyrannical and collectivist.

MacKinnon's remarks about the collectivity with respect to *Wanrow* are here revealing. The *Wanrow* decision, she writes, moves toward "a single standard from women's point of view." The defendant's subjectivity "is equated with the point of view from women's experience. What she actually perceived as an individual in that moment of threat is important, but without a collective context in which to interpret its meaning it is unintelligible and nondispositive. Here subjectivity does not mean personal except in the sense in which the personal is political."[9]

Catharine MacKinnon is dissatisfied with the law because the unit of the law is the individual. And her creed is that the personal— which means something individual—is in fact political, which is not individual but collective. MacKinnon's true agenda involves the replacement of the individual by the collectivity, which will be, inevitably, in the hands of the few who claim to speak for it.

To say, though, that "the personal is political" is a totalitarian premise yielding totalitarian law does not address the matter of whether the premise is true, and if it is false, of where exactly it goes wrong. The falsity of "the personal is political" is not discoverable as much by argument as it is by experience. And the precise point at which this dictum errs is discoverable only by the sort of reflection on the human lot to which—happily—many wise observers have already opened the door.

By looking at Eastern Europe—and by looking at our own lives as well—we know that although the personal is in some ways touched by the political, it is not only political, or even mainly political. Most of the personal is not political at all, which is why it is called "the personal." It is totalitarianism which tries to politicize the personal. Yet even totalitarianism must fight the personal's trenchant, sometimes involuntary resistance to politicization.

By looking at our own lives, too, we know that MacKinnon vastly oversimplifies power (at least, as it prevails in a free nation like the

United States). While there is considerable truth in her idea that politics have to do with power, power encompasses a great deal more than just politics. Power relations between men and women, in particular, encompass more than politics. And even to the extent that male-female relations are divisions of political power—to the extent, in other words, that the power we have or lack in our public lives does filter through to our personal lives and sexual relationships— that power is far more complex than the brute exploitation she assumes.

Catharine MacKinnon's mistake, in short, is in assuming that men are just beasts and women are just victims. In fact, we are all a lot more and a lot better than that. A short illustrative passage from Henry James's *Portrait of a Lady* wonderfully illustrates our true complexity. The characters are Isabel Archer, a young American, and Ralph Touchett, her English cousin. They are in a London square at dusk. Isabel tells her cousin, who is in love with her, that soon she will return to her hotel and have a simple dinner. Ralph asks if he may join her, and she answers him, "No, you'll dine at your club." James writes:

> They had wandered back to their chairs in the center of the square again, and Ralph had lighted his cigarette. It would have given him extreme pleasure to be present at the modest little feast she had sketched; but in default of this he liked even being forbidden. For the moment, however, he liked immensely being alone with her, in the thickening dusk, in the multitudinous town; it made her seem to depend upon him and to be in his power. This power he could exert but vaguely; the best exercise of it was to accept her decisions submissively—which indeed there was already an emotion in doing.

This paragraph throws the failings of radical feminism into sharp, clear relief. For what James understands, that radical feminists do not, is that people are complex, and the bonds between people are complex. Most of all, he knows that power is complex. James understands, as radical feminists do not, the various and beautiful shifts of power from protector to protected and back again, among decent, civilized men and women.

Notes

1. Catharine MacKinnon, "Feminism, Marxism, Method and the State: Toward Feminist Jurisprudence," *Signs* 8, no. 4 (1983): 638–39.
2. Ibid., p. 639.
3. Ibid., p. 651.
4. Catharine MacKinnon, "Feminism, Marxism, Method and the State: An Agenda for Theory," *Signs* 7, no. 3 (1982): 535.

5. MacKinnon, "Feminism, Marxism, Method and the State: Toward Feminist Jurisprudence," p. 644.

6. Ibid., p. 655.

7. Ibid., p. 652.

8. *State* v. *Wanrow*, 81 Wash. 2d 221, 559 P.2d 548 (1977); see pp. 285–87.

9. Catharine MacKinnon, "Toward Feminist Jurisprudence," *Stanford Law Review* 34, no. 3 (February 1982): 734.

14

Pay Equity for Women: Wage Discrimination and the Comparable Worth Controversy

Heidi I. Hartmann

COMPARABLE WORTH—the strategy that calls for the examination and realignment of the relative pay rates of predominantly female and predominantly male jobs—is an increasingly visible issue within the equal employment opportunity area. In this chaper, I first describe an emerging consensus among advocates as to what comparable worth is, then briefly outline recent developments in the area, and finally discuss some of the justifications for comparable worth as a strategy and several reactions to it. In particular, I offer an explanation of why some opponents resist the concept of comparable worth so strenuously.

In 1978 when I began work on the National Academy of Sciences study on comparable worth, the results of which have been published in *Women, Work, and Wages: Equal Pay for Jobs of Equal Value*, I interviewed labor union leaders to get their views on the subject.[1] Both in these interviews and in the course of conversation with colleagues and friends, I discovered that comparable worth was a relatively unknown concept; several labor leaders seemed not to have heard of it. But during the past eight years, public knowledge of the issue has increased tremendously. The phrase "comparable worth" is now generally recognized. Public service announcements appear in many newspapers and magazines stressing the importance of comparable worth for women workers. All the major Democratic candidates for president supported the concept of comparable worth, and the party platform endorses it. In recent years many labor union presidents have testified in favor of it in Congress. Comparable worth is now accepted by a large number of public leaders, at least as a concept that deserves exploration. Had someone asked me in 1978 whether this idea and strategy could have progressed toward public acceptance so rapidly, I would certainly have said no.

The Consensus View of Comparable Worth

Along with greater public acceptance, advocates of comparable worth have developed a consensus view of comparable worth as a particular set of strategies with a particular focus. The focus is on the employment practices of the individual employer; the set of strategies generally includes studies followed by bargaining or litigation (or both). Although opponents, particularly in the business press, still raise the specter of government-wide regulation of wage rates in all industries and in all firms, with wage tribunals or judges determining wages across the entire economy, much of the media and most proponents stress that what is being advocated is an employer-by-employer approach, much like that used in other equal employment opportunity approaches. It is also important to note that, like other equal employment opportunity policies, comparable worth is as relevant to jobs in which minorities predominate as it is to those in which women predominate, since such jobs may pay less because of the race or ethnicity of the incumbents.

The typical comparable worth strategy is developed by employees, generally unionized, who are concerned about the equity of wage rates at their workplace. It begins with a study of wage rates and job categories (often—in the public sector—mandated by legislation) in which some type of job evaluation system is used to measure the value of work according to such criteria as skill, effort, and responsibility. The study typically shows that jobs with similar evaluations have different wage rates, with jobs held predominantly by women paying less than jobs held predominantly by men. The suggested remedy is the realignment of the wage rates of those jobs. The results of the study can then be used to support collective bargaining or litigation (or both). Many of the employers involved are very large. They are state civil service systems that employ many thousands of workers. But small municipalities with only a few employees have also implemented comparable worth, thereby raising the wages of employees in predominantly female job categories.

In most lawsuits that have developed a comparable worth argument, the employment practices of the employer are thoroughly examined. The mainstay of an argument that discrimination has affected the wage rates of an *entire* occupation (as opposed to an argument that *individual* women have been discriminated against in pay in a particular job) is the existence of sex segregation in the firm's employment structure. If there were not extreme job segregation by sex in nearly all firms throughout the labor market such that some jobs are readily identifiable as female jobs and others are readily identifiable as male jobs, the issue of comparable worth could not arise. Hence, any showing that the employer has knowingly and intentionally maintained the sex segregation of jobs can certainly contribute to showing that the employer is also responsible for their relative wage rates. As Wynn Newman has put it so aptly, "comparable worth can be seen as garden variety, sex-based wage discrimination," and once put in the context of discrimination, the mode of attacking a comparable worth problem becomes clear. The comparable worth strategy, like other equal employment opportunity strategies, is employer-based, requires investigation and study, and points to an obvious remedy—wage realignment and back pay. It should also be clear from this approach that affirmative action, in opening up sex-segregated job opportunities, is also a critical component of redress.

Comparable worth legal cases operate in much the same way as cases based on equal access and equal pay for equal work. It is interesting to note that, conceptually, the vast problem of low-paid, female-dominated jobs—held by approximately two-thirds of all women workers—can be handled and dealt with in the same way as those problem areas that have been previously identified. In this view, comparable worth can be seen to be simply another application of relatively well-established equal employment opportunity law, particularly Title VII of the 1964 Civil Rights Act. Of course, advocates and opponents disagree about the extent to which the courts have accepted, or are likely to accept, comparable worth in this light.

Comparable worth is also being directly addressed in union negotiations, as it has been for years, though without the comparable worth label. Most unions are concerned with equity and fairness and sometimes assign particularly low-paying jobs a disproportionate share of the wage increase that results from any bargaining effort. The comparable worth movement, however, has heightened the awareness of unionized women workers about pay equity issues. Resolutions passed at annual union conventions and, in some cases, accompanying legal strategies, such as those within the American Federation of State, County, and Municipal Employees (AFSCME), have brought wage equity bargaining issues to the center of attention. Unfortunately most of the American labor force is not unionized, and so this remedy is not available to many women workers. Although in a bargaining context, wage equity or comparable worth can be pursued without elaborate job evaluation studies, simply by identifying some of the worst cases and stressing the reasonableness of the demand, the studies may have importance beyond their immediate results. If one looks at the wage determination process as essentially a political one where the outcome is determined largely by the power of various actors, then the supporting studies may be necessary to enhance the power of women workers within their unions. Supporting studies can legitimate the women's demands, help convince others, and strengthen their own convictions. Likewise, legal action can be seen as an attempt to enhance the power of the weaker parties in the wage bargain.

The continued application of these approaches over time would gradually result in a wage structure that might look significantly different from the wage structure we have today, yet the dire predictions of hardship, bankruptcy, and massive unemployment, should comparable worth take effect, seem unlikely to come true. These predictions seem to be based on a different conception of comparable worth from that which I am arguing has become the consensus view among those who advocate it and are indeed carrying it out today. Change will be gradual as one workplace after another alters its wage rates. In some current cases, the cost of change in women's and men's relative wage rates has been only 5 to 10 percent of the total payroll—hardly revolutionary. Over the past twenty years businesses and governments have institutionalized in their personnel practices what have come to be regarded as standard equal employment opportunity procedures: open announcements of jobs and promotion opportunities, salary reviews, and reporting and monitoring. The same will occur with comparable worth. For example, studies might be repeated at intervals in order to check on wage slippage and wage advancement of various jobs in workplaces. When new jobs are created, some detailed evaluation of them, particularly from the point of view of gender bias in their wage assignment, may be carried out routinely.

It is also important to note that comparable worth policies within firms, even if eventually enacted in all firms, are not a total solution to employment discrimination against women. Equal access to all occupations and all firms would still be necessary as would equitable promotion policies. There are wage leaders and wage followers in the labor market, firms at the high end of the wage hierarchy and firms at the low end. A computer operator in retailing, for example, is likely to continue to earn less than a computer operator in an engineering firm. Comparable worth within firms is not going to change that, but enforcement of equal access policies can ensure that the high-wage firms are equally open to women and men, minority members and majority whites. Likewise comparable worth will not aid women who want to be plumbers; equal access will. And equitable promotion policies, not comparable worth, will help secretaries become managers. Comparable worth could, however, help attain some of these goals.

If, like Rip Van Winkle, we could go to sleep for twenty years while comparable worth strategies progressed, we would wake up to see a labor market somewhat different from what we have today, particularly in the relative wage rates of men's and women's jobs. There would also be more integrated jobs and fewer sex-segregated ones, but the market would hardly be unrecognizable. If, for example, between now and then the comparable worth movement succeeds in having the secretarial job paid more like management jobs, no one would think it the least bit unusual. Such relative wages would have become an accepted aspect of the wage structure. (One remembers a time when all newscasters were white males; now it does not seem at all unusual to have black males and black and white females giving us the evening news.) Other secondary and tertiary effects may have occurred as well. Secretaries may be used more productively, for example, with greater use of and acknowledgment of their skills.

Recent Developments in Comparable Worth

In recent years numerous activities of different types have been generated around comparable worth issues, including legislation, studies, legal developments, and implementation. While the vast majority of the activity has been in the public sector, the private sector has not been completely untouched. A 1984 report by three organizations that seek to advance the cause of comparable worth—the National Committee on Pay Equity, the Comparable Worth Project, and the National Women's Political Caucus—identified over one hundred actions toward comparable worth taken at the state and local level alone.[2] I will provide a brief review of recent activities and comment on the federal role.

Legislation

Legislative bodies in several states and municipalities have passed laws or resolutions mandating studies of their public personnel systems. In Minnesota, legislation facilitated implementation of the results of a prior comparable worth study of the state civil service. Further legislation then required local governments in Minnesota to investigate their wage structures and implement comparable worth, if warranted. In the state of Washington, legislation authorized funding for significant comparable worth wage adjustments.

Statutes including language referring to equal pay for comparable work now exist in fourteen states and in some cases may apply to private employers as well as public ones.[3] Several different types of legislation can be relevant to comparable worth issues, including civil service laws, equal pay and fair employment practices laws, laws regulating government contractors, laws supporting collective bargaining, and equal rights amendments in state constitutions.

In Congress, both the House and the Senate have also been actively proposing legislation and resolutions pertaining to how the federal government, including Congress and congressional agencies, structures the wages of women's and men's jobs. The House has twice passed a bill (introduced by Representative Mary Rose Oakar, D–Ohio) requiring a study of the federal civil service system; at this writing, its future in the Senate is unclear. Representative Olympia Snowe (R–Maine) has introduced legislation to require a study of a legislative branch agency. In the Senate, Daniel Evans (R–Washington) introduced a concurrent resolution calling for a similar study.

Studies

Since a typical comparable worth action often begins with a study, the conduct of studies is particularly important. According to the National Committee on Pay Equity, as of April 1986, twenty-three states have completed job evaluation studies of all or part of their civil service systems with the goal of examining pay equity and developing comparable worth remedies. Many other government units are also engaged in studies (state university systems, local governments, etc.).[4]

Legal Developments

Some of these studies have led to lawsuits; some have led to complaints filed with the EEOC; more lawsuits and complaints are certain to follow. Despite a fair amount of litigation, however, the legal status of the comparable worth theory is unclear. In the best-known decision, *AFSCME* v. *State of Washington* (578 F.Supp 846), in the fall of 1983, a federal district judge, Jack Tanner, found the state guilty of failing to pay in accordance with its own studies, conducted in 1974 and 1976, and awarded back pay (estimated to amount to $500 million to $1 billion). The decision was then appealed to the U.S.

Court of Appeals for the Ninth Circuit. Judge Tanner found all three possible grounds for a punitive judgment identified in a recent Bureau of National Affairs report: failure to pay in accordance with the results of a job evaluation study; intent to segregate by sex and discriminate against women; and disparate impact of the employer's existing compensation system on women.[5] The Ninth Circuit, however, reversed the decision on all points of law and stated that, in its view, discriminatory intent is necessary for a finding in favor of a comparable worth case and discriminatory intent was not shown. In the Supreme Court's 1981 *Gunther* decision, which held that prison matrons could claim sex discrimination in wages under Title VII of the 1964 Civil Rights Act even though their jobs were not identical to those of higher-paid male guards, intent was suggested by the county's failure to pay according to its job evaluation results.

The Ninth Circuit, both in *Spalding* v. *University of Washington* (35 FEP Cases 217, 1984) and the AFSCME case, appears opposed to comparable worth; in *Gunther* the Justices say they are making no decision on comparable worth, but to some observers it seems a classic comparable worth case. Despite a few positive decisions (*Taylor* v. *Charley Brothers, Co.*, 25 FEP Cases 602, 1981; *Briggs* v. *City of Madison*, 536 F. Supp. 435; *International Union of Electrical, Radio and Machine Workers* v. *Westinghouse Electric Corp.*, 23 FEP Cases 588 and 25 FEP Cases, 1835), most decisions have been negative. The courts' reactions to employer defenses have also varied case by case. Most have found a market defense acceptable (we have to pay the men more because of the market; we simply follow the market in setting women's wages), but some have found the market defense unacceptable. For example, in *Kouba* v. *Allstate Insurance Company*, 523 F. Supp. 148, 1981, the employer was required by the district court not to use past salary elsewhere as a factor in setting starting wages unless it could show that those wages were not affected by discrimination. The Ninth Circuit, on appeal (691 F. 2nd 873, 1982), decided that Allstate had the right to a trial on whether their practices served a business purpose. (The case was resolved when it was settled during retrial.) Clearly, the available decisions are mixed and will probably continue to be so until more is heard from the Supreme Court or new legislation is created.

Implementation

Implementation of comparable worth to date has occurred more because of collective bargaining and negotiation than through suits and court decisions (though in some cases the threat of legal action may have contributed to the success of negotiation). The best-known negotiated settlement occurred in San Jose where, after a strike, an AFSCME local won substantial pay increases for predominantly female, underpaid job categories in the city civil service. A 1984–85 strike by recently organized clerical and technical workers at Yale University, who alleged comparable worth disparities, was settled with significant wage increases in women's jobs. In a recent study by Sorenson, the cost of achieving equity in three state systems, Michigan, Minnesota, and Washington, was estimated to range from 7.5 to 8.5 percent of each state's total annual payroll; since equity adjustments are phased in over several years, the cost in any one year is generally much smaller.[6] Idaho and Iowa have implemented wage adjustment plans. A number of smaller public units at the state and local level, such as Colorado Springs, have implemented pay increases because of comparable worth concerns.

The Federal Role

In contrast to federal activity in previous areas of employment opportunity law, the executive branch of the federal government has been particularly uninvolved in the comparable worth strategy. In 1984, some 260 cases charging lack of comparable pay were backlogged at the Equal Employment Opportunity Commission.[7] The EEOC has since adopted a policy on comparable worth that suggests it will enforce *Gunther* but will not investigate comparable worth claims generally. In 1985, the U.S. Civil Rights Commission issued a report stating its opposition to including comparable worth in equal employment opportunity strategies and urging the Justice Department to resist comparable worth via appropriate litigation.[8] In the face of the executive branch's lack of leadership, some of the legislation that has been introduced in Congress is designed to force the relevant agencies to take a more positive approach, such as monitoring developments in the area and reporting back to Congress on their own activities. Yet, as we have seen, a great deal of activity is taking place around comparable worth, regardless of the inactivity of the federal executive branch.

Underlying Bases of Comparable Worth Claims
and Related Opposition

I noted above that the progress that comparable worth has made in the public imagination seems fantastic especially considering the resistance that we have also heard during the same past eight years. In my view, three related developments account for the general public acceptance. The first is simply the women's liberation movement of the past fifteen to twenty years. Women are much more visible politically. Through a variety of organizations and channels, women have made their demands known, not only in the workplace, but also in political parties and civic organizations, and even within families. It is somewhat unusual, but nevertheless not unheard of, for a mother to go on strike against her family, picketing her own house. From the church to the army, from the office to the coal mine, from the country club to job training programs, women are demanding more access to the resources and benefits of full citizenship.

A second related development is the increased participation of women in the labor force, and along with that, their increasing responsibility for and contribution to the financial support of themselves and their families. As women have increasingly headed their own families and as their joint headship with their husbands involves a more substantial financial contribution to family income, women have come to recognize that they need money just as much as men do and have begun to demand higher wages. We are beginning to see increased organization among women workers, particularly among clerical workers.[9] Women began to have more experience with unionization after World War II when a major increase in unionization occurred in the public sector among teachers and other public servants. I think it is likely that we will see substantially greater unionization among women workers over the next ten to twenty years, as clerical workers in the private sector organize.

The third development that has contributed to a fairly broad acceptance of the comparable worth concept is the commitment that our society has made over the last twenty years to equality of opportunity, particularly in employment but also in such other areas of life as public accommodations, voting, and housing. Although we observe a backlash, we also observe a widely shared commitment to the concepts of fairness and equity. When the comparable worth issue is understood as one that comes about first of all because of inequality of opportunity via the extreme sex segregation of jobs, and then further because of a discriminatory wage-setting process that fails to remunerate the same job characteristics as highly when they are found in women's jobs as when they are found in men's jobs, support for comparable worth will be even broader. Let me expand upon this a bit. Once unequal pay for jobs of comparable worth is understood as sex-based wage *discrimination*, even arguments that redress would be costly or might lead to some unemployment won't hold up against the basic issue of fairness and the importance of removing discrimination.

When, however, the issue is posed, as it often is, as the overturning of the laws of supply and demand, the restructuring of the entire marketplace, and the setting of wages by the courts, the concept comes into opposition with another concept held very dear by the American public, namely, that the marketplace works. It is productive, efficient, and provides opportunity for upward mobility to those who work hard. Moreover, not only does it work, it's inviolable. If businesses are forced to pay more than the market dictates for women's work, they will go bankrupt. At the very least, they will hire fewer women. Either way unemployment of women will increase substantially. Interfering with the market can only lead to no good. In this way and others, it is argued, comparable worth will hurt women more than it will help.

Can the tension between these two very different principles—equal employment opportunity and the free market—that generates so much of the comparable worth controversy be resolved? I think it can. The resolution takes the form of understanding that comparable worth adjusts market wage rates and removes bias in wage rates that results from discrimination. In a sense, it makes the market work better. It does not totally eliminate the market and administratively determine the relative wages of jobs. Major league basketball players may always earn more than secretaries, and cleaning personnel may earn even less. Comparable worth is not going to change that, but it does seek to eliminate whatever effect sex discrimination has had in determining the relative wages of occupations that have been dominated by women or men.

Comparable Worth Improves the Market

The elimination of discrimination would distribute human resources more efficiently and productively as well as ensure equal opportunity. For example, if a commodity is overpriced because of a monopoly in production, less of that good is produced and used than would ideally be the case. Similarly if something is underpriced, we are likely to use more of it than we should. With respect to women secretaries, for example, we are using entirely too many highly skilled women with good verbal, human relations, and communications skills, in jobs that may, at times, underutilize those skills. We frequently hear someone say: I want to have a secretary who is a college graduate, even though it is not a formal requirement of the job. Why? Because we want those skills without having to pay for them. And, because of women's limited opportunities, we can get them. But if we, as a society, are using too many college graduates in this way, we are missing the opportunity to use them somewhere else more productively. Insofar as discrimination alters the relative wage rates of jobs that are typically held by men and women, men and women are not being utilized in the most efficient ways. Some reallocation of labor, some shifting of women and men from one occupation to another, some unemployment, may well result from a general re-alignment of the wage rates of men's and women's jobs. However, keep in mind that this realignment will occur over many, many years.

Most economists would accept the argument that discrimination results in a less than ideal allocation of human resources and human talent to the work of society, is therefore inefficient, and should be eliminated. Moreover, it is generally agreed that, although the elimi-nation of discrimination would result in some change in the way the market operates (for example, when blacks were finally hired to play on professional white baseball teams, professional black teams de-clined), these effects are in general transitory, small, and of minor cost relative to the benefit to be reaped from the better allocation of resources.

But there is little agreement on the extent of discrimination against women. In particular, there is disagreement about whether the lower wages of women's occupations are the result of discriminatory proc-esses or something else; and little research specifically on the relative wages of occupations has been done.

Some would argue that discrimination, more social and cultural, is so diffuse that there are no perpetrators but only victims. Some would say it is society that is responsible, not the employer, and some would even say women themselves are responsible. Women may choose occupations that pay less for a variety of reasons: they may have a greater commitment to marriage, to family, to raising children, to taking care of family members. Women may freely make these commitments acknowledging that this affects their labor market par-ticipation. Such a commitment to family may reduce their commit-ment to their jobs generally and result in their lower productivity on the job, which in turn accounts for their lower rates of pay.

In contrast, others would argue that women are tracked into a narrow set of occupations and denied opportunity. One can point to the fact that law schools and medical schools were virtually closed to women until quite recently, that engineering and coal mining and many of the better remunerated occupations such as carpentry, electrical work, and truck driving were closed to women and some still effectively are.

These differences of opinion among economists find their way into the courtroom as expert witnesses appear on both sides of any discrimination or comparable worth case. It is safe to say that there is no consensus within the economics profession (or within the social sciences in general) about how much discrimination exists in the labor market and particularly about how much it affects the relative wage rates of specific jobs. Very few empirical studies have directly focused on the comparable worth issue. Those that exist have often relied upon job evaluation methodology and have been carried out in conjunction with comparable worth cases or union bargaining processes. It is possible that after substantial study we will find that wage discrimination affects relative occupational pay rates less than comparable worth advocates think it does. It is also possible that we will find more wage discrimination than the "chamber of commerce" thinks exists. Nevertheless, if theoretical and empirical research determines that discrimination does affect the relative wage rates of occupations, agreement to seek the realignment of these wage rates within discriminating firms should be forthcoming. Presumably, that realignment would require a degree of interference with the behavior of employers.

Let us assume therefore that, even if we do not have consensus now about the extent of the problem, we could in fact have greater consensus at some time in the future. Such a consensus would include agreement on two aspects of the labor market: 1) sex segregation exists (a fact no one disputes), and it is not entirely the result of women's choices; and 2) discrimination in the labor market is widespread enough to affect the relative wage rates of occupations dominated by women or men. These key elements of a comparable worth strategy were supported by the National Academy of Sciences report on which I worked. Although the committee pointed out that evidence is rather sparse on the effect of discrimination on the wage rates of occupations, as opposed to the wage rates of individuals, it nevertheless concluded that it was highly likely that, given what we know about how the labor market operates, discrimination does affect the wage rates of women's jobs, depressing them below where they would be in the absence of that discrimination.[10]

Wage Discrmination

Conceptually, I have found it useful to distinguish two aspects of this discrimination. The first is what we might view as market-based discrimination, which comes about by tracking women into a restricted set of jobs and opportunities, thereby overcrowding a particular field. This concept was developed by Barbara Bergmann.[11] In the overcrowding model, equal access to all jobs would result in a realignment of wage rates. Wages of formerly women's jobs would increase because the supply of women to these jobs would decrease as new opportunities opened to women, while the wage rates of formerly men's jobs would decrease because the supply to these jobs would increase as women entered them. According to the overcrowding explanation, women, because of exclusion, are in oversupply to those occupations open to them, thus driving down their wage rates. In short, if equal opportunity existed in the labor market, a free market would be restored and would raise women's wages, both because the wage rates of women's jobs would increase and because women could earn better wages in the formerly male jobs they entered.

There could be a second source of discrimination in women's wage rates, however. Some part of the underpayment of women's jobs could be due to what we might call direct wage discrimination, above and beyond that resulting from overcrowding. Imagine that today's women's jobs were done instead by men and that there were just as many men available to do them as there now are women (the relative supply of men and women just discussed would *not* be an issue). The suspicion is that the same jobs when done by men would be valued more highly. Many women have come to believe that their work is undervalued precisely *because* it is typically women's work. They believe that such activities as caring, nurturing, and being polite and friendly are underpaid, at least when done by women. For example, if men were nurses, it is held, nursing would be paid more, not because there were fewer men than women available for nursing, but because men's skills are recognized and valued differently (or perhaps it would also be the case that men would define and do the job somewhat differently). It is quite likely, given what we know about social and cultural beliefs, that the devaluation of women's activities and characteristics is deeply imbedded in all our social practices and does indeed affect wage rates.

Studying these two aspects of wage discrimination is difficult, but not impossible. The extent of discrimination in the labor market due to overcrowding could be estimated, for example, by simulation studies that would move men and women around into different occupations with some varying assumptions of what free choice would look like. Using such models, new relative occupational wage rates could be derived. But such studies might not get at the second potential source of this wage discrimination. For this, job evaluation is needed.

The Role of Job Evaluation

Job evaluation attempts specifically to identify the components of jobs that are valued and asks what makes one job more valuable than another. What are the kinds of skills and effort demanded of the person doing the job? It is less intellectually demanding to collect tickets at a movie theater than it is to sell the tickets and make change, for example. It might, however, require more assertiveness and more physical ability to keep a customer without a ticket from entering the theater than the cashier must have to make change.

Job evaluation, developed in the 1930s and 40s as part of the general trend toward scientific management, was designed to compare and rank jobs in large workplaces. As workplaces grow larger in size, they grow more complex. More management is required to coordinate workers, to hire them, to pay them, to promote them, and to fire them. Systematic procedures also contribute to making workers feel justly treated. The general development of personnel offices, personnel procedures, and job evaluation brought order to haphazard personnel processes. Several major types of job evaluation systems exist, including broad classification schemes like the federal civil service system and more quantitative plans known as "point factor" plans. Most point-factor plans are "policy-capturing plans." They attempt to model or "capture" the firm's existing pay policy and to bring any outlying jobs into conformity with the firm's general policy.

Pay policies can and do differ among firms. It is widely held, for example, that at IBM, sales capability is well compensated relative to technical expertise in comparison to other high-technology firms. In the steel industry, the degree of responsibility in jobs is better compensated relative to other factors than in other industries. Why? Because steel making is dangerous and responsibility is important to prevent accidents and death. In general, we can expect that the relative wages of jobs within workplaces will differ according to the kinds of values that the employer has developed (sometimes in conjunction with employees).

Many, perhaps most, job evaluation systems are "installed" by consultants. A job evaluation consultant can come into any workplace and, by studying the existing pay structure, determine what it is that the employer implicitly values. A policy-capturing plan developed for the firm can make those values explicit. Typically each job will be described and rated, according to established criteria, on a variety of job factors thought to be related to pay: how many people are supervised, how long does it take to train for the job, how much physical effort is required. The measures of the job factors can then be regressed against the existing wage rates to develop a policy line, around which many of the jobs cluster. Of course, there will be outlyers and these are usually brought into alignment with the policy line over time or are exempted. In any case, however, these plans essentially use existing wages to determine the weights (the coefficients in the regression equation) of the factors identified, and the relationship of the total scores for each job in the plan (the sum of its weighted factor scores) will replicate the relationship among their wage rates. These plans do what they were designed to do: replicate and rationalize the internal wage hierarchy. Job evaluation consultants also come into firms with ready-made plans that establish the weights of the different factors and so determine what is to be valued in jobs. These are sometimes called a priori job evaluation systems. Of course, even these a priori evaluation systems have a relationship to market wages. They are often the result of many applications at many different workplaces having evolved, through trial and error, from what has replicated the marketplace best. Hence, job evaluation plans essentially attempt to identify what it is that is valuable about jobs, by measuring those aspects of jobs that currently give them value and then using those measures to bring all the wage rates into rational relationship with one another. The plans are then also used to determine the wage rates of new jobs created within the firm.

From this brief and schematic description of job evaluation systems, one would be hard pressed to see why or how these evaluation systems are used in comparable worth cases, since they seem designed to reinforce the status quo. The National Academy of Sciences report pinpointed several weaknesses in these evaluations: 1. the subjective nature of many of the judgments made in rating jobs, 2. the use of discrimination-tainted wages in the development of factor weights, 3. the tendency of many firms to use several different types of job evaluation plans for different types of work—blue collar, clerical, and management, for example, and 4. the lack of attention to the complexities of measurement and modeling. The report also concluded, however, that with proper attention to these problems, job evaluation plans could be used to determine the relative worth of jobs, without gender bias. Moreover, several completed studies of wage structures have used relatively "unimproved" job evaluation plans and have nevertheless determined that women's jobs were paid about 20 percent less than men's jobs with the same job evaluation scores. These results occurred for at least two reasons. First, all types of jobs were evaluated with one plan, rather than several. This alone forces a comparison of men's and women's jobs on their content. Second, these studies were usually carried out with the advice of a labor-management committee that was already attuned to comparable worth issues and monitored the consultants' decisions.

A great deal of attention has been paid in recent years to improving job evaluation plans. The NAS report discusses several techniques for eliminating the sex bias inherent in the use of market wages to derive factor weights. Recent papers by Leslie McArthur and her colleagues describe experiments conducted to test for rater bias in the more subjective aspects of job evaluation.[12] While this research will eventually pay off in better job evaluation instruments, it does appear that even the relatively unsophisticated plans now available can successfully identify instances of sex-based wage discrimination. What job evaluation plans do is identify and measure the characteristics of jobs that give them value. When used in a relatively unbiased manner they can get at what I called "direct" wage discrimination—the undervaluing of the characteristics found in women's jobs *because* they are in *women's* jobs. With job evaluation, characteristics of jobs must be valued the same regardless of what jobs they are found in.

Let me hasten to point out that despite its qualified endorsement of job evaluation, the NAS report is also careful to note that what *should* be valued cannot be scientifically determined. We can use science to identify and measure what currently gives jobs value; we can use it to determine what jobs *should be* paid *if* a set of value criteria has been established by other means.

I noted above that firms have discretion, within bounds, to set wages according to internal criteria. They do so, of course, with attention to going market wages. Job evaluation plans retain that same flexibility. They can adjust market wages to take into account the firm's policies and to remove the effects of sex bias. The standard job evaluation procedure for deriving weights essentially preserves many aspects of the market relationships between jobs. The comparable worth strategy, via job evaluation, is not an attempt to overthrow the market but simply to eliminate the sex-discriminatory component of market wages. Consequently, the conflict in the viewpoints identified at the outset of this section can be resolved by a proper understanding of the comparable worth strategy, along the lines suggested here.

This discussion of the role of job evaluation also makes clear that the comparable worth strategy is a gradual employer-by-employer approach. No one is advocating that a single job evaluation plan be foisted upon all employers. There are no universal criteria for job worth, and it is probably very good that there are not.

Other approaches to comparable worth and to job evaluation that seek to determine more directly the question of value have been suggested. Schwab, for example, suggests that a "value-capturing" plan analogous to policy-capturing plans could be developed by attempting to identify job values that most American adults agree on.[13] Although this may be a fruitful area for research, the development of such universally agreed upon standards is likely to be very far off in the future.

Women's Economic Independence

While the challenge to "supply and demand" that comparable worth poses can theoretically be resolved by more information about the extent and degree of sex-based wage discrimination, the challenge posed to another important cultural belief system may not be so easily met.

Comparable worth challenges the belief that women are secondary earners, that men are the only or rightful household heads, that women's primary commitment is to the family. When women demand comparable worth they are demanding wages equal to men's and an equal chance with men to be economically independent. Wages that assign greater value to what women do are *crucial* to women's ability to be financially independent. That women want economic equality with men does not mean that women no longer want to live with or marry men. But women's demands can be interpreted as a demand to eliminate men's unique privilege of having a wage large enough to support a family. A family wage should not be a matter of male privilege but should be equally available to women. Because family formation and household structures are changing, because women are very likely to have sole responsibility for supporting themselves and their children for some part of their lifetimes, because women's participation in the labor market is increasing, women—through comparable worth and other means—are saying they need and want a "family" wage just as much as men do.

Women's demand for the ability to support themselves and their families in a way equal to men's is a fundamental challenge to the nature of gender relations today. The economic dependence of women on men is both fact and norm, and is deeply imbedded in our social structure. But for women and men, the norm and reality of lifelong marriage and male support of women is disappearing. Equal earnings for women are both a cause of and a response to that disappearance. Comparable worth, which attempts to revalue what women do, may be a more fundamental challenge to these older notions of male economic superiority than even equal pay or affirmative action, because it is a strategy that implicitly challenges the worth of what men do. A woman who wants access to a male-dominated job conveys the message: I want a good job like yours. If she wants equal pay in a "male job" she conveys: I deserve equal pay because I'm doing men's work. But if she demands comparable worth she conveys the message: My job is as good as your job, your job is no better than mine, women's work is worth as much as men's. Comparable worth challenges the cultural devaluations of women and women's work. In doing so, it challenges the notion that women should be economically, socially, and culturally dependent on men. I suspect that much of the heat generated in opposition to comparable worth and the vocal defense of the free market is really a displaced response to this much more fundamental challenge that comparable worth poses to the status quo.

Because of the strength of the women's movement and the twenty-year legacy of equal opportunity in this country, opponents to comparable worth do not come out and say women belong in the home (or at least in low-paid jobs). Instead, Phyllis Schlafly is reduced to bemoaning the disruption of the marketplace and the potential threat of government regulation to the free enterprise system. That comparable worth has become as visible as it has is an indication of the strength of the civil rights and women's movements that have kept issues of equity and opportunity at center stage. That the opposition is as irrational, emotional, and vociferous as it is indicates that comparable worth challenges something more basic than the "laws of supply and demand." It questions the bases of our most intimate lives and says this too we must change.

Notes

1. Donald J. Treiman and Heidi I. Hartmann, eds., *Women, Work, and Wages: Equal Pay for Jobs of Equal Value* (Washington, D.C.: National Academy Press, 1981).

2. National Committee on Pay Equity, Comparable Worth Project, and National Women's Political Caucus, *Who's Working for Working Women: A Survey of State and Local Government Pay Equity Activities and Initiatives* (Washington, D.C.: Comparable Worth Project, National Committee on Pay Equity, and National Women's Political Caucus, 1984).

3. Bureau of National Affairs, Inc., *Pay Equity and Comparable Worth*, A BNA Special Report (Washington, D.C.: Bureau of National Affairs, Inc., 1984).

4. National Committee on Pay Equity, oral communication, May 23, 1986.

5. Bureau of National Affairs, Inc., *Pay Equity*.

6. Elaine Sorenson, "Comparable Worth Matures: Measurement Issues Under Pay Equity Implementation," paper presented at a conference on "New Directions for Comparable Worth," Minneapolis, Minn., October 18, 1985.

7. Bureau of National Affairs, *Pay Equity*.

8. U.S. Commission on Civil Rights, *Comparable Worth: An Analysis and Recommendations* (Washington, D.C.: U.S. Commission on Civil Rights, June 1985).

9. Heidi I. Hartmann and Karen Nussbaum, "The Clerical Workers' Movement in the U.S.," published in German in *Dollars and Trauma*, a journal of American Studies (Fall 1983).

10. Treiman and Hartmann, eds., *Women, Work, and Wages*.

11. Barbara R. Bergmann, "Occupational Segregation, Wages and Profits When Employers Discriminate by Race or Sex," *Eastern Economic Journal* 1 (April/July 1974): 103–10.

12. Leslie Z. McArthur, "Social Judgment Biases in Comparable Worth Analysis," paper presented at the Seminar on Comparable Worth Research sponsored by the National Academy of Sciences Committee on Women's Employment and Related Social Issues, October 1983; Leslie Z. McArthur and S. Obrant, "Sex Biases in Comparable Worth Analysis," Department of Psychology, Brandeis University, unpublished paper, 1984.

13. Donald P. Schwab, "Job Evaluation Research and Research Needs," paper presented at the Seminar on Comparable Worth Research sponsored by the National Academy of Sciences Committee on Women's Employment and Related Social Issues, October 1983.

15

The Economics of
Comparable Worth:
A Comment on Hartmann

Mark R. Killingsworth

ECONOMISTS OFTEN PERCEIVE comparable worth as antithetical to wage determination by market supply and demand. That may be why their reaction to comparable worth is often negative. Ironically, however, in a sense, the concept of comparable worth may be traced to no less a figure than Adam Smith. In Book I, Chapter 10, of *The Wealth of Nations*, Smith wrote:

> The five following are the principal circumstances which, so far as I have been able to observe, make up for a small pecuniary gain in some employments, and counter-balance a great one in others: first, the agreeableness or disagreeableness of the employments themselves; secondly, the easiness and cheapness, or the difficulty and expence of learning them; thirdly, the constancy or inconstancy of employment in them; fourthly, the small or great trust which must be reposed in those who exercise them; and fifthly, the probability or improbability of success in them.[2]

In words only slightly different from Smith's, comparable worth proponents such as Heidi Hartmann define comparability in terms of the same factors Smith enumerated: skill ("the easiness and cheapness, or the difficulty and expence of learning [jobs]"); effort and working conditions ("agreeableness or disagreeableness," "the constancy or inconstancy of employment," "the probability or improbability of success"); and responsibility ("the small or great trust which must be reposed").

In a sense, then, comparable worth amounts to nothing more radical than an insistence that the economic theory of compensating wage differentials be taken seriously. If two jobs *are* comparable in terms of Smith's factors but pay different wages, is the pay differential justified? If the differential favors the job with greater male representation, is that not gender-based discrimination?

Preliminaries

At the outset, it is helpful to dispose of the naive "free market" argument that comparable worth is ill-advised because it would interfere with the so-called free interplay of supply and demand in the labor market.

This argument is fallacious for two reasons. First, it ignores one of the main points raised (if only implicitly) by comparable worth: whether or not the "free interplay" of marketplace supply and demand has been affected by the impermissible influence of employer discrimination. Unlike some economists, who are unwilling to say whether any portion of the female-male wage gap observed at particular employers might be attributable to discriminatory employment practices, based on my own research, I agree with Hartmann that employer discrimination is a serious problem.[2]

A second difficulty with the "free market" argument against comparable worth is that it simply asserts a distaste for market intervention without examining the conceptual basis or likely effects of intervention. In evaluating a proposed intervention, one should instead ask both whether the factual and analytical premises on which the intervention is based are sound and whether the consequences of the intervention are likely to be favorable.

Unfortunately, Hartmann does not seriously tackle either of these questions. Just as opponents of comparable worth typically reject it on a priori grounds because it would entail intervention in the labor market, proponents typically support comparable worth simply because they judge its objectives to be laudable. However, good intentions are not enough. In commenting on Hartmann, I argue as follows:

> The concept of comparable worth suffers from a fundamental misunderstanding of the way in which real-world labor markets operate and of how employer discrimination harms women. There is nothing inherently discriminatory about *unequal* pay for supposedly comparable jobs, and there is nothing inherently nondiscriminatory about paying jobs according to their "worth," as advocated by proponents of comparable worth.
>
> Viewed purely from the pragmatic perspective of its likely effect on women workers, comparable worth will be a mixed blessing. In practical terms, comparable worth amounts to a tax on predominantly female low-wage labor whose revenues would go not to the Treasury but

rather to those workers fortunate enough to keep their jobs after the tax takes effect. Some women workers—those who enjoy wage increases brought about by comparable worth—will gain, but other women workers will lose.[3]

The Rationale for Comparable Worth: Was Adam Smith Right?

Adam Smith and present-day advocates of comparable worth such as Hartmann are mistaken. There is no necessary relationship between the "worth" of a job—as measured by skill, effort, responsibility, and working conditions—and what it will pay, or even what it ought to pay in the absence of labor market discrimination.

The basic reason for this is that tastes and preferences are heterogeneous: different people can (and do) evaluate the same job quite differently. Thus, the "job worth" and "comparability" advocated by the proponents of comparable worth are inherently subjective. Neither concept necessarily conveys any useful information, either about the way the current discriminatory real-world labor market works, or about the way a nondiscriminatory real-world labor market would work.

To see why, consider an example provided by Sharon—not Adam—Smith. An employer asks us to evaluate the comparability of the jobs of Spanish-English translator and French-English translator.[4] Most job evaluations would probably find these two jobs comparable: it would be hard to argue that one requires more skill, effort, or responsibility than the other; and both presumably involve the same working conditions since they are with the same employer. Under comparable worth, then, both jobs would receive the same wage.

Now suppose we learn that the employer in question is located in Miami. Even if all employers of translators were gender-blind, would it be very surprising if the two jobs received different pay? Hardly. Would it even be possible to predict which job would get the higher wage? Probably not. Relative to demand for French-English translators, demand in Miami for Spanish-English translators may be very high. Even if all employers are gender-blind, that would tend to raise pay for Spanish-English relative to French-English translators. However, the *supply* of Spanish-English translators in Miami may be much greater than the supply of French-English translators. Other things being equal, that will tend to reduce pay for Spanish-English relative to French-English translators, even if all employers are gender-blind.

Thus, even if two jobs involve exactly the same skill, effort, responsibility, and working conditions, there is no reason to expect that they would receive the same pay—even in a completely gender-blind labor market.[5]

By the same token, there is no reason to expect that jobs of different "worth," as defined by advocates of comparable worth, should necessarily receive *different* pay, even in a completely gender-blind labor market. For example, police work is generally regarded as arduous and dangerous. It would therefore not be surprising if a job evaluation awarded more points—and higher pay—to police work than to clerical work.

Would such a pay differential really be necessary, however? If different people evaluate clerical and police jobs differently, it might not be. Indeed, if enough people think of police work as exciting and clerical work as dull, it would be possible to fill all police jobs without any wage premium, even in a gender-blind labor market.

Of course, in the discriminatory labor market of the real world, comparable worth here would merely justify and protect the practice of paying premium wages to police work, a job still held mostly by men, even if there were no rational basis for such a differential. If Caspar Weinberger finds out about comparable worth, then the statement Hartmann attributes to Wynn Newman—"comparable worth can be seen as garden variety, sex-based wage discrimination"—may turn out to be devastatingly accurate instead of merely poorly expressed.

It is certainly true, as some advocates of comparable worth point out, that job evaluation and "job worth" have long been in use in parts of private industry. However, this ignores an essential distinction between the kind of job evaluation typically used in private industry and the kind of job evaluation advocated by proponents of comparable worth. Commercial job evaluations are generally based explicitly on market considerations: for example, commercial job evaluation firms often "benchmark" wages for "key jobs" on the basis of labor market surveys and use procedures such as regression analysis of existing salary structures to determine the weights that are given to the different factors considered.

In contrast, comparable worth advocates argue that market-generated wage structures are likely to be contaminated by discrimination. They therefore advocate "bias-free" job evaluations, derived at least to some extent from a priori, ad hoc considerations independently of the existing wage structure.[6] As Schwab has observed, such evaluations would differ substantially from those now in use.[7]

A problem with bias-free evaluations is that, as Hartmann notes, they are inherently subjective. How, then, can one distinguish between bias-free evaluations that are truly bias-free and those that are not? Arguments in support of bias-free evaluations contain a dismaying element of circularity. For example, consider Hartmann's expla-

nation of why even "relatively 'unimproved' job evaluation plans . . .
have, nevertheless, determined that women's jobs were paid about
20 percent less than men's jobs with the same job evaluation scores":
not only were men's and women's jobs evaluated using the same
plan, the evaluations "were usually carried out with the advice of a
labor-management committee that was already attuned to comparable worth issues and monitored the consultants' decisions." In other
words, one can be sure that the evaluations were bias-free because
they had been designed to increase wages in women's jobs!

Comparable worth advocates are on seemingly firmer ground in
arguing that, regardless of the merits of comparable worth in the
abstract, there is something inherently suspicious about a situation in
which predominantly female jobs tend to be paid less than predominantly male jobs that have been deemed comparable. However, just
as the abstract case for comparable worth ignores the heterogeneity of
tastes in the general population, this specific argument for comparable worth ignores systematic gender-related differences in tastes.

The National Academy of Sciences/National Research Council report on comparable worth—which, it should be noted, endorsed the
general concept—provides an admirable summary of many of the
reasons why women may be overrepresented in low-wage jobs: they
may be "socialized to believe that some types of jobs are appropriate
. . . and . . . others are inappropriate for women"; they may not have
chosen the education or training that would qualify them for other
jobs; they may lack information about other jobs; they may be aware
of other jobs, "but because of actual or expected family obligations
may structure their labor force participation in particular ways" that
reduce their earnings possibilities.[8]

This is in no sense an attempt to "blame the victim"; discussion of
gender differences in field of study or career need not (and in this case
does not) entail the assumption that such "choice" is "free." Economists realize that the essence of choice is *constraints*, including constraints that individual decision makers may bear quite unwillingly. A
woman's labor market success may be critically affected by the way
she is socialized by her parents, discrimination against her within the
school system, or the roles her husband imposes on her.

However, this does not dispose of—indeed, it underscores—a
point that many advocates of comparable worth overlook: factors
other than employer discrimination contribute substantially to the
male-female pay gap and to the concentration of women in low-wage
occupations. This being the case, there is simply no reason to ascribe
all of the difference in pay between "comparable" predominantly

female and predominantly male jobs to employer discrimination, as comparable worth implicitly does.

The Labor Market Consequences of Comparable Worth

Although comparable worth is conceptually specious, it might still deserve support on pragmatic grounds. If employer discrimination is a serious problem, and if comparable worth will increase wages in predominantly female jobs, aren't conceptual objections to comparable worth rather unimportant?

Unfortunately, even from a purely practical standpoint, comparable worth is likely to prove a mixed blessing. Suppose that a public servant were to advocate that the labor market status of women could be improved by putting a tax on female labor, and using the revenues derived from the tax to reduce the budget deficit or to increase military spending. Most sensible people would find this proposal hard to take seriously. However, what Hartmann and other proponents of comparable worth are advocating is not terribly different: comparable worth amounts to putting a tax on labor in predominantly female jobs and distributing the revenues to the workers in those jobs who are fortunate enough to *remain* employed *after* the tax is imposed!

Because comparable worth would increase the cost of employing low-wage predominantly female labor, it will reduce employment of such labor (other things being equal).[9] To the extent that it raises overall labor costs, it may also reduce employment in other categories, e.g., predominantly male or integrated jobs.[10] Thus, comparable worth "solves" the problem of women's low wages only to aggravate others.

To her credit, Hartmann (unlike many other advocates of comparable worth) recognizes at least the possibility that comparable worth will have adverse side-effects. However, she argues (emphasis original): "Once unequal pay for jobs of comparable worth is understood as sex-based wage *discrimination*, even arguments that redress would be costly or might lead to some unemployment won't hold up against the basic issue of fairness and the importance of removing discrimination."

This statement suffers from severe confusion. First, as noted above, unequal pay for jobs of comparable worth is *not* inherently discriminatory; and equal pay for jobs of comparable worth—and different pay for jobs of different worth—is *not* inherently nondiscriminatory or "fair." Second, comparable worth will do nothing to attack discrimination outside the labor market—in education, in the household, etc.—though many observers (including, apparently, Hartmann) would agree that a significant part of women's economic disadvantage stems from this kind of discrimination rather than from discrimination practiced by employers. Third, even if literally all of the female-male pay gap *were* the result of *employer* discrimination, requiring equal pay for jobs of comparable worth would *not* succeed in "removing discrimination." Under comparable worth, discriminatory employers would remain free to give preference to men, relative to qualified women, in their hiring and promotion decisions. Thus, comparable worth would *redirect* employer discrimination, not "remove" it.

Hartmann argues—correctly, in my view—that, because of discrimination (both in employment and elsewhere in society), women workers are not employed as productively as they could be. She is also correct in implying that comparable worth will lead to "some reallocation of labor." Unfortunately, such changes are unlikely to be ones that she would find desirable. Comparable worth will reduce employment opportunities for women in so-called traditional jobs (because it would increase the cost of employing workers in such jobs) without creating any new opportunities in so-called nontraditional jobs. Indeed, to the extent that comparable worth raises overall labor costs, it is likely to reduce employment in nontraditional as well as traditional female occupations.

Finally, although Hartmann remarks that comparable worth policies "are not a total solution to employment discrimination against women" (indeed not!), she apparently does not realize that the drive to implement comparable worth policies diverts attention, effort, and resources away from antidiscrimination programs that can provide substantial benefits with few or no adverse side-effects. If it were necessary to choose between adopting comparable worth and doing nothing, the adverse side-effects of comparable worth would even then raise doubts about its desirability. In fact, however, there are several important alternatives to comparable worth; and it is these alternatives, not comparable worth, that have the greatest potential for improving women's labor market status.

Alternatives to Comparable Worth

Measures that attack "societal" discrimination—e.g., in schools—are one very important alternative to comparable worth. As Hartmann notes, there is little agreement on just how much of the overall female-male pay gap is attributable to such discrimination rather than to employer discrimination. At a minimum, however, most of the available evidence suggests that societal discrimination is profoundly important even if it is hardly the sole source of women's economic disadvantage. Policies that attack such discrimination—e.g., Title IX of the Civil Rights Act—have a very important role to play.

A second alternative to comparable worth is the "old-time religion" of Title VII of the Civil Rights Act. The essential difference between comparable worth and Title VII is very simple. Comparable worth makes it costly for all employers, whether or not they discriminate against women, to employ low-wage predominantly female labor. In contrast, Title VII makes it costly for discriminatory employers to treat equally qualified men and women differently with respect to employment, promotions, or pay. Comparable worth raises women's wages while reducing women's employment opportunities. In contrast, Title VII—since it focuses on discriminatory employers and penalizes unequal treatment of equally qualified men and women at any point in the employment relation—can reverse all of the adverse effects of discrimination.

Nor is it possible to object to Title VII, as with comparable worth, on the grounds that it imposes serious costs on employers. What is costly is discrimination, not Title VII antidiscrimination remedies. A firm that discriminates in favor of men, hiring them in preference to comparably qualified women, paying male employees higher salaries and putting them in better positions than comparably qualified female employees, is obviously not operating at the lowest possible cost. Requiring equal treatment of equally qualified people without reference to gender—the Title VII remedy of discrimination—not only improves the labor market status of women with respect to hiring *and* promotions *and* pay, it also *reduces* discriminatory firms' costs and improves their efficiency. In contrast, comparable worth simply increases employment costs still further.

Although simple discrimination probably lies at the root of many claims by comparable worth advocates that wages in predominantly female jobs are "artificially depressed," another possible factor also deserves investigation: cartelization. The nursing labor market is quite literally a textbook example of a cartelized labor market.[11] According to one witness at recent congressional hearings, hospital administrators in Denver—the site of one notable comparable worth court case—have colluded to fix nurses' wages.[12] Likewise, another witness testified that employers of clerical workers in cities such as Boston and San Francisco have formed "consortia" or "study groups" whose actual purpose is collusive wage-fixing.[13]

It is well known that the monopsony model provides a simple

explanation of precisely the situation that is said to exist in labor markets for certain predominantly female jobs such as nursing: widespread shortages, coexisting with low wages that do not seem to increase in response to shortages. (With wages held below the equilibrium level by employer collusion, *individual* employers naturally want to hire more workers than they are able to attract, but cannot raise wages in order to do so.) However, the actual extent of employer wage-fixing in such markets is not known at all. The potential importance of such wage-fixing deserves serious study; application or expansion of the antitrust laws to address such wage-fixing deserves serious consideration.

Notes

1. Adam Smith, *The Wealth of Nations*, 1776. Reprint edition, E. Cannan, ed. (New York: Modern Library, 1937).

2. See John M. Abowd and Mark R. Killingsworth, "Sex Discrimination and Atrophy: A Case Study of the Male-Female Wage Differential," *Industrial Relations* 22 (1983): 387–402; Mark R. Killingsworth and Cordelia W. Reimers, "Race, Ranking, Promotions and Pay at a Federal Facility: A Logit Analysis," *Industrial and Labor Relations Review* 37 (1983): 92–107.

3. Further discussion of many issues related to comparable worth can be found in my recent papers: "Heterogeneous Preferences, Compensating Wage Differentials and Comparable Worth," unpublished manuscript, Rutgers University, 1984; "Statement on Comparable Worth," in Joint Economic Committee, U.S. Congress, *Women in the Work Force: Pay Equity* (Washington, D.C.: U.S. Government Printing Office, 1984) (S. Hrg. 98–1050), pp. 87–127; "The Economics of Comparable Worth: Analytical, Empirical and Policy Questions," in *New Directions for Research on Comparable Worth*, edited by Heidi Hartmann (Washington, D.C.: National Academy Press, forthcoming); and "Economic Analysis of Comparable Worth and Its Consequences," in Industrial Relations Research Association, *Proceedings of the Thirty-Seventh Annual Meeting* (Madison, Wis.: Industrial Relations Research Association, forthcoming).

4. Michael Evan Gold, *A Dialogue on Comparable Worth* (Ithaca, N.Y.: ILR Press, 1983), pp. 43–44.

5. Likewise, consider the jobs of Homemaker One and Park Ranger, which were found to be comparable in a study of state government employment in Washington State (ibid., p. 49). Is there any reason to expect that, even in a nondiscriminatory world, Washington State would pay the same wage to persons in both jobs?

6. See Donald Treiman and Heidi Hartmann, eds., *Women, Work, and Wages: Equal Pay for Jobs of Equal Value* (Washington, D.C.: National Academy Press, 1981), pp. 81–82.

7. Donald P. Schwab, "Job Evaluation and Pay Setting: Concepts and Practices," in *Comparable Worth: Issues and Alternatives*, edited by E. Robert Livernash (Washington, D.C.: Equal Employment Advisory Council, 1980), pp. 49–78.

8. Treiman and Hartmann, *Women, Work, and Wages*, p. 53.

9. In theory, comparable worth need not require *increases* in pay for predominantly female jobs found to be comparable to, but lower paid than, other predominantly male jobs. For example, pay in the male jobs could be reduced until it equals the pay in comparable predominantly female jobs. However, comparable worth advocates appear to equate "fair" with "more" and—not unmindful of the need to enlist as much support as they can get—often specify that under comparable worth no job's pay would ever be reduced.

10. Note that reductions in employment in predominantly male jobs would be certain to occur if the substitution toward them, induced by the increase in the cost of predominantly female jobs due to comparable worth, were smaller than the reduction in scale induced by the rise in labor costs and, hence, prices. In the nature of the case, substitution between male and female jobs is probably small, so adverse effects on predominantly male jobs seem quite likely. See Killingsworth, "Heterogeneous Preferences," for details.

11. Ronald Ehrenberg and Robert S. Smith, *Modern Labor Economics* (Homewood, Ill.: Scott, Foresman and Company, 1982), pp. 65–66.

12. Committee on Post Office and Civil Service, U.S. House of Representatives, *Pay Equity: Equal Pay for Work of Comparable Value*, Parts I and II, Serial No. 97–53 (Washington, D.C.: U.S. Government Printing Office, 1983), p. 70.

13. Ibid., pp. 88, 96.

Index

Abowd, John M., 194*n*
Abuse of women: and socio-political structure, 153
Affirmative action, 10; "color-blind" policies, 74*n*; comparable worth, 169; consensus, 56–57, 77; current status of, 26; defined, 73*n*; equality of opportunity and results, 39; Executive Order 10925, 40; goals v. predictions, 7–8; individual responsibility, 82–83; measured by equal opportunity, 106; moral costs and benefits, 93; National Labor Relations Act of 1935, 13*n*; preferential treatment, 6–9, 99; private v. public interests, 66–67; reality alteration through behavior changes, 104; results and opportunities, 64–65; rights based arguments, 57–60; risk aversion, 74*n*; self-determination, 81–82; seniority, 21–22; two cases of, 7; white women, 32
Age Discrimination in Employment Act of 1967: job protection for the elderly, 22*n*
Albemarle Paper Company v. *Moody*: articulating "make-whole" theory, 113*n*
Anderson, Monroe, 26
Aristotle, 125; concept of equality, 118; *The Generation of Animals*, 142*n*; *The Nicomachean Ethics*, 124*n*; justice, 127*n*; male standard of comparison, 120–21; women as inferior, 126–27
Augustine, 82

Barnett, Ross, 3
Barry, K.: on prostitution, 158*n*

Bell, Daniel: on the private household, 83
Bergmann, Barbara R., 185*n*
Bickel, Alexander: *The Morality of Consent*, 11, 14*n*
Bittker, Borris: compensation of victims, 68, 76*n*
Blackmun, Harry: in *Regents of the University of California* v. *Bakke*, 73
Black Panther Party: and the Los Angeles police, 91–92
Black vote; decline of, 32–33
Bona Fide Occupational Qualification (BFOQ), 156*n*; sex as a valid job qualification, 145; under Civil Rights Act of 1964, 117
Brennan, Teresa, 142*n*
Brown v. *Board of Education*, 27, 73; balance between legal authority and morality, 18; school desegregation, 3, 15; and the challenge of Communism, 29
Burger, Warren: in *Franks* dissent, 43

Calvinism, 82
Chaney, James, 16, 22*n*
Children: as sexual assault victims, 152
Civil rights: moral v. legalistic view of policy, 16; need for persuasion, 72
Civil Rights Act of 1964, 3, 27, 96; and comparable worth, 169; consequences of, 15–16; on gender, 117; reduced enforcement of, 32; Title VII application using quotas, 106. *See also* Title VII
Civil Rights Cases, 23*n*; invalidation of civil rights laws, 33; and public accommodities act, 19

197

Contributors

DERRICK BELL is a professor in the University of Oregon School of Law, and its former dean. One of America's foremost scholars on race and the law, his book *Race, Racism, and American Law* (Little, Brown, 1981 [2nd ed.]) is a standard text in law schools.

DREW S. DAYS III, associate professor of law at Yale Law School, was Assistant Attorney General for Civil Rights during the Carter administration. He recently published "Seeking a New Civil Rights Consensus" in *Daedalus* (Fall 1983).

CHRISTOPHER EDLEY, JR., is an assistant professor at Harvard Law School. Formerly he served in the Carter administration as Assistant Director of the White House Domestic Policy Staff, Special Assistant to HEW Secretary Patricia Roberts Harris, and Associate Assistant to the President in the Office of the Chief of Staff.

RACHEL FLICK is with the Washington Bureau of the *New York Post;* formerly she was with the White House Office of Planning and Evaluation.

ROBERT K. FULLINWIDER is a research associate at the Center for Philosophy and Public Policy. He is the author of *The Reverse Discrimination Controversy* (Rowman and Littlefield, 1980).

HEIDI I. HARTMANN is Study Director of the Committee on Women's Employment and Related Social Issues, National Academy of Sciences, and is co-editor of *Women, Work, and Wages: Equal Pay for Jobs of Equal Value* (1981).

MARK R. KILLINGSWORTH is associate professor of economics at Rutgers University and a research economist at the National Bureau of Economic Research.

CATHARINE A. MACKINNON is visiting scholar at Stanford Law School. She is a leading feminist theorist on women and the law, and author of *Sexual Harassment of Working Women* (Yale University Press, 1979).

CLAUDIA MILLS is editor at the Center for Philosophy and Public Policy.

SUSAN MOLLER OKIN is associate professor of politics at Brandeis University and author of *Women in Western Political Thought* (Princeton University Press, 1979).

ORLANDO PATTERSON is professor of sociology at Harvard University. A noted scholar of slavery and of black-white relations, he is the author of *Slavery and Social Death: A Comparative Study* (Harvard University Press, 1982).

WM. BRADFORD REYNOLDS is Assistant Attorney General for Civil Rights in the U.S. Department of Justice.

RICHARD WASSERSTROM is a professor of philosophy at the University of California at Santa Cruz. His books include *The Judicial Decision* (Stanford University Press, 1961) and *Philosophy and Social Issues* (Notre Dame University Press, 1980).